INDUSTRIAL SUNSET

The Making of North America's Rust Belt, 1969–1984

Plant shutdowns in Canada and the United States from 1969 to 1984 led to a ravaging industrial decline of the Great Lakes region. *Industrial Sunset* offers a comparative regional analysis of the economic and cultural devastation caused by the shutdowns and provides an insightful examination of how mill and factory workers on both sides of the border made sense of their own displacement. The history of deindustrialization rendered in cultural terms reveals the importance of community and national identifications in how North Americans responded to the problem.

Based on the plant shutdown stories told by over 130 industrial workers, and drawing on extensive archival and published sources as well as songs and poetry from the time, Steven High explores the central issues in the history and contemporary politics of plant closings. In so doing, he poses new questions about group identification and solidarity in the face of often dramatic industrial transformation.

STEVEN HIGH is an assistant professor of history at Nipissing University.

INDUSTRIAL SUNSET

The Making of
North America's Rust Belt,
1969–1984

Steven High

UNIVERSITY OF TORONTO PRESS
Toronto Buffalo London

ISBN 0-8020-3738-0 (cloth)
ISBN 0-8020-8528-8 (paper)

Printed on acid-free paper

National Library of Canada Cataloguing in Publication

High, Steven C.
Industrial sunset : the making of North America's rust belt, 1969–
1984 / Steven High.

Includes bibliographical references and index.
ISBN 0-8020-3738-0 (bound)   ISBN 0-8020-8528-8 (pbk.)

1. Deindustrialization – United States.   2. Deindustrialization –
Canada.   3. Plant shutdown – United States.   4. Plant shutdowns –
Canada.   5. Displaced workers – United States.   6. Displaced workers –
Canada.   7. Industries – Social aspects – United States.   8. Industries –
Social aspects – Canada.   I. Title.

HC95.H54 2003   338.6'042   C2002-905291-2

University of Toronto Press acknowledges the financial assistance to its
publishing program of the Canada Council for the Arts and the Ontario
Arts Council.

This book has been published with the help of a grant from the Humanities
and Social Sciences Federation of Canada, using funds provided by the
Social Sciences and Humanities Research Council of Canada.

University of Toronto Press acknowledges the financial support for its
publishing activities of the Government of Canada through the Book
Publishing Industry Development Program (BPIDP).

Contents

List of Tables and Figures

Tables

Figures

Acknowledgments

This book began its life in 1995 as a doctoral project. At that time, the massive job losses from the recession earlier in the decade were fresh in everyone's mind. By the time the thesis was completed in 1999, however, these memories were fast fading. Yet as I write these acknowledgments, North America is once again being rocked by plant closings. The Ford Motor Company recently announced that it was laying off 10 per cent of its North American work force. By late 2002, the announced plant closures in Canada and the United States will be taking effect. The issue of worker dislocation and job loss, sadly, is as relevant today as it was during the 1970s and 1980s. We can therefore learn much from past experience.

I could not have written this book without the support of a large number of amazing people. I would first like to thank Don Davis, whose constant encouragement and open-mindedness made him a superb thesis supervisor. This project also owes a considerable debt to Michael Behiels, Chad Gaffield, Greg Kealey, and Jeff Keshen, whose insightful comments helped turn the thesis into a book. The book benefited from the comments of the two anonymous reviewers, as well as from my editor at the University of Toronto Press, Len Husband. Margaret Tessman's thorough copy editing of the book manuscript is also greaty appreciated. At various stages in my writing, I was aided by the comments of friends and colleagues at the University of Ottawa: Kimberley Berry, John Bonnett, Guy Chiasson, Jamie Disbrow, Brian Locking, JoAnne McCutcheon, Jean Manore, David Moorman, Linda Quiney, Pam Roper, Jarret Rudy, John Vardalas, and Don Wright. My use of the term community in this book owes much to my collaboration with John Walsh. Ken Clavette of the Heritage Committee of the Ottawa District Labour Council also provided contacts and encouragement. Most of all I would like to thank my partner-in-life, Barbara Lorenzkowski, whose incisive comments on my work make such a vital contribution to everything that I do.

Special thanks to Barry Cottam, Rob Dobrucki, Joel Duff, Greg Duggan, Ernie Epp, Patricia Jasen, Linda Kealey, Bruce Muirhead, Sergio Piccinin, Helen Smith, Vic Smith, John Topping, Jeff Webb, the Workers' Arts and Heritage Centre, the Windsor Municipal Archives, and the Walter Reuther Library at Wayne State University in Detroit. My parents, Carolyn and Gerald High of Thunder Bay, Ontario, have been the source of both inspiration and assistance. Their enthusiasm is very much appreciated!

The research phase of this project benefited enormously from the archivists and librarians at thirty-three American and Canadian institutions. The folks at the Inter-Library Loan Office at the University of Ottawa were especially helpful. The illustrations were identified with the assistance of Gerald High, David Rosenberg, Martha Bishop, Mary J. Wallace, Mike Smith, Lorraine Endicott, Jane V. Charles, Beth Greenhorn, Kathleen Goray, Anne Chetwynd, and the Ontario Federation of Labour. Three labour photographers kindly agreed to the reproduction of their work in this book: Frank Rooney, David Smiley, and Jim West. Poet Tom Wayman similarly permitted the use of his words. Access to restricted material was granted by the United Steelworkers of America, the Canadian Auto Workers, and the International Association of Machinists and Aerospace Workers.

As the financial burden of doing extensive research in the United States was nearly prohibitive for a Canadian lucky to get sixty cents on the dollar, I am particularly indebted to the Canadian Labour Congress for awarding me an A.A. Heaps scholarship early on in my research. Financial support also came from the University of Ottawa, the Ontario Graduate Scholarship program, and the Social Sciences and Humanities Research Council. Sean Cadigan and the Public Policy Research Centre at the Memorial University of Newfoundland kindly gave me a computer and an office in the final stages of preparing this manuscript. Parts of *Industrial Sunset* were originally published in *History Workshop Journal*, the *Journal of the Canadian Historical Association*, the *Canadian Review of American Studies*, and in *Canadian Issues.*

My decision to include an oral history component in this book was triggered by the inspiring work of Donna DeBlasio and Michael Frisch. A number of people assisted me in my efforts to identify interviewees:

Bill Scandlon and Bill Fuller in Hamilton, Nelson and Betty Sheehan in Buffalo, Dan McCarthy in Detroit, Les Dickirson in Windsor, Martin Hanratty of the Canadian Labour Congress, the Canadian Auto Workers, the United Food and Commercial Workers, UAW Local 417, the Steelworkers' Organization of Active Retirees, and the *Detroit Sunday Journal* newspaper. Above all, I owe a debt of gratitude to the men and women who agreed to share their stories. This book is dedicated to them.

INDUSTRIAL SUNSET

The Making of North America's Rust Belt, 1969–1984

Introduction

A siren wailed twice. Two more blasts shattered the silence. A minute passed before the siren sounded the last warning. A voice crackled onto the loud speaker for the final countdown and the four old blast furnaces were lifted by a series of thuds before they fell crashing to the ground. A huge red plume of iron ore rose up, threatening to shower the crowd of onlookers who had come to witness the demolition of the Ohio Works in Youngstown. It was a spring day in 1982.[1]

Watching the explosion, spectators arrived at different conclusions. Charles Horne, vice-president of U.S. Steel, celebrated the demolition as the dawning of a 'whole new era' of industrial diversification for Youngstown and the Mahoning River valley in northeastern Ohio.[2] Steelworker Clem Smereck, who had fed the blast furnaces for thirty-two years, called it the 'second saddest day' of his life, the first being the day the mill closed. 'I have a lot of memories, a lot of good friends, in that dust there,' he said.[3] Was the demolition a brave step forward into a post-industrial future? Or did it represent the end of a way of life? However one might answer this question, there was no escaping the fact that steel-making was coming to an end in the Steel Valley after more than a century of production.

The end of an era is frequently marked by the ritualized toppling of the symbolic markers of the old regime. One example that comes readily to mind is the enthusiasm with which Eastern Europeans knocked down the statues of Karl Marx and Vladimir Lenin during the early 1990s. The end of the industrial era has been similarly, if less obviously, dramatized in North America. Public demonstrations such as the one in Youngstown communicate to us that North America is changing in new and important ways. While many onlookers lamented these changes,

Blast furnace demolition in Youngstown, Ohio.

the orderly destruction of old economic landmarks was carefully choreographed to engineer consent and legitimate the economic changes underway. The familiarity of these public spectacles, repeated in towns and cities across the continent, reinforced the sense that older industries were literally vanishing before our eyes.

This book traces and compares the processes of industrial transformation in Canada and the United States. It addresses central issues in the history and contemporary politics of plant closings during the fifteen years between 1969 and 1984, a period beginning and ending in recession. It represents both a regional analysis of the economic and cultural devastation of the Great Lakes region and a study of how mill and factory workers made sense of their own displacement. The cross-national comparative perspective taken in this study permits the exploration of the similarities and differences in Canadian and American responses to the accelerated pace of industrial transformation. To better situate job loss in its social context (see Map I.1), this book lingers in Youngstown and Detroit, both of which experienced early decline in the perceived core of the Rust Belt, as well as Hamilton and Windsor, Ontario, two cities located on the belt's periphery. Drawing cross-border comparisons reveals how perceptions of, and responses to, plant closings varied across regional and national boundaries. Youngstown

Map I.1

may have symbolized the transformation that was underway, but it was not an isolated case.

Youngstown had once been part of the industrial heartland of North America that stretched from western Pennsylvania to Wisconsin, and from the Ohio River to the Canadian Shield. This industrially diverse heartland region, which straddled the Canada–United States border, produced most of the consumer goods bought by North Americans. The region was home to the auto, steel, rubber, and agricultural machinery industries, and its great cities of Cleveland, Detroit, and Chicago were the wunderkinds of the late nineteenth and early twentieth centuries.[4] Indeed, their strutting self-confidence was legendary. Yet industrial towns were rarely regarded as subject to the same destructive boom and bust cycles commonly associated with resource towns. Mills and factories were presumably semi-permanent fixtures in stable towns and cities, whose central location in the industrial heartland made them seem indestructible.

In reality, many heartland towns and cities were wholly dependent on a single industry or a single employer for their existence. As journalist William Serrin wrote, Homestead, Pennsylvania, 'existed because of the mill.'[5] In the United States, there were steel towns such as Youngstown, Lackawanna, New York, and Gary, Indiana, auto towns such as Kenosha, Wisconsin, and Flint and Detroit, Michigan, and towns such as Akron and neighbouring Barberton, both in Ohio, that produced rubber products. Ontario, had the auto towns of Windsor and Oshawa, the steel towns of Sault Ste Marie and Hamilton, the rubber factories of Kitchener, and the textile centres of Paris and Cornwall.

The towns and cities of Southern Ontario had, as a whole, a more diversified industrial base than did cities across the border. Even in Hamilton, where the two steel mills dominate the city's skyline, there were dozens of other factories producing farm implements, electrical equipment, auto parts, textiles, clothing, shovels, and candy. Canada's textile and electrical industries were located mainly inside the heartland region; this was not the case in the United States. As a result, the more specialized industrial structure of American cities made them more vulnerable to dislocation.

Two great waves of plant closings inundated the region between 1969 and 1984, washing away millions of jobs. While job losses were staggering on both sides of the border, Canadian industry appeared to be situated on higher ground, as no steel mills or auto assembly plants closed during this period. Laid-off workers were thus more likely to have a plant to return to. In the industrial Midwest, by contrast, dozens of these sprawling mills and factories went down. The number of Americans employed by the steel industry dropped 40 per cent from 1979 to 1984, and 300,000 auto workers lost their jobs between 1978 and 1982.[6] In some areas of the heartland, entire industries disappeared. Steel production ceased in Pittsburgh, tire production ended in Akron, and the auto industry shifted much of its production out of Detroit. Few industrial towns and cities were spared.

The disappearance of industrial Ohio was particularly striking. The changing cityscape was reflected in the oral history interviews. George Richardson, a displaced foreman of the open hearth department at Youngstown's Campbell works remembers: 'When I read those headlines [about the mill closure in 1977] it made me sick. It makes me sick now to drive down Poland Avenue to see those empty spaces where the blast furnaces used to be.'[7] Gaping holes could be found in cities across the region and mirrored the emotional loss felt by residents and industrial workers. As always, emptiness disturbs and empty spaces beg for explanation.[8]

The debate over the meaning of industrial transformation is fundamentally about who is going to control the future. Economic decline has typically been set against an ascendant other: sunset versus sunrise industries; industrial versus post-industrial eras; and the old versus the new economy. Each dual metaphor encloses and structures our understanding of economic change.[9] The post-industrialism/deindustrialization debate of the 1970s and 1980s, for example, defined the ideological struggle over the meaning of industrial transformation. Political conservatives took their cue from sociologist Daniel Bell, who wrote *The Coming of Post-Industrial Society* in 1973.[10] Bell interpreted the vast changes sweeping the industrialized world as evidence of an emerging knowledge-based economy of computers and telecommunications. Bell's sweeping interpretation underpins present-day distinctions between the old and new economies.

In another explanation for this transformation, Joseph Schumpeter characterizes capitalism as a gale of 'creative destruction' that sweeps the globe devouring the old in order to create the new.[11] These opposing forces take on a spatial fix as old and new geographic areas change shape, and entire regions become redundant to the needs of capitalism. Thus, the creation of new economic spaces and the destruction of old ones have been endemic to capitalism. The 1970s and 1980s saw the birth of the Sunbelt and Rust Belt labels to describe the geography of economic rise and decline in the United States. For those living in these blighted areas, discourses of rise and decline conveyed a sense of collective powerlessness and inevitability.

By contrast, the 'deindustrialization thesis' was first proposed by Canadian economic nationalists such as Robert Laxer in the early 1970s to explain the high price apparently paid by workers for Canada's dependent relationship with the United States.[12] They argued that, for reasons of patriotism, American-based multinational corporations closed their Canadian branch plants to save jobs at home. The nationalist Canadian line sometimes reached dizzying rhetorical heights. Historian Wayne Roberts wrote: 'With the frostbite of international recession, the blood money of multinationals flowed back to protect the internal organs at corporate headquarters. The outer limbs of branch plants were cut off.'[13] The rhetoric of the deindustrialization thesis advocates tapped into a deep wellspring of national anxiety in Canada. At a time when plants were closing in record numbers, Canadians worried that vital economic decisions were being made outside the country. Central to this nationalist discourse was a binary opposition between Canadian workers on the one hand and American bosses on the other.

The deindustrialization thesis was subsequently adopted in a revised form by plant closing opponents in the United States. Instead of pitting one country against the other, American proponents of the thesis such as Barry Bluestone and Bennett Harrison defined the struggle as communities against capital.[14] The American plant-closing opponents thus were able to draw a line between community members hurt by economic dislocation and outsiders closing mills and factories. Historian John Cumbler, in his social history of industrial decline in Trenton, New Jersey, showed that the city's decline paralleled the decline of civic capitalism, and the concurrent rise of national capitalism. This loss of local economic control had far-reaching implications for Trenton: 'When decisions are made at national headquarters removed from traditional production sites, there are few local constraints. Decisions are likely to be made on the narrowest of economic grounds, and these affect all segments of the society.'[15] The loss of local control mirrored the loss of national control identified in Canada.

Both versions of the thesis blamed deindustrialization on the 'widespread, systematic disinvestment' of multinational corporations in the basic productive capacity of Canadian and American industrial cities.[16] Deindustrialization did not just happen. Rather, conscious decisions were made by corporate executives to shift production from one location to another or to diversify out of certain industries. The corporation's private interest thus took priority over the public's interest, whether that imagined public was a local community in the United States or, in the case of Canada, a national community.

It is now clear that the deindustrialization thesis is part myth and part fact. Robert Z. Lawrence, for example, uses aggregate economic data to show that manufacturing employment in the United States did not decline but actually increased from 16.8 million in 1960, to 20.1 million in 1973, and 20.3 million in 1980.[17] However, manufacturing employment was in relative decline. Barry Bluestone noted that manufacturing represented a decreasing proportion of the U.S. labour force, from 26.2 per cent in 1973 to 22.1 per cent in 1980.[18] Studies in Canada have likewise shown that manufacturing employment was only in relative decline during these years.[19] Yet mills and factories did close, and towns and cities lost their industries. John Cumbler submitted that 'depressions do not manifest themselves only at moments of national economic collapse' such as in the 1930s, but 'also recur in scattered sites across the nation in regions, in industries, and in communities.'[20] It is in this regional and local sense, then, that deindustrialization is used in this study.

It is useful to read deindustrialization as an anthropological exercise, with broader cultural meanings embedded in mill and factory closings. Anthropologists have long been immersed in the vanishing ways of life of those people caught on the wrong side of history. It is highly significant that anthropologists should have discovered industrial workers in the 1990s. In her insightful study of deindustrializing Kenosha, Wisconsin, Kathryn Marie Dudley noted that a cultural transformation accompanied the closing of the American Motors auto assembly plant in 1988. Displaced auto workers stood to lose much more than their jobs. They lost a social structure on which their collective integrity depended. The workplace culture that had sustained and legitimated individual pride and dignity was replaced by a post-industrial culture that measured hard work by educational credentials rather than seniority and physical prowess. Industrial workers, who had once stood at the centre of local life, now seemed out of place.[21]

There was also a gendered dimension to the changes underway. The auto, steel, and rubber industries employed the classic male proletarians who formed the centre of traditional working-class identity.[22] Anthropologist Tom Dunk once asked working-class men in Thunder Bay, Ontario, what made their city different. He was told that it was a place where 'men go to work in work clothes, work boots, and hard hats, and carry a lunch box.'[23] But as male breadwinners lost their jobs, this sense of place began to change. The new jobs being created were mainly in the service and public sectors, two areas in which women have traditionally found employment.

The importance of community and nation are central to how North Americans responded to the problem of plant closings. The motive power of these two concepts provided a shared sense of purpose and meaning and validated the efforts of plant closing opponents to save plants and to win new legislation. What this book seeks to discover is whether, in building these solidarities, plant closing opponents in Canada and the United States invoked sufficiently empowering myths. Was the universalizing impulse behind the appeals to community and nation able to mobilize large numbers of people? Did these hopeful appeals fulfil their promise as a base for collective action? A history of deindustrialization rendered in cultural terms might demonstrate the importance of group solidarities – of an imagined us against a symbolic them – in understanding a topic that is too often analysed exclusively in economic and individualistic terms. Nonetheless, the story is a gloomy and often discouraging one.

To understand how North Americans responded to plant closings, it is necessary to evaluate and analyse the origins and political effects of the universalizing impulse behind local and national communities. 'There can be no collective purpose without myth,' wrote Anthony D. Smith.[24] Myths bind individuals together or keep them apart; they can represent a magnificent fiction or an ugly stereotype.[25] This book employs myth in the same sense that historian Jonathan Vance uses the term in relation to the public memory of the First World War, as a 'combination of invention, truth, and half-truth.'[26] This study delves into two empowering myths – community and nation – invoked by plant closing opponents at a key transitional moment in the economic, social, and political history of North America.

Communal identification has been a source of resistance for centuries. In an influential essay, historian E.P. Thompson showed how bread riots in eighteenth-century England enforced what he called a 'moral economy' in times of shortages and high prices.[27] A merchant's decision to increase the price of bread above what was thought reasonable could spark a violent mob confrontation. Rioters believed that they were justified in taking these actions because they were 'supported by the wider consensus of the community.'[28] A popular notion of just prices legitimated the use of force to regulate the price of bread.

E.P. Thompson's notion of community is a place-bound one, as is often the case. On the whole, community is used synonymously with a geographic place: a city, town, or neighbourhood. Community is also used to identify a recognizable group of people that have something in common such as language, religion, ethnicity, or even professional occupation. This common sense approach treats community as a static category rather than a fluid process undergoing constant change.[29] Community might best be defined as social interaction, as spatial process, and as imagined reality.[30] In the first sense, community identity develops out of the face-to-face social interactions of everyday life. In the spatial process, places develop, institutions form, and local identities are constructed.[31] Finally, community is an imagined reality where people associate themselves with others they have never met. This third element allows community to extend well beyond personal social networks and local places to encompass a region or a nation.

The cultural approach to the study of nationalism has shifted the focus of research from the nation building of political elites to nation as a product of collective invention and cultural expression.[32] Benedict Anderson's 1983 definition of nation as an imagined political community has become generally accepted in academic circles.[33] Nationalism first arose in the late Enlightenment as an integrating political ideology. 'The nation is always conceived as a deep, horizontal comradeship,' Anderson wrote.[34] The striking ability of nationalism to bring people of diverse backgrounds imaginatively together – in spite of differences of ethnicity, gender, class, and region – has been well-documented. As Eric Hobsbawm indicated, 'where ideologies are in conflict, the appeal to the imagined community of the nation appears to have defeated all challengers.'[35] In short, there were any number of communities of identification available to plant shutdown opponents: communities imaginatively tied to place, occupation, region, or nation. Each of these solidarities had the ability to mobilize people for political purposes.[36]

The pivotal role local and national communities played in providing legitimacy and purpose to those who defied the economic decisions of others is crucial to understanding the opposition to plant closings during the 1970s and 1980s. The motivating power of local and national solidarities was tested repeatedly as mills and factories closed, leaving workers with little or nothing. In an influential article entitled 'The Great Disruption' published in the *Atlantic Monthly*, Francis Fukuyama wrote that the bonds of community that once constrained destructive behaviour have been cut by a series of 'liberation movements.' The political left espoused freedom from social values and morality while the political right pushed freedom from economic constraints. Voluntary community membership, in turn, has left human communities 'smaller and weaker than most of those that have existed in the past.'[37] The rise of moral individualism narrowed the circle that people trust, freeing corporate managers from any moral obligation they may have had to their employees while restricting the possibilities of collective resistance.

This book posits that the Great Disruption was filtered through national contexts. In the United States, the fears and anxieties engendered by industrial transformation turned workers into metaphorical gypsies, encamped on an emptied industrial landscape. Under the banner of local community, plant closing opponents in the United States proved unable to save factories from closing or to soften the blow of displacement. Ultimately, the identity of many Americans was irrevocably altered by the experience of displacement. Canadians felt deeply threatened by plant shutdowns as well, but were able to marshal nationalist claims as rhetorical weapons against plant shutdowns and lobbying tools. Canadian politicians were convinced to legislate advance notice of layoffs, severance pay, pension reinsurance, job placement assistance, and preferential hiring rights.

Why did plant closing opponents in Canada and the United States choose different communities of identification? The 'cult of the little community' in the United States has its origins in the Vietnam War and the New Left.[38] The patriotism and support for the Democratic Party of the mainstream union movement, compounded by the unions' political purges during the Cold War era, all led to union support of the war in Vietnam. For the young people who opposed the war, the union movement became part of the problem. Anti-war activists turned to local community instead as a non-hierarchical alternative to nationalism. Since that time, historian Christopher Lasch argues, their 'little community' has become so entrenched in the United States that 'we find it more and more difficult to conceive of any form of social solidarity that does not rest on shared values and spontaneous cooperation, on the one hand, or an engineered consent, manipulation, or outright coercion on the other.'[39] An atmosphere of sentimental regret thus surrounds the nostalgic local communities invoked by American critics of plant closings.

Recent scholarship relating to deindustrialization reflects the trend to localism. In the United States, there has been a flurry of local community studies of the hardship and hurt caused by mill and factory closings.[40] Many of the authors of these studies rely on a combination of oral history interviews and photographic images to convey the enormity of industrial transformation. With their tape recorders and camera lenses directed at displaced workers, scholars succeed in personalizing a process that is usually debated in the abstract or the aggregate. At its best, oral history can cut through abstraction to a 'complexity grounded in location, in history, and in the lives, labor, and communities of the people.'[41] The haunting *Portraits in Steel* is a case in point. Documentary photographer Milton Rogovin photographed steelworkers at home and at work in Buffalo in the mid-1970s. Insofar as Rogovin let his subjects choose the time and the place, these photographs were given as much as taken. When many of these same men and women lost their jobs in the mill closings of the 1980s, Rogovin teamed up with oral historian Michael Frisch to record the effects of job loss. Another photograph was taken and added to the first, and Frisch interviewed the former steelworkers about the intervening years. The resulting visual and oral portraits resonated, but this approach is not without its problems.

Historian William Westerman astutely observed that North Americans are more willing to listen to personal experiences than they are to political discussion.[42] Perhaps with this in mind, Rogovin and Frisch have tried to humanize job loss via personal stories in the hope that readers would be moved to act. Yet, personal narratives sometimes leave the impression that job loss was an individual experience, not a collective one, and that displaced workers were innocent and passive victims of deindustrialization. The irony here is that in an effort to inspire collective action in the future, the authors have minimized the collective action of the past.

Other scholars, especially those writing in the 1980s, have focused instead on the fight-back campaigns against plant shutdowns in Youngstown, Pittsburgh, and the Calumet region of northwestern Indiana.[43] Several of these authors were participants in the events they wrote about. The most prominent historian of American resistance to plant closings is undoubtedly Staughton Lynd. An activist historian-turned-lawyer, Lynd was integrally involved in the well-publicized effort to reopen the Youngstown area's Campbell works under community ownership after it closed in September 1977. His extensive writings on the campaign stressed worker solidarity and militancy, as well as community defiance. For Lynd, the Youngstown story became a heroic struggle against impossible odds, and eventually resulted in the defeat of community. The scholarly penchant for local community sometimes results in the suggestion that resistance failed because there was not enough community identification.[44] A more important contributing factor in the failure of resistance in the United States was which facet of community had been invoked.

Much of the American literature on plant closings and deindustrialization turns on the contrast between capital and community. In recent years, these studies have emphasized personal loss over collective resistance. They have also focused on a single closed factory or a lone city. As a result, many deindustrialized cities now have their own biographer who has recorded their life and death. Local studies do reveal larger processes and the contribution these authors make in drawing attention to the human cost of deindustrialization is clear. There is, however, a set of assumptions about community and labour that needs to be acknowledged. Virtually none of these studies have much to say about the wider trade union movement or the role played by state and federal governments. What has been written is intensely negative and, in many instances, national unions are removed from the equation altogether. As historian Elizabeth Faue has suggested, community has become a strategy for class organization for New Left activists and scholars alike.[45] The struggle between community and capital is thus frequently played out on a local stage.

Given the large number of locality-based community studies in the United States, it is telling that no comparable literature exists in Canada. This absence results in part from the fact that deindustrialization in Canada has not been extensively studied. Yet almost without exception, those who have studied plant closings and job loss have situated their work in a national context. Rianne Mahon's study of the decline of the textile industry called for an industrial strategy for Canada.[46] Plant closing studies by J. Paul Grayson and Daniel Drache, and the Canadian contributors to Jane Jenson and Rianne Mahon's *The Challenge of Restructuring* have also taken a nationalist line.[47] Even studies of a single plant closing, such as David Sobel and Susan Meurer's *Working at Inglis*, have tied these Canadian factories to a national community of identification.[48] Shutdown dynamics are still generally seen as pitting Canadian workers against American bosses. Accordingly, the approaches taken by historians of industrial transformation in Canada and similarly in the United States have mirrored the national and local strategies adopted by plant closing opponents themselves.

Archival sources available in Canada and the United States also reflect the divergent responses of government agencies, unions, and community organizations to the plant shutdown problem. In Canada, government records reveal an active and sustained interest in these matters including attempts to track the numbers of workers losing their jobs. By contrast, federal and state governments in the United States played little or no role in plant closings. Divergent responses can likewise be seen in the sources of resistance. Evidence of opposition to plant shutdowns in the United States can be found mainly in the archival records of local fight-back campaigns such as those led by the Ecumenical Coalition in Youngstown or the Denominational Ministry Strategy in Pittsburgh. In Canada, this story is largely preserved in the archival holdings of the trade union movement. The widely scattered records of the United Auto Workers, United Steelworkers, United Rubber Workers, United Electrical Workers, Canadian Auto Workers, International Union of Electrical Workers, and various union centrals were examined for this study. Without exception, these unions generously opened restricted records. The location of sources provides further evidence that the locus of resistance and the political ramifications of protest differed substantially on either side of the Canada–United States border.

More than twenty major corporations were asked to provide conditional access to their records. All politely declined. What remained for research purposes were published sources and corporate records that have found their way into public archives. Special thanks go to the intrepid archivist at Kettering University in Flint who drove to Dayton in 1979 to save the splendid Frigidaire collection. The book was also the beneficiary of records of Beach Foundry, B.F. Goodrich, Goodyear, Youngstown Sheet and Tube, and several smaller concerns. This fragmentary record still leaves some important questions unanswered: How far in advance did corporations know that they were going to close mills and factories? Who made these decisions and why? Did political considerations influence plant closing decisions? Were corporations headquartered in other cities or other countries more willing to close plants? No attempt is made here to determine whether individual plants should or should not have been closed. Nor is it suggested that companies must operate unprofitable factories indefinitely. Rather, this study focuses on the lessons learned by North Americans at this critical juncture.

To explore the meanings of job loss, this book draws from 137 oral history interviews conducted with displaced workers in Canada and the United States. Most interviews were conducted by research projects headed by Donna DeBlasio and Youngstown State University in Youngstown and by Ken Clavette in Ottawa. One of the first oral histories found was that of Sam Donnorummo of Youngstown. Sam had been head stocker at the Brier Hill mill before it closed in 1979. The pain of the mill's closing was still evident: 'Everybody felt bad. I felt bad and I knew it. I put all them years down. Where would you get another job? I couldn't get another job ... Ya, I really felt bad when they shut that place down. Everybody did, believe me. It was a good place to work. And them kinda jobs, you can't get them kind of jobs today. That pay, that kind of money. And they come up with minimum wage, how can people live like that?'[49] To these pre-existing oral history collections, twenty-six individual interviews were added from Hamilton, Windsor, and the metropolitan Detroit area in February 1998. In April 1998, seventeen members of the Steelworkers Organization of Active Retirees chapter in Buffalo agreed to be interviewed in short sessions.

The interviewees were secured by a variety of means. The few men and women who responded to public service announcements published in community newspapers regarded our conversation as a political act. Their enthusiasm for the project originated in their desire to tell their stories so that others would not have to experience what they went through. The majority of those interviewed were identified with the help of the union movement and through word of mouth. Still others agreed to participate after being identified from newspaper coverage of plant closings. These strategies have produced a broad range of plant shutdown stories from both Canadian and American men and women, including racial minorities.

The interviews were arranged to elicit a spontaneous type of reply. Questions were open ended and interventions were minimal. The conversations that resulted generally followed the life story of the interviewee (see Appendix I). The two hour interview was often half over before a discussion of the plant's closing had even begun. Whenever possible, the interviewee was encouraged to take the lead. Bill Scandlon's fascinating memories of the 1946 strike at the Steel Company of Canada in Hamilton enriches the understanding of a significant labour struggle even if his story fell outside the parameter of this project. All of the interviewees welcomed the donation of the videotaped recordings to an archives located in their hometown.

From this diverse assortment of sources, the following chapters highlight the dynamic tension between communities and capital, resistance and loss, Canada and the United States. Each chapter examines the plant shutdown process from a variety of vantage points: the factory floor, the corporate boardroom, the union office, and the political capital. Chapter 1 explores how North Americans interpreted industrial decline through the filter of popular regional identities and the memory of the Dust Bowl of the 1930s. Although the American industrial Midwest transmuted into the Rust Belt, no similar stigma attached itself to industrial Ontario. The Golden Horseshoe, it appears, did not rust. Chapter 2 examines the world that workers lost, as narrated in the oral history interviews of displaced workers. Through the recurring metaphors of home and family, we come to see how workers on both sides of the border developed associational ties and familial identification with their mill and factory. The subjectivity of oral history also allows for questioning the meanings derived from job loss. Workers inverted the meaning of familiar cultural symbols of loyalty and service and even began to identify with their displacement. Here, the concept of liminality proves crucial to our understanding of the cultural implications of deindustrialization.

Chapter 3 charts the emergence of a new post-industrial aesthetic in mill and factory architecture. Under pressure from the environmental movement, and wanting to abandon their association with the old economy, executives sought to retool their corporate images. Yet, this post-industrial facade masked the growing detachment of employers from the factory floor. Chapter 4 reconsiders the usual distinction between plants that relocate and those that close. Through an examination of runaway factories and obsolete mills, this chapter situates job loss in the context of the waning importance of industry and its spatial reorganization. This dramatic backdrop allows another opportunity to compare the uneven pattern of industrial transformation in both countries.

Chapters 5 and 6 examine the degree to which workers' collective responses were embedded in distinct national contexts. Chapter 5 examines the business-as-usual attitude of the mainstream union movement in the United States when faced with massive job loss and plant closings. It goes on to show that the divergent trajectories of trade unionists and the New Left fatally divided plant closing opponents. Both the 'buy Americanism' of the AFL-CIO and the New Left's community strategy failed to rally public opinion. Chapter 6 finds that a national community in Canada proved to be far more effective in pushing reluctant politicians to regulate plant shutdowns, thereby mitigating some of the worst effects of job loss. The book concludes that only the nationalist resistance to plant shutdowns in Canada enforced a 'moral economy' on industrial firms operating there.[50]

Drawing on a wide range of sources including song and poetry as well as archival material and oral history interviews, this study finds that Canadian workers proved far more successful than American plant-closing opponents in softening the blow of job loss. Canadian economic nationalism acted as a kind of ideological rustproofing that denied the Rust Belt – the image and the reality – entry into the country and mitigated the social and cultural effects of plant closings during the two waves of dislocation. Most of all, the goal of this book is to show that in spite of the aura of inevitability that surrounds industrial transformation working people can and do make a difference. In the final reckoning, as worker-poet Sue Doro once wrote, 'survival's a victory to be counted.'[51]

1 Gold Doesn't Rust: Regions of the North American Mind

Roger and Me, Michael Moore's irreverent 1989 film documentary about corporate greed and the hollowness of the American Dream, propelled Flint, Michigan, into the North American limelight.[1] The fall of Moore's hometown was a decidedly sharp one. To the upbeat music of the Beach Boys' 'Wouldn't It Be Nice,' Moore showed his audience what Flint had become: a town of abandoned homes, vacant lots, boarded-up businesses, and empty streets. Interspersed with these scenes of urban decay were newspaper headlines announcing the closure of one General Motors plant after another. Moore's technique of juxtaposing contrasting images produced a devastating indictment of GM's relationship to Flint. The most damning example occurred at the end of the film, when Moore overlaid GM Chairman Roger Smith's Christmas message of human fellowship with visual images of a family being evicted from their home on Christmas Eve. As carollers sang 'Santa Claus Is Coming to Town' in the background, the family's meagre possessions were piled onto the curbside. Even their Christmas tree was added to the pile. The impact of the film owed not only to the creativity of Michael Moore, but also to the fact that North Americans were already primed to interpret the history of Flint, and of other industrial cities in the Great Lakes region, in terms of decline. Had Moore made such a negative film at the outset of the 1969 recession about a city in the industrial heartland, he would have been dismissed as an alarmist. By the 1980s, however, North Americans had become used to thinking pessimistically about the Great Lakes region. As the industrial heartland transmuted in the minds of Americans into the Rust Belt, its cities became ideal targets for black humour.

The focus of this chapter is the transformation of the image of the

Great Lakes basin from industrial heartland to Rust Belt in the United States and the resilience of the Golden Horseshoe label in Canada. American geographer Wilbur Zelinsky defined these so-called vernacular regions, or popular regional identities, as shared spontaneous images of territorial reality represented by ordinary people.[2] The ambiguity surrounding the meaning of region is due largely to the many purposes the term has been asked to perform by North American scholars. 'Its content will vary with the purposes and standards of those using the concept,' cautioned Frederick G. Luebke.[3] A new cultural conception of region emerged in the scholarship of the 1970s and coincided, in Luebke's mind, with a fresh emphasis on pluralism. Region became increasingly seen as a complex and fluid mental construction rather than an objective spatial entity.[4] Indeed, new regional images have evolved from and eventually supplanted previous ones.[5] To understand the making of the Rust Belt, this study must go beyond the prevailing image of region and study the interaction of competing regional identities. How did the Rust Belt enter our everyday vocabulary and what did it signify? Did its social construction follow or precede regional industrial decline in the Great Lakes basin? Did the international boundary make any difference to how North Americans understood industrial decline?

This chapter explores the social construction of the Rust Belt as revealed in four magazines (*Time*, *Maclean's*, *The Nation*, and *Canadian Forum*), and in film, art, photography, literature, song, and dictionaries. Two older, agreeable landscapes of the mind in the United States – the 'Middle West' and the 'Heartland' – were transformed by the deteriorating economic position of the United States during the 1970s and into the 1980s. Derived from the symbolic legacy of the Great Depression's Dust Bowl, and the desire for a Northern counterpoise for the pre-existing Sunbelt symbol, the Rust Belt emerged from, and eventually supplanted, previous vernacular regions in the early 1980s to become the primary regional label for the industrial cities on the American side of the Great Lakes basin. But the Rust Belt did not extend into Canada. North of the border the Golden Horseshoe and the industrial heartland of Canada could still be found. Why did these Canadian regions of the mind never metamorphose into the stigma of the Rust Belt? A different understanding of the North American recession originated, at least in part, from the relatively more favourable economic situation in Southern Ontario, one that allowed earlier notions of Canada's industrial heartland and the Golden Horseshoe to persist.

The Middle-Western Heartland

The Middle West has been a place where Americans imagined the essential characteristics of the nation resided, although where that place might actually be has shifted over time. The precise configuration of the Middle West has been elusive. As geographer James Shortridge details in a 1989 book, when the term first arose in the 1880s, it signified Kansas and Nebraska; it then had an exclusively pastoral connotation. Subsequently, the boundaries of this vernacular region expanded northward and eastward to include the northern plains and the Old Northwest, the states carved out of the territory between the Appalachians and the Mississippi River, north of the Ohio River and south of the Great Lakes. Shortridge explains the shift eastward as a consequence of the hard times of the 1930s: 'The disaster of the Dust Bowl was probably a factor in the original perceived migration of the cultural core of the Middle West eastward from the [stricken] plains.'[6]

The Middle West, as it made its journey eastward and northward across the continent, added an industrial dimension to its original pastoralism. Under the rubric of Industrial Midwest, the heavily industrialized states of Ohio, Indiana, Illinois, Michigan, and Wisconsin were simultaneously associated with, and differentiated from, the rest of the Middle West. This great industrial complex acted as the hub of the United States economy. Wallace Akin, writing in 1968, claims that the region's success derived from the optimism and hard work of its inhabitants. The industrial dimension of the Middle West drew from the same wellspring of images commonly associated with the breadbasket, with Chicago as the metropolitan capital of the Midwest, and Detroit as its industrial engine. The Motor City was, for Akin, where 'mass production and industrial technology have reached their highest development.'[7] A certain nostalgia about the post-war period of prosperity in the industrial Midwest permeated the scholarship of the 1980s. Photographer Michael Williamson and journalist Dale Maharidge began their 1985 *Journey to Nowhere* with a chapter entitled 'How It Was.'[8] The photographs and text revealed a golden age where the steel and auto industries symbolized American might and a time when industrial workers were honoured. Life was good for steeltowns such as Youngstown. Michael Moore similarly began *Roger and Me* with his own childhood remembrances of Flint, where 'every day was a good day.' Americans had grown accustomed by the early 1960s to seeing the Midwest as the dynamic heart of the industrial economy of the United States.

The heartland is another vernacular region whose boundaries and location have shifted over time. Though not entirely coterminus, the Middle West and the heartland were intimately tied together in the minds of Americans. This link can be seen in *MidAmerica*, a literary journal that has provided an important forum for exploration of the literary images of the region. Its editor, David D. Anderson, frequently has evoked the heartland in his own writings. He wrote in 1973 that just 'as the Midwest is for [Frederick Jackson] Turner the interaction of frontier, nation, and democratic philosophy in microcosm, it is also the American heartland, as demonstrated not only by its geographic position, but by its political and social reality and by the inevitability of its future.'[9] The association of heartland with the Midwest also surfaced in Lucien Stryck's 1975 poetry anthology, *Heartland II: Poets of the Midwest*.[10] Implicit in these images of heartland was the sense of a region's cultural, political, geographic, and economic centrality. The heartland has been presented as the centre of an authentic Middle America: the mythical heart of the nation.

Origins of the Rust Belt Label

In 1969, the industrial cities of the Great Lakes basin had a positive image. They were heartland. They were Midwest. But over the next fifteen years, the cumulative impact of plant shutdowns in the auto, rubber, and steel industries devastated the region, and transformed its prevailing image. By the 1980s the hard times evoked memories of, and allusions to, the Great Depression of the 1930s and it was increasingly used as a reference point for explaining industrial decline. One image of the economic crisis in the Dirty Thirties seemed to have particular salience in the early 1980s: the Dust Bowl. This image still had a powerful grip on the imagination of Americans thanks to John Steinbeck's classic, *The Grapes of Wrath*, the folk music of Woody Guthrie, the painting of Grant Wood, and the documentary photography of Arthur Rothstein, Walker Evans, and Dorothea Lange. Dust storms and the sight of desperate families moving west made an indelible impression on the popular imagination.

There was more than one dust bowl in the historical memory of North Americans, and more than one image which connected past and present distress.[11] These images are worth noting in detail because the symbolic legacy of the Dust Bowl influenced how Americans perceived industrial decline during the 1970s and 1980s. The Dust Bowl referred to a specific area of the southwestern United States particularly devastated by drought and depression. The *New Century Cyclopedia of Names* located that area between 'a line near the 100th meridian, on the E., and the Rocky Mountains, on the W. More particularly, it applies to the high plains of the Southwest.'[12] A mental image was thus superimposed onto a specific geographic area. Dictionaries increasingly provided both generic and capitalized versions that retained the historic and geographic associations of the term. The fifth edition of the *Columbia Encyclopedia* (1993) suggested that the Dust Bowl maintained its spatial association with the Southwest until government intervention and sustainable farming practices in the 1960s made the phenomenon 'a historical reference.'[13]

The Depression imprinted the symbolic cover, or composite image, of the Dust Bowl onto the popular imagination, such that whenever an agricultural crisis loomed, commentators were quick to warn of another dust bowl. As a result, North Americans were constantly being reminded of the term after the Second World War.[14] This recourse to Great Depression imagery led to the dislodging of the symbol from place, as it no longer necessarily referred to the southwestern United States. Amid the economic turmoil of 1979, North Americans were deluged with a wave of commentary about the Great Depression in general, and the Dust Bowl in particular, as the continent commemorated the fiftieth anniversary of the Stock Market Crash. Donald Worster wrote that the Dust Bowl was 'a place – a region whose borders are as inexact and shifting as a sand dune.'[15] Like the dust storms themselves, it was more of an experience than a precise place. Oral histories by Studs Terkel and Barry Broadfoot further ensured that most North Americans were well acquainted with the symbolic legacy of the Depression at the outset of the recession of 1980–3.[16] The persistence of the Dust Bowl region, even as its frontiers drifted across the imaginary landscape of North America, was one factor in the eventual creation of the Rust Belt, for it provided the play on words for one half of the name.

The other half was derived from a new vernacular region, the Sunbelt. The Sunbelt did more than provide part of the terminology for describing the decline of an industrial region no longer deemed worthy of such honorifics as Midwest and heartland; it also provided a foil to that region. During the 1970s, the supremacy of the Industrial Midwest was increasingly challenged by the ascendancy of the Sunbelt. Etymological dictionaries suggest that the term Sunbelt was coined by American

Selling out-of-town newspapers to unemployed Detroit residents at the corner
of Six Mile and Woodward, March 1981.

writer Kevin Phillips in 1969, patterned after the Bible Belt and Corn
Belt. The *Second Barnhart Dictionary of New English*, published in 1980,
indicated that the region stretched from Virginia to Southern California. A somewhat more precise location was given in the dictionary's
third edition, wherein it was identified as the southern tier of the
United States 'focused on Florida, Texas, Arizona, and California, and
extending as far north as Virginia.'[17]

The economic and cultural ascendency of the Sunbelt states casts a
shadow over the old industrial heartland of the United States. Southern
culture blossomed to such an extent during these years that historian
James Cobb proclaimed the 'Southernization of America' in 1982.[18] A
growing number of Americans tuned into country-and-western radio
stations, saw *Coal Miner's Daughter* and *Urban Cowboy* on the big screen,
and waited impatiently over the summer of 1980 to find out who shot
the Texas oilman J.R. Ewing.[19] Even though the stereotypical fan of
country-and-western music was, until the 1970s, the Southern redneck,

musicians such as Bobby Bare, whose song 'Detroit City' recounted how Southerners were drawn into the auto plants of the Motor City, held enormous appeal to blue-collar listeners in the North. As the image of the South and Southwest was reborn with the Sunbelt, country-and-western music's newfound respectability allowed it to go mainstream with a new generation of singers such as Kris Kristofferson, Willie Nelson, and Crystal Gale. Waxing eloquent over the brash upstart, print and electronic media were impressed by the region's rapid economic growth and remarkable sense of optimism. *The Nation* editorialized in December 1979 that the 'American future, it has been said, has picked up and moved to the burgeoning cities of the Sunbelt.'[20] Further evidence of the shift in the relationship between North and South could be seen in Bob Seger's 1982 album *The Distance*. His song 'Boomtown Blues,' about a homesick Michigonian forced to work in one of these rapidly growing Sunbelt cities, came full circle from Bobby Bare's 'Detroit City.'[21] The view from the South, on the other hand, did not dwell on things lost. In an opinion piece entitled 'The Divided States of America,' Bernard Weinstein, a paid Sunbelt lobbyist, credited the region's apparent success to its entrepreneurial spirit.[22]

The ascent of the area was synchronous with a reassessment of the industrial, urbanized region north of the Ohio River. Race riots, urban decline, environmental concerns, and a wave of plant shutdowns in the late 1970s and early 1980s produced intensely negative images that made the positive connotations of the Middle West and heartland labels anachronistic. In response, the Middle West began moving west to Nebraska and Kansas in people's minds. James Shortridge used the results from a 1980 questionnaire administered to students in thirty-two states to chart this westward shift in the cognitive map of the Middle West. When asked to locate its core 70 per cent of the respondents selected Kansas, Nebraska, Missouri, or Iowa.[23] The incompatibility of the hearth-like image of the Middle West and the negative images emanating from the industrial cities divorced the rural and industrial dimensions of the region in people's minds. Why would anyone 'want to lump Ohio and Nebraska in the same region?' asked Joel Garreau in 1981.[24] The imaginative boundaries of the heartland also drew away from the troubled industrial cities of the Great Lakes basin. The core of the heartland had shifted northwest to Minnesota and northern Wisconsin by the time John Borchert wrote *The Northern Heartland* in 1987.[25] The bond between rural and industrial dimensions of the Middle West and the heartland was severed by the end of the 1970s, and new, negative regional labels became attached to the industrial cities in the Great Lakes basin.

The Meaning of the Rust Belt

The life-cycle metaphor was central to the discourse in the early 1980s over industrial decline in the United States. The Industrial Midwest and the northeastern United States had, for Allan Ornstein, become 'aged America.'[26] *Time* magazine also explained industrial decline in terms of old age: 'Like an aging heavyweight gone to flab, US industry has fallen behind some of its world-class competitors,'[27] and 'probably will take it on the chin' from the booming Sunbelt powerhouse. Historians such as Jon C. Teaford adopted the life-cycle metaphor to explain the rise and fall of the *Cities of the Heartland*.[28] The frequent recourse to this metaphor by media commentators and scholars reflected the pervasive sense of the inevitability of industrial decline in the United States.

By 1979, the automobile, symbol of the American Dream, mass production, and conspicuous consumption, had come to symbolize what was wrong with the old industrial heartland. Detroit and the auto industry were represented as one by the national media. Crisis in the auto industry and the near-bankruptcy of the Chrysler Corporation in 1979 were also projected onto the image of the Motor City itself. The negative connotations attached to Detroit can be demonstrated by the shifting literary image of the city during the 1970s and 1980s. The shutdown of many of the city's automotive plants put tens of thousands out of work between 1979 and 1984. The social consequences were represented in a 1984 short story, 'The Empty House,' by Earl Shorris. The story is told from the perspective of a woman whose life is shattered when Chrysler lets her go. Alone in her home, the narrator sees a new meanness from her window: 'Houses crouch on the flat land, row after row, relieved only by the empty places where the fires are burned out and the rubble is bulldozed. There are few cars in the streets. There are no people walking, nothing moves except the dogs prowling inside the chain-linked fences.'[29] The climax is the sheriff's auction of the woman's home, which adds one more empty house to an already silent street.

Demolition of part of Chrysler's McGraw glass plant, Detroit, 1992.

Canada's foremost poet of the working class, Tom Wayman, also evoked the devastating impact of industrial decline on Detroit. Wayman wrote in 1983:

A Detroit poem has to have holes in it:
places where the words have been cleared out
by Housing and Urban Development
and a sparse white wooden fence
erected, that soon weathers into dirty grey

. . .

Larger themes have to be forgotten, too,
like the big factories on Jefferson
and elsewhere, standing empty
with as much damage done to their outsides
as can be humanly accomplished
and then ignored.[30]

Detroit had indeed fallen victim to what economists euphemistically called post-industrialism. If this city and its region could no longer be called the American heartland, what should they be called?

For the sake of symmetry, the mass media and academics searched for a symbolic northern counterpoise to the Sunbelt, settling on the Frostbelt and Snowbelt by 1977. These two new mental constructs ostensibly stretched from coast to coast in the northern tier of the United States. The *Second Barnhart Dictionary of New English* (1980) submitted that the two new vernacular regions were interchangeable and were referential to the Sunbelt. Ironically, the example cited in this dictionary for the Frostbelt was drawn from a highly critical 1978 *Harper's* magazine article that questioned the accuracy of the Frostbelt/Sunbelt analogy. Even though economists Barry Bluestone and Bennett Harrison adopted the antithesis between the Frostbelt and Sunbelt in their influential 1982 monograph *The Deindustrialization of America*, they warned that these large vernacular regions were not homogeneous entities.[31] The spatial boundaries of rise and decline, in their minds, were not co-terminant with one or the other. Hence, almost immediately, the symbolic covers of the Frostbelt and Snowbelt came under attack for their imprecision. The debate revealed the need for a more precise label to identify the part of the North that was being associated with industrial decline. The ambiguity of the Frostbelt and Snowbelt labels resulted in such awkward or geographically vague adaptations as industrial Frostbelt, traditional Midwest Industrial America, Smokestack America, and The Foundry.

The social construction of Smokestack America was an attempt to tie to place the industries of steel, rubber, and auto. The industrial smokestack symbolized heavy industry's pollution of the environment. Environmentalists used dramatic images of steel plants belching black smoke in their campaigns for stricter pollution standards. Environmental degradation became part of the emotional baggage carried by the industrial cities of the Great Lakes basin after Love Canal, the Cuyahoga River fire, the near-death experience of Lake Erie, and acid rain all

Beginning phase of Dodge Main's demolition, with the Chrysler sign still visible, January 1981.

blackened the reputation of the area. By the end of 1981 Smokestack America had almost completely supplanted the industrial heartland in the pages of *Time*. Janice Castor dryly observed in the magazine that the decline in America's smokestack industries was such a popular topic it was proving a boon for book publishers.[32]

The projection of the heavy industry image onto an entire region reached its apex in the coinage of the term The Foundry. In *The Nine Nations of North America*, newspaper editor Joel Garreau rewrote the map of the continent in favour of 'understandable concepts' that rely 'on a certain intuitive, subjective sense of the loyalties that unify it.'[33] Garreau's nine vernacular regions ignored the international border entirely: The Foundry encompassed all of the industrial communities of the Great Lakes basin. Symbolized by the industrial smokestack, this mental map lumped Southern Ontario and parts of Northern Ontario including Sudbury and Sault Ste Marie in with the Great Lakes states and the Northeast. The gritty industrial cities of the area evoked unpleasant associations in the minds of North Americans. Garreau wrote that their 'names mean one thing: heavy work with heavy machines. Hard work for those with jobs; hard times for those without.'[34] The reputation of the industrial region was being undermined by images of environmental degradation, brute labour, and most forcefully, industrial decline.

Depression talk in the United States escalated dramatically in 1982 as the economy fell deeper into recession. Twelve million Americans, 10.8 per cent of the national workforce, were without work by October 1982. The recession ravaged the Industrial Midwest, pushing official unemployment figures up to 17.2 per cent in Michigan and 14.2 per cent in Ohio.[35] In the depths of recession amid fears of a new depression, the American media began referring to the devastated Great Lakes states as the Rust Bowl, and a new vernacular region was born. The Dust Bowl had symbolized dust storms and abandoned farms in the southwestern plains; the emerging Rust Bowl became associated with rusting machinery, abandoned factories, the demolition of old mills, locked factory gates, and urban blight. The theme of abandonment permeated both mental constructs.

The social construction of the Rust Bowl can be seen in the business pages of *Time* magazine from 1980 to 1982, a period in which reporters grasped for a central idea, or symbolic cover, to encapsulate what they saw happening to the industrial cities of the Great Lakes basin. As early as May 1980, reporters described the devastated geographic area as a 'crescent encompassing the aging industrial cities tied to the auto in- dustry – Pittsburgh, Detroit and Chicago.'[36] The calamity had befallen an even larger spatial area in the mind of Christopher Byron: 'Stretch- ing across the nation's manufacturing heartland from the foothills of the Alleghenies, west to the Mississippi River and north to Michigan's Upper Peninsula, stands an idle army of jobless.'[37] The transformation of the industrial heartland from economic powerhouse to basket case was even more apparent in labour reporter Charles Alexander's obser- vation in December 1981 that 'with each passing day, the industrial landscape is increasingly marred by padlocked factory gates and smoke- less smokestacks.'[38] Few could deny that something had gone terribly wrong.

The deepening of the recession in late 1982, and the many compari- sons made to the Great Depression, gave *Time* journalists the symbolic cover they were searching for. In a December 1982 article aptly entitled 'Booms, Busts and Birth of a Rust Bowl,' Christopher Byron proclaimed the death of the region's economy. Battered by mass lay-offs and falling demand for metals, 'the once pulsing industrial belt that stretches from Illinois across to western New England took on the grim, ground-down demeanour of a half century earlier, acquiring the glumly descriptive epithet of Rust Bowl.'[39] The Rust Bowl struck a popular chord due to its historic association with abandonment and regional crisis. Expanding on its meaning in a subsequent article, Byron painted a very bleak picture indeed. 'Like mausoleums of a passing age,' he wrote 'they stand shuttered and empty. They are the padlocked steel mills of what has come to be known grimly as the American Rust Bowl, and from the rail sidings of East Chicago to the icy waterways of western New York State, they offer mute testimony of the industrial damage that has been done by the longest economic decline in half a century.[40] The Rust Bowl signified the apparent death, some would say due to old age, of the industrial heartland.

The associated images of rusting machinery, padlocked gates, and abandoned and demolished factories attracted the interest of documen- tary photographers in the United States. Photographic images of the remains of abandoned mills were common fare in popular magazines, in television news reports, and in monographs about deindustrialization. The 1988 *Historical Atlas of the United States* selected a photograph of a demolished blast furnace in Pittsburgh to illustrate the 'Postindustrial Revolution.'[41] In *Journey to Nowhere*, Michael Williamson and Dale Maharidge record the brutality of industrial decline. Chapter 2, 'The

Rust Bowl,' includes Williamson's haunting photographs of the dead hulks of abandoned steel mills in Youngstown – silent testimony to the physical and human devastation wrought by plant shutdowns. Photographs of the cathedral-like shell of the Brier Hill steel works, two ex-steelworkers sifting through the rubble of what once had been U.S. Steel's Ohio works, and the ghostly interior of a dead factory where time seems suspended, capture the death of the steel industry in that city. Historian James Guimond commented that almost 'every image' of the Rust Bowl in the book 'is an inversion of motifs from the 1940s and 1950s mass media': 'Instead of glistening production lines and glowing blast furnaces in Life's hymns to American "productivity," Williamson photographed the "dead hulk" of Youngstown Steel and Tube's Campbell Works, the ruined interior of the Brier Hill steel mill, and the wreckage of US Steel's Ohio works, which was dynamited and looked very similar to the ruins in Europe at the end of World War II.'[42] Maharidge's text contributes greatly to the powerful effect of this monograph. He quotes an unemployed steelworker, for example, who observed that the steel companies achieved, in the destruction of the city's steel plants, what Hitler had failed to do.[43] *Journey to Nowhere* documents this 'achievement' in the tradition of the hard times photographers of the Great Depression.

While photography captured moments in time, moving images recorded the process of industrial decline itself. To demonstrate the disastrous effects of disinvestment from the United States by multinational corporations, *Controlling Interest*, a 1978 documentary, showed abandoned American plants, broken windows, padlocked gates, and barbed wire. The 1984 film *The Business of America* superimposed the opening credits over the demolition of a U.S. Steel blast furnace to dramatic effect.[44] Other film-makers have recorded similar spectacles. In *Roger and Me*, Michael Moore showed a GM water tower at an auto plant fall slowly to the ground after being dynamited. Even Hollywood feature films, such as *All the Right Moves*, *The Deer Hunter*, and *Slapshot*, were set in dying industrial towns.[45] In *All the Right Moves* (1982), the film-maker focused on a youth's eventually successful efforts to escape a dying Pennsylvania steel town through high school football.[46] The demise of the steel industry also provided the backdrop for NBC's short-lived 1980 drama series *Skag*, about a middle-aged foreman at a steel mill in Pittsburgh.[47]

Meanwhile, popular musicians, politicized by the recession, exposed North Americans to the plight of millions of people in the Rust Bowl. In

Brier Hill Works, Blowing Engine House, 1981.

the depths of the recession, Bob Seger, Billy Joel, and Bruce Springsteen wrote songs that expressed the anger, disillusionment, and confusion felt by blue-collar workers who had lost their jobs. In 'Makin' Thunderbirds,' Bob Seger captured some of the anger felt by autoworkers in the early 1980s.[48] Billy Joel's 1982 popular song 'Allentown' dealt with disillusionment in a dying Pennsylvania industrial town.[49] The musician most closely associated with the Rust Bowl was Bruce Springsteen, who gained international acclaim in 1975 with his *Born to Run* album.[50] According to Bart Testa, a music reviewer for *Maclean's* magazine, Springsteen 'played to his working-class roots years after rock had become middle-class celebrity music.'[51] With his album *The River* (1980), Springsteen moved beyond his earlier emphasis on working-class rebelliousness and young love to explore the effects of the economic crisis on local communities.[52] This shift in emphasis was even clearer two years later in 'Johnny 99,' a song about a laid-off autoworker who turned to violence.[53] By the time that Springsteen's hit record *Born in the USA* appeared in 1984, the singer had become thoroughly associated with the cause of working people. In 'My Hometown,' Springsteen sang lamentfully about a father who is showing his eight-year-old son their hometown.[54] When the son grows to manhood, however, the town is dying. 'My Hometown' ended with the young man in turn showing his son the shut factories before the family migrated to find work. Springsteen's music of the dispossessed, written and performed during the recession, made him the modern-day equivalent of Woody Guthrie.

The upturn in the U.S. economy in 1983 made such comparisons to the Great Depression seem overwrought, and by the end of 1984 Rust Belt had supplanted Rust Bowl. The new expression had the advantage of being a counterpoise to the idea of the Sunbelt and a more accurate representation of the spatial distribution of heavy industry in a belt running from Chicago and Milwaukee in the west, to Buffalo and Pittsburgh in the east. The *Oxford Dictionary of New Words* (1991) credited U.S. Democratic Party presidential candidate Walter Mondale for the 'coinage of the term' in 1984.[55] It seems more likely, however, that Rust Belt had become commonplace long before Mondale's remarks.

The Rust Belt was defined by American dictionaries as stretching across the Great Lakes states and the Northeast. The association was strongest, however, with the steel-producing areas of the Great Lakes states. According to the 1993 edition of *The Columbia Encyclopedia*, the Rust Belt 'focused on the Midwestern ... states of Illinois, Indiana,

Michigan, and Ohio, as well as Pennsylvania.'[56] The *Oxford Dictionary of New Words* submitted that the term was: 'humorously formed by compounding: a belt or zone where once-profitable industry (in particular the metals industry) is left to rust away.'[57] Ohio writer R. Douglas Hurt allowed that 'by the last quarter of the twentieth century, Ohio was known more for being part of the "rust belt" than the corn belt.'[58] The making of the region in the minds of Americans produced a stigma that attached itself to the once mighty industrial heartland, hastening its decline.

Canada's Golden Horseshoe

Would Canada's industrial heartland be similarly stigmatized? What label would be attached to Ontario, in particular? Ontarians historically have been so convinced that their province was, to all intents and purposes, Canada itself that they have not devised many regional labels.[59] The national mythology spun by J.M.S. Careless, Donald Creighton, and others further ensured that Canada's image of Southern Ontario has usually been juxtaposed with hinterland areas rather than seen as an autonomous region. A booklet produced by Ontario's Department of Travel and Publicity in the early 1960s boasted that the province was the 'Heartland of Canada' and exalted in Ontario's proximity to the industrial heartland of the United States.[60] The completion of the St Lawrence Seaway in the mid-1950s had also reinforced this sense of centrality. *Seaway to the Heartland*, a documentary film produced by the National Film Board in 1975, depicted the seaway as the realization of an age-old desire to extend the water lifeline to the heart of the continent.[61] Ontario's sense of itself as Canada's heartland reflected not only the northward drift of an American regional construct, but also Canada's own tradition of conceptualizing its space in terms of metropolis and hinterland, core and periphery, and heartland and hinterland.[62]

Geographer L.D. McCann's classic *Heartland and Hinterland* explored the relationship between staples-producing hinterlands and the industrial heartland.[63] Canada's industrial heartland, located in the Quebec City–Windsor corridor, was integrated, McCann found, into an American heartland stretching from Wisconsin to the Atlantic Ocean and as far south as Kentucky. Canadian manufacturing activity was concentrated in 'a crescent around the western end of Lake Ontario' from

Oshawa to Niagara Falls, and 'a broad belt extending from Toronto to Windsor. These two zones comprise the Western Axis Manufacturing Area.'[64] Canada's heartland was, unlike America's, industrial from the start.[65]

Competing with the heartland as a positive vernacular region was the Golden Horseshoe. The latter term had been used since at least 1959, when a *Canadian Geographic* article identified it as 'a popular name given to the urban complex around the western end of Lake Ontario.'[66] Similarly, R. Douglas Francis saw it as a product of post–Second World War prosperity in the 'band of industrial sites' from Niagara Falls to Oshawa.[67] The construction of the Queen Elizabeth Way (QEW) in the 1930s was crucial in the making of the Golden Horseshoe according to John C. van Nostrand, for this superhighway generated an urbanized corridor from Toronto to Fort Erie on the Niagara River and provided access to the United States as well.[69]

Those who wished to challenge the dominance of the regional label tended to manipulate the Golden Horseshoe image rather than the heartland image. Growing public concern over the environment led the Nature Conservancy of Canada to warn in an April 1970 issue of *Maclean's* that rapid urban sprawl threatened to turn the Golden Horseshoe into the 'Asphalt Horseshoe.'[69] Geographer Maurice Yeates rejected the accuracy of the label in 1982 because the 'image it creates is that of a beautiful, well organized, and planned environment. If the word "golden" refers to anything, it is money, for the population within the region has the highest standard of living in the country. The word "golden" can hardly refer to the environment.'[70] The political left also attacked the positive connotations of the label. John Bachar and Wayne Roberts suggested in a 1981 article entitled 'The Unlucky Horseshoe' that life in Southern Ontario's Golden Horseshoe 'has turned to dross. The Midas touch that kept this area bustling with activity is working in reverse.'[71]

Despite these criticisms, the Golden Horseshoe continued to act as symbolic cover for the wealth and industry of Southern Ontario. A 1982 multimedia teaching kit for intermediate English as a second language students, 'Canada's Golden Horseshoe,' characterized the region as a wealthy industrialized area.[72] The authors of the kit explained that the area acquired its name 'because of its horseshoe shape and the rapid growth of its businesses and industries.' The continued popular identification with the Golden Horseshoe was reinforced as industry in Quebec declined, and the imaginative boundaries of the industrial heartland

Molten steel being poured from a giant ladle into 17-ton capacity moulds at the Steel Company of Canada in Hamilton, Ontario.

became even more closely tied to Southern Ontario. Canada's industrial heartland, according to geographer W.P. Anderson in 1987, had shifted from the lower St Lawrence to Ontario.[73] The decline of Montreal and the concomitant ascendancy of Toronto as Canada's first city in the late 1970s reinforced the heartland's association with Southern Ontario.[74] Though environmental concerns tarnished the Golden Horseshoe by the 1970s, they did not obscure this region entirely in the imagination of Canadians.

Would that still be the case if one of Ontario's post-1969 recessions had caused Canada's own Dust Bowl imagery to blow eastward from the Prairies, carrying with it the besmirching Rust Bowl analogy? Canadians, like Americans, knew their country had once had a dust bowl. Historians David Bercuson and J.L. Granatstein found that the idea of the Dust Bowl had been applied to Canada's three Prairie provinces during the 1930s.[75] The 1991 *Dictionary of Canadianisms on Historical Principles* located the Dust Bowl in a Dry Belt of low precipitation roughly bounded by Moose Jaw, Saskatchewan, and Medicine Hat, Alberta. The concept of a Dry Belt in Western Canada seems to have preceded the Great Depression by at least twenty-five years. Certainly, the area bore this epithet during the drought of 1917–26.[76]

Canada thus had its own Dust Bowl imagery available to attach to the Golden Horseshoe. There was some risk of this happening. Canadians – especially those urging more interventionist government – tended throughout the period from 1969 to 1984 to exaggerate the difficulties of their economy and society and to seek parallels with the rusting reputation of the erstwhile industrial heartland of the United States. The powerful influence of the United States on the Canadian imagination was demonstrated by the changing perception of the city. Contributors to the liberal journal *Canadian Forum* contested the relevance of the so-called urban crisis to the domestic situation after the debate spilled over from the United States in 1969.[77] However, the spectre of urban decline did compel the Canadian federal government to form the Task Force on Housing and Urban Development.[78] The diagnosis of urban decline may therefore have preceded the disease in Canada. When the debate turned away from the cities and towards industrial decline, Canadian attitudes parted ways with what was considered public knowledge south of the border.

This differing attitude was reflected in the word play used to describe the changes that were happening. Plant closing was the term of preference in the United States, whereas Canadians appear to have used shutdown much more frequently in the national print media. The nuances between the two may appear insignificant, but they reveal different mind sets. According to *Webster's Ninth New Collegiate Dictionary*, closing meant 'an act of closing: the condition of being closed,' whereas shutdown was defined as 'the cessation or suspension of an operation.'[79] The apparent natural predestination of the former contrasted sharply with the human action and sense of reversibility implicit in the latter.

There are remarkable differences in how industrial decline was explained to the public in Canadian and American magazines between 1969 and 1984. *Time* desperately hoped for a recession in 1979 to cool off the economy and fight inflation; contributors to *Maclean's*, its Canadian counterpart, consistently cast the impending recession in a negative light. The wave of plant shutdowns that struck Southern Ontario particularly hard in the first six months of 1980 was likewise interpreted differently. American journalists and economists conceded the inevitability, and frequently even the desirability, of the closures in sunset industries. Canadians, in contrast, blamed their shutdowns on American multinational corporations. Nationalism helped defuse the sense of crisis in Canada by giving people hope that the shutdowns were not part of the natural order but rather a foreign virus that could be suppressed without killing the host. A reading of *Maclean's* and *Canadian Forum* from 1969 to 1984 uncovers no instance where writers applied the Rust Bowl or Rust Belt analogies to Canada.

The confidence of Canada's heartland was, as in the United States, shaken by the economic challenge of another region. Alberta and the Western oil patch. Yet frosty Alberta was no Sunbelt. Canada's heartland, unlike that of the United States, had the political power to transfer resources from Alberta to itself through oil-pricing policies including the National Energy Policy. Raw political power was used to contain Alberta oil profits through parliamentary statutes. In sharp contrast, the Sunbelt transferred vast resources from the heartland of the United States, especially through defence spending. Consequently, the ascendancy of Alberta only haltingly challenged the centrality of Southern Ontario in the Canadian economy. For John Richards and Larry Pratt in their 1979 monograph *Prairie Capitalism*, the 'shift in power is not as far advanced in Canada as it is below the 49th parallel – the periphery does not become the centre overnight – but it certainly has begun.'[80] This shift was demonstrated by the relative decline of the central Canadian heartland and was borne out, to a certain extent, by patterns of migration at the height of the recession in 1980–1. A 1980 University of Windsor sociology team studying the effect of lay-offs on autoworkers discovered that while ex-autoworkers in Michigan headed for the Sunbelt, their Canadian counterparts headed to Alberta. The movement of capital and people to the West from Ontario proved short-lived, as the flow actually reversed itself by 1982.[81] Western Canada was unable to effectively challenge the industrial hegemony of Central Canada before 1984. As R. Douglas Francis wrote in 1993, Alberta and the other Prairie provinces have continued to be an economic hinterland to the central Canadian heartland. Anti-Americanism, the faltering rise of Canada's frostier sunbelt, and the relative health of Southern Ontario's economy staved off the corroding effects of the Rust Belt, as both a myth and a reality.

The paintings of Alma Duncan support the idea that industrial decline failed to take hold in Canada to the same degree as in the United States. Her series of industrial landscapes of Stelco's new Erie Works at Nanticoke, Ontario, in 1985 provide a startling counterpoint to Williamson's photographs of the dead steel mills on the other side of Lake Erie. Done in pastel on paper, Duncan's portraits communicate the still-impressive power of the steel mill. Glen Norcliffe observed that the Erie Works depicted in Duncan's 'Steam, Clouds and Blast Furnace' resemble a rocket-launching pad.[82] Duncan's decision to paint the newest steel mill in North America reflected a different mindset from the one that had brought Williamson to Youngstown a year earlier.

The literary images of the industrial cities of Ontario, though exceedingly rare, were also sympathetic. W.J. Keith's 1992 Ontario Historical Series monograph, *Literary Images of Ontario*, included only three pages dedicated to the industrial communities of the province.[83] The inclusion by Keith of David McFadden's observations about his hometown of Hamilton was a telling choice. Though McFadden recognized that Hamilton was 'not considered a great place to live,' he nonetheless wrote about the 'incredible beauty of steel mills, all the more beautiful because it wasn't intended to be and is not widely considered to be.'[84]

The visual images of abandoned steel mills and urban blight that signified industrial decline in the United States did not resonate in Canada, but the image of the padlocked factory gate certainly did. Canadian television reporters were often shown in front of locked factory gates for dramatic effect during the recession of the early 1980s. The 1980 NFB documentary film *Shutdown* focused vividly on a Canadian flag viewed through a chain link fence. The flag is lowered as local union activists outside the padlocked gate blame 'the Americans' for closing a branch plant in Sarnia.[85] A special issue on plant shutdowns in *Our Times*, an independent labour magazine, featured a photograph of a padlocked factory gate on its October 1984 front cover.[86] Canadian images of padlocked sites were clearly meant to energize, not enervate, and to complement the language of shutdown, not closing. The almost supernatural post-industrial landscapes of Youngstown reinforced the pervasive sense of irreversible decline in the United States; the locked gate and the shut down plant in Canada implied human agency and reversibility.

Although Canadians were affected by developments in the United States, they were able to distinguish between the projected images of industrial decline emanating from the United States and the more favourable situation in Canada. As a result the stigma of the Rust Belt did not attach itself fixedly to Southern Ontario, which continued to be associated with Canada's industrial heartland and Golden Horseshoe in the 1969–84 period.

Conclusion

Region and regionalism are mindsets rather than fixed realities in relation to the transformation of the prevailing image of the Great Lakes states – from the Midwestern industrial heartland to Rust Belt – in the period 1969–84. The same economic criteria that once made the Great Lakes states the industrial heartland eventually stigmatized the area with the Rust Bowl and Rust Belt labels. If the Dust Bowl symbolized the failure of rural society on the southwestern plains in the 1930s, the Rust Bowl signified the death of the Industrial Midwest fifty years later. The Rust Belt, which soon supplanted the Rust Bowl in the national media, more permanently signified regional decline in the United States.

The imaginative boundaries of the Rust Belt did not extend into Canada, though earlier images had entered Canadian consciousness. Industrial decline in Canada was not considered to be inevitable. The locked factory gate symbolized the dangers of direct foreign investment instead of regional abandonment. Canada's industrial heartland and the Golden Horseshoe continued to signify the wealth and industry of Southern Ontario, but they were not the only regional images of the area. In fact, Canadians' sense of regional identity has rarely been defined exclusively in economic terms. The recession of the 1980s, for example, did little to undermine Central Canada's association with regional political, social, and cultural power.

2 Transplanted Identities

'I heard about the closure on television on the six o'clock news. Then a couple of weeks later they phoned me up and said, "You got a thirty-five year pin that we have here. We'd like to give it to you." I said ok. He said, "Meet us at the front gate." You know, everything was closed, so the fellow, our superintendent at the time, he gave me the thirty-five year pin. You can picture a chain link fence; he handed it to me through the fence. "Here is your thirty-five year pin."'

Bricklayer, Lackawana, New York, 1998[1]

The cultural implications of deindustrialization surface repeatedly in the plant shutdown stories told by displaced industrial workers in Canada and the United States. In some cases, as in the above story told by a former steelworker from Buffalo, the sense of displacement was expressed by inverting the meaning of a familiar cultural symbol of loyalty and service. In others, workers experiencing joblessness for extended periods of time eventually came to identify with their displacement. All agreed, however, that the ordeal of having a plant go down was profoundly different from the layoffs, or down times, that have always been part of working-class life. Detroit foundry worker Diane Garner succinctly explained the distinction: 'When you're laid off ... [you think] "I'm going back to work." In plant closings, you don't have anything to go back to.'[2] Jim McHale, a tool-and-die maker, also from the Detroit area, said it was as though: 'You're in a little world. Then you leave that world.'[3] Having passed through the factory gate for the last time, many displaced workers waited months or years to re-enter another. Some never did.

This chapter examines the emotional impact of job loss on those industrial workers who never felt at home again in the mill or factory.

By examining the narrative paths blazed by 137 workers who endured job loss in the 1970s and 1980s, this chapter will chart a chronology of job loss: the factory as home and family; rumours running at a fever pitch; workers looking for signs of reassurance; the news brutally revealed; the shock of displacement and its aftermath.[4] The oral testimony of displaced workers in Canada and the United States does not diverge significantly until the workers begin to relate the aftermath of the plant closing announcement.

This chapter integrates multiple perspectives by including the voices of other narrators. How the past is remembered and by whom are questions that lie at the centre of the oral historian's work. In order to respond to lingering concerns about the representativeness and reliability of interviews, oral historians have begun to stress the subjectivity of each narrative – 'their truths,' as Studs Terkel once wrote. Although each story is unique, patterns of experience, shared meaning, and collective memories emerge.[5] Taken together, these stories represent a sad chapter in North America's economic and social history.

North Americans who lost their jobs to plant shutdowns had to adjust to an abrupt new reality. They did so, as always, in a variety of ways and with divergent results. Some workers, usually younger ones with much of their working lives ahead of them, found the transition to new jobs relatively easy. Sociologist Ruth Milkman has recently shown that former employees at a General Motors plant in Linden, New Jersey, did not share in the 'nostalgia' for the 'bygone glory days of industrial America.'[6] In fact, many of the workers she interviewed had even come to see deindustrialization in a 'positive light.' However, as Milkman is quick to add, her study group was composed of mainly younger employees in their thirties who had accepted a generous GM buy-out package in 1987 rather than continuing to work at the plant.

By contrast, *Industrial Sunset* records the plant shutdown stories of those who experienced involuntarily job loss. These men and women tended to be older workers with long service histories. Many of them did not find full-time remunerative work again. Unionized workers, mainly in the automotive sector, were also unable to put plant closings behind them. Because these workers had recall rights with their employers, their plants' closings did not immediately sever their employment relationship. However, in the depressed 1980s, these autoworkers had to endure often lengthy waits to be recalled to another assembly plant, sometimes in another city or state. The emotional loss that they continue to feel from this upheaval, even decades later, illustrates the devastating impact of plant closings.

Although most workers interviewed agreed that they lost money in a shutdown, long-time employees placed far greater emphasis on more intangible losses. It was as if they had lost 'something internal' or a piece of themselves. 'You get that worthless feeling,' sighed Ed Lawrenson of Windsor. Gabriel Solano of Detroit expressed his sense of loss in the profoundest possible terms: 'I lost part of me. Me as a person who said "I have a goal. I have a dream" ... To come home and say "I no longer have a job." The wife looks at you. You're looking at this baby. You're looking at this house and you're realizing that something is missing and it is a part of me. I don't so much feel that I was missing GM but I was missing a part of me. Something internal. It's hard to explain because it's an emotion. It's a feeling. Because it took all those years to build this emotion and this feeling and then it's not there. So you end up with a blank in your life.'[7]

Stunned by the suddenness of job loss, North American workers had their 'very self-concept ... shaken and stolen from them.'[8] The narratives that emerge from the interviews indicate that some workers' identities were redefined in distinctive ways. Whereas the emotional impact of job loss was great for workers on both sides of the border, the transplantation was more extreme and persisted longer in the plant shutdown stories told by displaced American workers. In fact, these Americans began to think of themselves as displaced persons or gypsies, moving across an abandoned industrial landscape of rusting monoliths and empty spaces.[9]

For many displaced American workers trapped inside the partitioned and emptied heartland, insecurity and uncertainty became the constant around which their identities coalesced. In identifying themselves as 'I-75 gypsies,' 'Flat Rockers,' or 'transplants,' interviewees revealed the often profound personal cost of industrial transformation. The anthropological concept of liminality proves invaluable in interpreting their stories. Originating in the work of Belgian folklorist Arnold Van Gennup in the early twentieth century, and reinvigorated by Victor Turner in the 1960s and 1970s, liminality refers to the passage between one world and another.[10] As applied to displaced industrial workers, it relates to the time a worker separated from his or her employment took to be reincorporated physically and emotionally into another workplace. Much like uprooted immigrants who crossed great distances and national frontiers to come to North America, displaced workers found their 'older roots were sundered, before the new were established.'[11] This liminal existence, as Victor Turner pointed out, can become a 'way of life' in itself rather than a mere transitional phase.[12] This attitude was demonstrated by displaced industrial workers such as Diane Garner and Gabriel Solano. Having seen the gates of the plant close on them before, they fully expected to go through the same experience again. To borrow a phrase from Oscar Handlin, these liminal people existed in an 'extreme situation.'

Home and Family on the Factory Floor

Soon-to-be empty spaces were once vibrant places where an intricate web of relationships had bound factory and home together. Memories of factory work tended to be framed around the metaphors of home and family. Working in the mill or factory was invariably described in interviews in familial terms: 'a home atmosphere,' 'a second home,' or 'a family affair.' After spending much of their adult lives working on the factory floor, blue-collar workers such as Ruby Kendrick, who worked at Al-Craft Manufacturing in Troy, a Detroit suburb, stressed their attachment to old work sites: 'We were like a family. We did a lot of things together. Just everything.'[13] This theme surfaced time and again during oral history interviews with working people in Canada and the United States.[14]

Heavy industry and mass production have often been described as dehumanizing and alienating. Iron and steel towns were so frequently compared to hell that it is hard to imagine how workers in these 'satanic mills' could equate factory with home and co-workers with family. Industrial smokestacks, once icons of prosperity, later images of pollution, towered over steeltowns along the Mahoning River in northeastern Ohio, where residents had to inhale smoke-filled air while their houses bore the black stains typical of mill towns.

Although visitors to industrial towns such as Youngstown might have noticed only the blemished houses, workers recall growing up in close-knit neighbourhoods where factories represented community institutions. Youngstown, which with a population of 140,000 was the largest city in the Mahoning Valley, emerged as the second-most important steel-making region in the United States, after Pittsburgh. Here, factory and home were closely intertwined, and the sight of these mills left an indelible impression. James C. Davis learned numbers as a child by 'counting the stacks' of the Brier Hill mill near his home.[15] Reverend Fred Williams grew up just down the river in the shadow of the Republic Steel plant in Niles, Ohio.[16] As long as he could remember, Williams

Youngstown Sheet and Tube's Campbell Works.

had seen 'the workers going back and forth to work in the morning.' When he joined the workforce himself, he became part of the fourth generation of steelworkers in his family. The symbiosis of the valley's social life with iron and steel over many generations made the industry a central reference point in the identities of residents.[17]

Until the 1950s, mills and factories were frequently located in and around residential areas. In Detroit, Marilyn McCormack fondly recalls how she used to visit her father at work in a small factory just around the corner from where they lived.[18] Jim McHale, also of Detroit, remembers how his father, a machine assembler at Burroughs Adding Machines, used to walk home every day for lunch and catch a ten-minute nap.[19] In Hamilton, the physical proximity of working-class neighbourhoods to mills and factories provided daily clues as to the nature of the products. David Christopherson's family lived so close to the Life Saver factory that he could tell what they were producing by the smell: 'It was either butterscotch or strawberries. You could smell it. Some days it was beautiful. Some days it was annoying. But it was part of [us].'[20] In this sense, something many people might have described as ugly, or a nuisance, could represent home.

Factory and mill work represented a way of life in many towns and cities across the industrial heartland. It was common for multiple family members to work in the same plant. John Livingstone, a Scottish immigrant to Canada, secured employment at True Temper in 1965 'through the influence of Father and Uncle Jimmy.' When asked whether many people were hired at True Temper's Hamilton plant through family connections, he replied, 'Ya, it was a family thing. You can say that you're in the family. There were a lot of my relatives in there at one time.'[21] Having followed his father and uncle into the plant, John subsequently got his three sons hired there as well. For a time there were three generations of Livingstone men working side by side at True Temper, a plant that employed only 109 people.

The same pattern was present, albeit on a much larger scale, in steel mills. When asked whether he had wanted to work in steel as a youth, one former Bethlehem steelworker responded matter-of-factly: 'My father worked there. His father worked there ... It was like your family. All my uncles worked there. All my relatives. All my friends. Everybody I knew. When you were from Lackawanna or Hamburg, the steel plant was the livelihood for the whole area.'[22] Family momentum, the lack of other jobs, and limited formal education restricted the choices available to young people. When young men, and

Youngstown community members wearing shirts promoting the city.

a growing number of women, chose to work at the mill, they frequently found themselves working among relatives and friends from
school and the neighbourhood.

This metaphorical bond between home and factory became a real one
when co-workers decided to marry. One of six children born to farming
parents, Dorothy Routenberg left home at age sixteen to start a new life
in the big city. After a short stint working in a Hamilton restaurant,
Dorothy was drawn into International Harvester's twine mill in 1946
by the good wages. Laughing, Dorothy recalled that the twine mill 'was
smelly, oily, hard work. And I told Bob Kerr, that was my foreman, I
says, "I am going to stay until one good pay and then I'm quitting."
Twenty-five years later I was still there.'[23] Dorothy's reminiscences
revealed a close-knit workplace composed overwhelmingly of women
working as spinners, cutters, and inspectors. Men worked as machinists and mill foremen. It was in her recollection 'a big happy family.'
Dorothy remembers the little things during her night shift such as the
coffee trolley that made its rounds of the factory floor at two a.m. It was

terrible coffee, but Dorothy remembers it fondly; it was during a coffee break that she met her second husband, Bernie.

The plant shutdown stories told by men and women had much in common, but there were some key differences. The memories of the working-class neighbourhoods of their youth had a strong gendered dimension. Ruby Kendrick, Diane Garner, Bernice Adams, and Marilyn McCormack all remembered Detroit neighbourhood matriarchs who protected children. Marilyn McCormack recalled a world where 'everybody knew everybody. Everybody watched everybody else's children.' All the children in her old neighbourhood used to play games under one street light: 'There was one lady, an elderly woman, that lived right by that street light, and everybody called her Grandma Kercha. She had no children we knew of and she lived by herself ... She was everybody's grandma.'[24] Diane Garner similarly recalls a world where 'I couldn't stand Miss Evelyn. She'd stand on the street and see everything that went on ... My mother could be away, if it started to get dark, we knew to get on the porch. Nobody had to tell us ... Everybody hated Miss Evelyn, but as I look back we need more people like that today.'[25]

Several women interviewed also faced discrimination in the workplace. Diane Garner got hired into Ford's Flat Rock, Michigan, foundry through an affirmative action program in July 1973. As one of the first women working in the foundry, Diane's male co-workers resented her at first. 'Some men felt that we had invaded their territory,' she recalled. One nasty incident in the cafeteria still stands out in her memory. After a male co-worker had been told to watch his language, he said 'these aren't women. If they were, they wouldn't be here.'[26] Remarkably similar stories were told by other women who crossed the frontier between the world of neighbourhood streets and front porches and the world of the factory floor. One Buffalo steelworker recounted with a laugh that she had a 'tough transition because the men didn't want us there at the time.'[27] Later, she found her male co-workers helpful, but they would sometimes 'stand back just to see what I would do under certain circumstances.' Years later, with the mill closed and demolished, she continues to attend meetings of the local retired steelworkers' chapter and to speak of her experience in the mill with pride.

By contrast, in their early memories male interviewees were much more closely identified with their fathers and with factory work. David Christopherson remembers his east end Hamilton neighbourhood as a homogeneous working-class area where most people worked in the

The assembly line at Inglis Appliance Factory in Toronto, Ontario.

steel industry. According to him, 'every street had a teacher or the cop. Some neighbourhoods were lucky enough to have *the* doctor or *the* lawyer, we didn't. It was very, very blue-collar. But by the same token, there wasn't any abject poverty nearby either. Very, very working-class in the very traditional sense of the word.'[28] Fathers loom large in these narratives. While he was growing up, Gabriel Solano's father – 'a steelworker for Great Lakes Steel. A union man. Put in his thirty years' – taught him two things: that he had to 'work for a living' and that 'nothing was given to you.' From the male perspective, and in spite of the growing number of white-collar workers and women in the workforce, these were areas where men went to work in hard hats and work boots.[29]

The narrative paths of interviewees also diverged between skilled tradespersons and unskilled assembly-line workers. Skilled workers not only missed people and place, but work as well. Basil Adili, a Hamilton foundry worker, took out his home-made coremaking tools during the course of the interview: a fifty-year-old pigskin mallet, patching tools, slicks, metal clamps, wood screws, and a vent wire.[30] Jim McHale also proudly displayed some of the dies that he had designed. Assembly-line workers, however, went to great lengths to avoid speaking of their work. When asked directly what they did in the plant, they dismissed the work as unimportant or 'the usual thing.'

In their stories, workers displayed an intimate knowledge of the inner geography of the factory floor. Every mill or factory had its own vernacular geography. Workers described directions within the Kelsey-Hayes factory in Windsor, for example, in terms of 'down the hill' or 'up the hill,' referring to the three-foot grade-level change between the old and new parts of the plant.[31] In his autobiography, Ben Hamper gave readers a tour of the General Motors assembly plant in Flint where he worked in the cab shop, known simply as 'the Jungle': 'It wasn't difficult to see how they had come up with the name for the place. Ropes, wires and assorted black rubber cables dropped down and entangled everything. Sparks shot out in all directions – bouncing in the aisles, flying into the rafters and even ricocheting off the natives' heads. The noise level was deafening.'[32]

Memories of work were often rooted in different combinations of sense perception. It is surprising how frequently interviewees recalled sounds, smells, and even tastes.[33] These sensations were often remembered more vividly than the sights in the mill or factory, even though 'what did the plant look like?' was often the point of departure for these recollections. In describing Detroit's Northland Plastics as a newcomer, Marilyn McCormack remembers it as 'just huge and noisy. Very noisy ... It was a plastics plant. And the stink. The smell was awful.'[34] David Christopherson similarly described working at True Temper in Hamilton as 'a *real* experience' because it was 'very loud.' He also recalled the pungent smell as he dipped shovels into a large molten vat of lead: 'You lifted them and, by hand, drove them into the molten lead. The only distance between your [asbestos] gloves ... and the molten lead was probably the better part of a foot of coals.'[35]

Working in the mill or factory also provided tangible benefits. Industrial cities such as Detroit and Hamilton were widely regarded as having the highest levels of home ownership in North America. Owning a house was one of the most powerful markers of workers' entry into the middle class. Willy Eugene Eady said with evident pride that, 'the house that I bought in Highland Park, Michigan, is the same house that I used to deliver the *Shopping News* newspaper to. I always dreamed as a young fellow that "one of these days when I get older I'm going to buy a big house like this over here." And the lord blessed me and I was able.'[37] Dorothy Routenberg derived a similar sense of achievement and satisfaction from owning a house in Hamilton.

I decided to buy a house. Don't ask me what on. I phoned this real estate guy and asked him about a house. He took me down and showed me this house on Superior Street. All I had was five dollars in my purse, going out to look at a house. I had nerve I'm telling you. I liked the house. And he said, 'How about a down-payment?' I said, 'Well, not tonight, we'll have to talk this over. I'll see about it.' I went into work the next day and I wanted that house but I thought, 'How can I get a house with five bucks?' My foreman then was Scotty Wilcox. So I went and talked to Scotty and I told him I had to have a house. He agreed with me. He knew everything about me and I never missed a day of work. He said, 'Go over and see the credit union.' I said, 'I got nothing in the credit union to buy a house.' He said, 'I'll give you time off of work. Go on.' I went over ... and talked to the guy. He said, 'You hardly have any money in here.' I said, 'I know but I want to buy a house.' So he told me, 'You got more nerve than anything I ever seen! Well, if you can get somebody to co-sign for you I'll give you the money for the house.' I [went] back over to see Scotty. Talked it over with Scotty. Scotty says, 'I'll tell you what I'll do. I'll sign for you. Where's the papers?' I had the papers all ready. I says, 'Here they are.' He says, 'Oh my god, you have nerve.' He signed them ... I never missed a day off of work. I worked in there and I got that house paid for ... 'Five buck house' I called it. That's all the money I had.[37]

Dorothy was justly proud of her home. Like the twine mill where she worked, her 'five buck house' signified security and rootedness. Dorothy's second home at work had begotten her first.

What does it mean to equate a mill or factory with home, and co-workers with family? Historian Lisa Fine has suggested that recourse to the family metaphor by industrial workers reflects the paternalism of their employers.[38] Though there is no disputing that paternalistic employers tried to instill such a hierarchical world-view, few large employers bothered to cast themselves in the role of the father figure by the 1970s. By then, the formalization of labour–management relations, combined with a growing number of corporate mergers and acquisitions, had further depersonalized the workplace. Indeed, the working people interviewed for this project usually placed management and the company outside the family unit. For example, when asked whether the sense of family dissipated at Dominion Forge in Windsor once labour–management relations took a sharp turn for the worse in the 1970s, Paul Hansen claimed they did not. For him, the workplace became 'a more solidified family because of the tactics of management.

They made the workers get tighter together.'[39] When questioned about the meaning of family, working people frequently pointed to the special bond among unionized workers.[40]

Home and family usually surfaced as metaphors for close-knit workplace relations. When industrial workers recalled past associational ties with co-workers and familial identification with mill and factory, they did so from the perspective of a sometimes-lonely present. The mill evoked a familiar atmosphere where displaced workers had once felt secure and rooted. Workers rarely invoked community explicitly; they preferred to use more intimate family metaphors. In all, workers' familial identification with mill and factory is an evocative symbol of their solidarity, and their strong attachment to place and identification with others was grounded in spatial relationships. As one Lackawanna steelworker said, everyone working in a steel mill 'had something in common. We had steel in our blood, that's what it was ... The people made that steel plant, not the steel companies.'[41]

When Canadians employed in large and small plants summoned up the metaphors of family and home, they also identified themselves as Canadians against their mainly American employers. Ed Lawrenson recalled that when it came time to negotiate a collective agreement at Bendix Automotive in Windsor, the union dealt 'with the Canadians on the little stuff.' But when it came down to 'the crunch' the 'guys from the States' appeared on the scene.[42] Lawrenson claimed that on more than one occasion, U.S. companies operating in Windsor threatened to 'pull out' and 'go to the States' unless Canadian workers agreed to their final offers. Other interviewees chose to emphasize the differences between Canadians and Americans. 'We're not the same people,' summed up Floyd Harris.[43] Whether interviewees extended familial metaphors to encompass a class community bounded by the plant or by the nation, their choice of language underlined the full import of job loss.

There are few more important touchstones in North America today than home and family. In an increasingly secular, market-driven society, family has come to signify an oasis of security, belonging, and rootedness, and a source of refuge and defence.[44] These are the same notions projected by displaced workers onto their old workplaces. These idealized plant families bear little resemblance to their actual co-workers, but they are no less real in the minds of the men and women interviewed. It is clear from their plant shutdown stories that many of those displaced became less at home in the world around them once their mill or factory closed.

Where people work and where they live are generally separate spheres. Yet these oral narratives suggest that the two were physically and psychologically interconnected. Like the church and the tavern, the factory represented a communal institution, a world that grew more complex as generation after generation of family members entered the factory gates.[45] Industrial workers developed strong attachments to co-workers and identified with mill and factory.[46] In their narratives, plants were filled with the sounds, smells, and sights of work – the very antithesis of empty spaces. Industrial workers recall a rich social world on the factory floor. When Canadian workers such as Dorothy Routenberg, Basil Adili, and John Livingstone introduced group photographs or seniority lists into the conversation, they did so in order to tell stories of others. Their plant shutdown stories were not theirs alone but stories of collective belonging and eventual collective displacement.

Reading the Writing on the Factory Wall

As their sense of security began to erode, North American workers sought signs of job security in their physical surroundings. Not being privy to the intentions of top management, workers attempted to anticipate job loss. On the factory floor, they weighed and considered rumours of mill or factory closings: a new piece of expensive equipment or an addition to the factory building was assumed to be concrete evidence that the company intended to continue operating the plant for the foreseeable future. If the company failed to modernize, something quite common in the aging industrial heartland, workers worried that closure rumours might be true. Every worker understood, as did Windsor tool-and-die maker Peter Wirth, that when production drops 'there is a reason for it.'[47] Workers also found significance in overtime and new hiring on the one hand, and the frequency and duration of layoffs on the other. With one eye on their work and the other on their surroundings, they tried to divine the intentions of management.[48]

Factory shutdown was frequently foreshadowed in the interviews by observations of the plant's advancing age. One of the most memorable descriptions of an obsolete factory was provided by Ed Lawrenson, who worked at the Bendix Automotive plant on Argyle Street in Windsor's old industrial belt. According to him, 'it was an old plant ... part of the plant was originally stables for Hiram Walker's animals. There was huge oak beams, solid white oak beams ... In the cement floors you could see the urinal troughs where they ... had cemented it in.'[49]

Several scholars have recently expressed incredulity that displaced workers failed to foresee the closure of their plants.[50] In theory, at least, there should have been less surprise. The signs of obsolescence had been all around them. Aging equipment, for example, made it nearly impossible for Mahoning Valley mills to compete. It is hard to imagine a more tenuous situation than the one described by Frank Farizo, who recalled these old plants as kept together 'with baling wire and masking tape.'[51] Mechanical breakdowns had become commonplace. The stress of it all made George Richardson sick with worry:

> Well, right off you could see that they were not maintaining the mill, they were not maintaining the machinery ... they were not maintaining the cranes. At that time, I was scheduling the operation of twelve open hearths ... I would break my neck every day I put on a big schedule for the twelve furnaces what I wanted ... And I would break my neck, to make my next heat up and I'd come out the next morning. Well, 'we have a breakdown in the bloom mill, they couldn't roll the steel.' They were down for eight hours; maybe a pit crane was down for four hours and that slowed up production. And here's my schedule all up in the air. I had to do it all over again. And that went on, day after day after day. That's what forced me out – I retired at 60 ... It got so bad I spent more time going up and down stairs to the john every day with an upset stomach. Just trying to make things work and everything was broken down. If you got one mill satisfied for their steel for the next week's rolling, it would break down. It got so bad that finally I said to my wife, 'I got cancer, there's something wrong with me, I think I got cancer in my stomach.'[52]

It was the stress of the job that had made George Richardson sick. His feverish attempts to keep the mill alive reflected the high personal stakes invested in the mill, and made the deep shock workers experienced in the wave of plant shutdowns all the more incomprehensible. As industrial workers tried to divine the intentions of top management by reading their surroundings, all the signs in Youngstown, at least, pointed towards an end to steel-making in the Mahoning Valley.

Yet in the dark days of the 1970s and early 1980s, physical signs of job security, sufficient to notify workers of trouble in good times, often failed them. Many workers drew the wrong conclusion from the appearance of new equipment and machinery, not anticipating how much financial incentive existed for management to abandon older facilities and costly long-service employees. Nor could workers know which managers were controlling decisions. Conveying his surprise about the closing of his Hamilton plant, Basil Adili remembered: 'We couldn't believe it. How can that be? They just spent three-quarters of a million dollars on an overhead crane for the furnace that spring, and February they were shutting down ... They thought, "How can this be? We're busy. We're negotiating. How can this possibly be?" But some guy in the corporate office says, "The foundry has got to go." Whether he was newly appointed ... we don't know who the heck put the finger on the foundry division. There was no sign, "For Sale," they just crossed it. I don't understand the reason.'[53] Similarly, in Buffalo, employees of Republic Steel pointed to a brand-new basic oxygen furnace when recalling their disbelief that their plant would soon close.[54] Workers on both sides of the border were unprepared for the psychological costs of job losses that had come as a surprise to many, who were used to reading the industrial landscape for signs of job insecurity.

Rumours of plant closures reached a fever pitch by the mid-1970s, with almost daily threats to the fragile hold working people in the industrial heartland had on middle-class status. Ironically, longstanding rumours of layoffs and closures fostered a sense of invulnerability among long-service employees who had heard it all before. Yet workers were 'shocked as hell,' even at plants like Continental Can in Hamilton where they had 'talked' about closure for years.[55] Evidently, the longer employees had worked in the plant, the less willing they became to entertain the idea of its closure.

Denial was well-nigh universal in Youngstown. Despite the ominous signs in the mid–1970s that the steel mills of the Mahoning Valley were going down, most workers continued to believe otherwise. As an employee at the mammoth Campbell Works, Johnny Holmes, noted, rumours had circulated for twenty years, 'ever since I'd been in the mills.' In practice, Holmes shared the attitudes of many of his co-workers: 'I'll believe it when I see it.'[56] Disbelief was general. Youngstown steelworker Francis McHugh recalled the blank expressions on everybody's face during the final shift: 'It was devastating, without a doubt. You were so close to the people, you just get engulfed in it and when it happened to Campbell, you thought it was down the road a ways. When you saw the last heat blow out and saw the last ingot roll and then you see the blank expression on these people's faces. Well, it happened, how the hell ... It's like facing death. You know it's coming, you know it is going to happen, and when it happens, it is almost like a relief.'[57] Even at the height of the wave of shutdowns that struck Southern Ontario, workers responded in disbelief. David Christopherson recalled that the closing of auto parts maker Allen Industries in Hamilton in 1983 'just blew us away' despite the signs around them: 'Rumours floating around for the longest time, people trying to decipher what's in crates and invoices that are coming in; strange people walking through the plant looking very worried or very decisive or very analytical and they weren't just studying for the usual reasons ... It was [all done] under a cloak of secrecy. The rumour mill was churning,'[58] yet nobody quite believed the calamity would actually happen.

Unionization could make hitherto idle threats appallingly real. The danger lurking at Al-Craft Manufacturing came to the attention of Ruby Kendrick when the company president threatened to close the Detroit-area plant after employees voted in 1967 to unionize. Although the owner cited 'economic reasons' for his decision to relocate production to Hialeah, Florida, in 1970, Kendrick remains convinced that he had it in for the union: 'I didn't believe [his threat]. I didn't believe it. And as things progressed, I didn't think that was going to happen because after ... two years, three years, I thought he was full of baloney. But he did do it. And when he did it, he told us, "It took a little bit longer but I did it."'[59] Many other companies closed plants because they wanted to rid themselves of unionized employees.

Some companies shamelessly fed the rumour mill. In public they vehemently denied any intention of shutting down a factory; in the plant itself, they threatened to do exactly that. When Great White Electric suddenly announced the closing of its Detroit factory in May 1987, the employees initially dismissed this announcement as yet another company threat. According to electrical worker Bernice Adams, 'You [heard] it every three years [so] you think "well let them go." But, then, it changes when they actually are going.'[60]

The News Revealed

On 'Black Monday,' 19 September 1977, 5,000 Youngstown Sheet and Tube employees came to the realization that the Campbell Works would close. When company officials met with local politicians the morning of the announcement, John Palermo, a Mahoning County commissioner, claimed that nobody knew why they had been summoned: 'Some had

The last shift at Inglis, 1989.

ideas, possibly, there may be a cutback announcement, possibly, of some standards, [Environmental Protection Agency] rules, regulations.'[61] The closing stunned those in attendance. 'I don't think the impact was really felt until a few minutes later, until you really heard or digested what was said,' Palermo explained. Michael Katula, a Campbell town councillor later recalled: 'One trouble with those of us that live in this area, we have lived in a dream world, a dream world that the Sheet and Tube is always going to be there. We don't have to worry about anything. "Those mills are never going to shut down." Who could comprehend the shutdown of such a great complex? And if we were told two years ahead of time ... There were – I never heard them myself, personally, from any official but I heard it through rumor, through discussions of steelworkers and so on – a possibility of the mills shutting down in the future, but as I said, who would have believed it anyway? Nobody would have taken steps to try to prevent it.'[62] Residents of the Steel Valley could hardly believe that the dam had burst.

This highly charged emotional experience bound workers together creating what almost everybody conceded was a 'collective catastrophe.' Workers' perceptions were later described in their oral narratives through the recurring metaphor of the flood, mirroring the enormity of the situation and its disastrous consequences. Steelworker staffer Marvin Weinstock said, 'It sort of makes me think of Bangladesh in the flood. It just felt like people were dying. All of their hopes were dying ... Nobody really knew where to turn. They were looking for answers and nobody really could come up with an answer ... It was a very traumatic experience and heart-rending. It hurt me not to be able to say there's a way we could do something.'[63] Had the Mahoning River actually overflowed its banks, inundating the valley, disaster relief would have been rushed into the area. But there was no national rescue for those uprooted by the metaphorical flood of the plant closure.

Following the closing of the Campbell works, the story of rumours, disbelief, and shock repeated itself in the Brier Hill works in 1979, U.S. Steel's Ohio and McDonald works in 1980, and Republic Steel's Youngstown facility in 1985. *Warren Tribune*'s Gregg Garland reported disbelief and anger in the steelworker bars on Steel Street when news of the closing of the Ohio and McDonald Works came down. '"It's like finding out you're going to die on a certain date,"' one steelworker told him. '"When that day comes, it doesn't make it easier to accept."'[64] The closing of a mill or factory, though not always unexpected, nonetheless delivered a devastating emotional blow to longservice employees.

Exacerbating matters further, the suddenness of job loss gave workers little time to adjust. Employees with decades in the plant found themselves displaced in a matter of minutes, hours, or days. The rapidity with which companies disposed of employees sometimes verged on cruelty. At age 62, Youngstown Sheet and Tube veteran George Chornock heard on a Monday that his plant would close that Thursday.[65] The Detroit Manufacturing Steel Supply Company abruptly ended operations after fifty years of continuous operation by having the manager distribute final cheques one hour before quitting time.[66] Meanwhile, in nearby Pontiac, employees of Seamen Manufacturing arrived at work in February 1979 to find the gates padlocked, the plant equipment already moving down Interstate 75 to Indiana. Across the St Clair River in Windsor, Ed Lawrenson recalled that the end came just as suddenly at Bendix Automotive: 'I thought: "Oh man, there's something up here." And sure as shootin' they says, "As of nine o'clock the people in the plant are being told that the plant is closing. They've got

15 minutes to clear their stuff out – any personal items – and the place is being closed." That's it. [Hand movement underlining the finality of the decision] ... It was panicsville.'[67] After decades in a plant, employees were curtly told to clear out their personal belongings. Former employees resented the rapidity of it all, comparing it to the sneak attack at Pearl Harbor in 1941. Yet these workers at least heard the word in person. Others had to read it on a bulletin board.

More confrontationally, firms notified their unionized employees of an imminent plant closing across the bargaining table during the collective agreement negotiations. Seeking retirement, the owner of the small Detroit-area electrical plant where Bernice Adams worked unexpectedly withdrew his investment. Notified at the bargaining table, Bernice had the unpleasant task of informing her co-workers that the plant would close on 15 May 1987.[68] Caught in a similar situation, Bill Scandlon, a staff person for the United Steelworkers of America in Hamilton, did what he could to soften the blow. He remembered when International Harvester's twine mill went down in 1970: 'When it was going to happen they let me know the decision was made in Chicago. They told me so I could prepare them. "How do you want to handle this?," they said. And I said, "Well, I guess the only thing to do is to tell them right up front." But, automatically they will be [saying] "What about my pensions, benefits, so on and so forth." So let's talk about that. They prepared something, a handout for me. I then brought the president in [who] was a very good guy ... He understood. It was a sign of the times. He wasn't going to fold up and cry.'[69] Dorothy Routenberg was one person who lost her job when the twine mill closed. Just six weeks shy of qualifying for early retirement, Dorothy had to start again elsewhere.

When they informed their employees of plant closings and job loss, many companies followed the pattern of Youngstown Sheet and Tube, where union officials and community leaders were brought to corporate headquarters to hear a short statement from the company. The Steel Company of Canada, without a word of explanation, herded almost three hundred Hamilton steelworkers onto buses destined for an undisclosed location. Finding themselves at the botanical gardens, they were then told that the Canada Works, a small finishing mill, would close.[70] Apparently, company officials hoped that the peaceful green surroundings would calm their employees. Instead, the stratagem added insult to injury.

The Shock of Displacement

With so many plants closing in the industrial heartland, many families had to contend with more than one job loss. In Windsor, Paul Hansen saw his own plant close in 1990, and his wife, son, eldest daughter, and brother-in-law also lost their jobs in separate plant closings. 'It hit home,' Paul poignantly observed.[71] To make matters worse, it was the early 1980s, and jobs were scarce at the height of the recession. As Ed Lawrenson recollected: 'There was no other work out there, man. There was nothing. Everything was falling apart. Places were closing up left and right.'[72]

In part because of the treatment they received, displaced workers protested the unfairness of the closings. Ralph Brubaker went through two plant closings: a Detroit Chrysler missile plant that relocated to the southern United States in the 1950s, and Sahlin Engineering of Clawson, Michigan, on 2 November 1972.[73] He recollected: 'I always felt I did my best. I always felt I did a good job. Being put out is hard to take. It's like saying "we used you, good bye. You're nothing to us. You don't mean nothing. We're in business, we're not in the good guy stuff. You're gone" ... You feel you don't have to worry and all of a sudden it is taken away from you. I didn't treat them that way. I wasn't the kind of guy that took time off. I was the kind of guy who came to work on time. When I was there I did my job. In fact, I always felt I did a little extra.'[74] Like many workers, Ralph felt that his loyalty to the company had not been reciprocated. He clearly had expected more respect. A similar story unfolded at the Ford Motor Company when it moved the production of engine blocks across the St Clair River to a much older facility in Windsor in December 1981. Diane Garner noted that everybody appeared to be walking around in a daze, wondering 'What do I do? What do I do?'[75] Being a divorced single mother, Diane had to break the news to her three dependent children. 'I always let my kids know how things were. I told them my plant was going to close and I would be laid off. "There's certain things we can't do. Certain things you can't have because I won't have the money that I had before." And they understood.'

Many interviewees recall moments of personal protest. Jim McHale, an employee of W.H. Chase in downtown Detroit, was asked to pick up his severance pay. 'The lady that was the secretary called me up to get that big cheque and I actually said to her "instead of this cheque I would rather have my job." But I knew it was futile to say that, but I wanted to.'[76] These small acts of defiance included letter writing. Personal letters mailed to Ohio governor James Rhodes and Michigan governor Peter Milliken during the 1970s provide an interesting counterpoint to the remembered experience of displacement recorded in oral history interviews.[77] In notes and letters ringing with emotion, workers revealed their fears about the future: non-existent job prospects, troubles paying off the mortgage, mental depression, fear of having to uproot their families in search of work out of state.

Having spent much of their lives in the closed plant, older workers naturally felt the loss of their jobs most deeply. They also found that few other employers were willing to hire them. As a result, many displaced workers in their late forties or fifties could not find work. One unemployed Detroit resident with over sixteen years of service wrote to the governor of Michigan, 'I am a very old man at 49, or so it seems.'[78] Faced with a similar situation at the age of fifty-five, Raymond J. Boza of nearby Harper Woods figured he was 'too young to retire and too old to get another job.'[79] Speaking for many of these older workers, one displaced Michigan worker looked back on thirty-five years of service and said, 'Now I have nothing.'[80]

The wives of displaced workers penned almost half of the letters to the two governors. In heartbreaking letters, these women revealed the devastating effect of job loss on their husbands and families. One woman wrote that the closure constituted 'Fraud on the working man ... I feel my husband has been cheated out of his pension. Words cannot explain the feeling I have to see [my] dear husband come from a meeting and say "Plant Closing moving to Tenn[essee]. Briggs Manufacturing." Had worked 32 years faithfully steady employe dedicated to his job. Could describe him man of the year. He has been everything a husband & father [should be]. Waited for the time when he will retire & now all dreams are gone.'[81] The author of this letter was telling both her husband and the governor that job loss was not her husband's fault. Her conviction that both her husband and her family had been betrayed was shared by many. One woman told the governor of Ohio that her fifty-six-year-old husband, married son, and twin daughters all now faced unemployment. Others drew the connection between the poor treatment of an older generation of workers and the rebelliousness of a younger generation of Americans: 'These men are all in their late 40's and 50's. Too old to even think of getting another job ... No wonder the young people of today have no pride in doing a good job for any business or company, when they see what is happening to their fathers and mothers after they have worked faithfully and with pride for so many years for one company.'[82] Repeating a familiar response to bad times, women looked for relief when men were without jobs. In adopting this traditional feminine voice, the wives of displaced workers hoped to prompt the government to intervene, yet they also readied themselves to be disappointed. These letters were modest and personal and unfortunately their misgivings were in large part realized.

Although the governors of Michigan and Ohio determined the tone and content of standard responses, they did not have the time to read incoming correspondence. In 1975, for example, nearly 68,000 citizens wrote to the governor of Michigan on a variety of issues.[83] In this pre-computer era, Michigan's correspondence unit was equipped with five electric typewriters to rap out form letters that would then be fed into a signature machine. To be sure, the governor received regular tallies of the number of letters received for or against specific issues. Of the huge volume of letters received and dutifully deposited in state archives, remarkably few dealt with plant shutdowns and displacement. A search uncovered only fifty-nine such letters, hardly enough to influence the direction of public policy. The responses sent out by the state in the governor's name were worded in soothing tones designed not to ruffle feathers.

Was it any more useful to appeal to corporate management? Some workers hoped so. In Detroit, the displaced employees of the Federal Mogul Corporation sent management an anonymous letter: 'Have either of you two gentlemen walked through the two plants and spoken to any of your employees? Why not take this walk and judge for yourselves, what your decision to close those two shops is doing to over 2000 of your fellow men. There are men with families who are in their 50's with over 20 years of seniority who stand to lose everything. They will receive not one cent of severance pay or Pension. Put yourself in their shoes. How would you feel?'[84] The unnamed authors of this letter framed their appeal for compassion by calling on managers to identify with the plight of hourly employees. The real problem, in their minds, was that managers did not understand the lives of ordinary employees.

None of the letters from workers in the United States were as explicit as one sent by a long-service employee with Wheel Trueing in Windsor:

> Having been an employee of Wheel Trueing Tool Co for the last thirty-three years my fellow co[mpany] workers and I cannot understand the

Closed Cadillac plant, Detroit, 1992.

thinking of closing the Windsor plant. Here you have had workers that were proud to work for W.T.T. Co. Most of us [have] 25 to 43 yrs service. We were not even asked to take concessions to better or save this plant. This to us shows you have no feeling for humanity, to the point, workers under you mean nothing. Just like Detroit you have put a lot of people, families & children through a lot of anxiety and misery through no fault of their own, only your ambition to make yourself look good in somebody else's eyes. I hope and pray these eyes will put you through the pain someday. The original men that started W.T.T. Co had in their minds to have good honest and sincere workers for a good living and retire in dignity. You have taken this away. Thanks for nothing.[85]

Clearly, the writer is too angry to feign a tone of patience, politeness, and deference. Instead, the letter is explicit in its condemnation of greedy owners who have 'no feelings for humanity' and the effect of their actions on 'good honest and sincere workers.'

Oral narratives of work on final shifts lingered on feelings of silence and emptiness. Most distressing was the silencing of the familiar every-day clatter of the shop floor that had surrounded workers for much of their adult lives. At some plants, in what Dan McCarthy describes as 'slow death closings,' layoffs gradually reduced the workforce until no one was left.[86] At Al-Craft Manufacturing in Detroit, Ruby Kendrick recalled, 'It was very depressing, very depressing' to see old friends leave one by one until the plant closed completely on 1 June 1970.[87] Across town at W.H. Chase, Jim McHale looked up from his tool-and-die grinder one day to find he was alone: 'It seemed it was like a ghost building.'[88] The mill and factory, once enlivened by co-workers at work and play, had been emptied.

The Aftermaths of Displacement

As suggested above, until they address the issue of the aftermath of plant shutdowns, the Canadian and American oral history narratives show few differences. Thereafter, they diverge dramatically. In the United States, familiar lines dissolved and old categories of gender, race, and class collapsed in the wake of major mill and factory closings. The disruption of the social boundaries that had long demarcated people's place in the world left local residents disoriented. In one industrial town after another, 'people who once stood at the centre of things now seem[ed] out of place.'[89] Autoworkers in Kenosha found themselves displaced to the periphery as civic leaders helped transform the industrial city into a post-industrial playground of marinas and cappuccino bars. A similar redefinition of place occurred in Barberton, Ohio, where the Labour Day parade, once a celebration of organized labour in the town's rubber industry, became the Mayor's Autumn Festival shortly after the plants closed down.[90]

By all accounts, the Rust Belt became a sweeping metaphor enclosing and structuring debate on deindustrialization in the United States. As Michel Foucault has argued, human societies spatially confine their problems.[91] In the last quarter of the twentieth century, industrial decline was one problem that apparently needed containment. Given the context of the accelerating shift in industrial production from the North to the South, and the emergence of the Rust Belt label, the metaphor of emptiness proved central to the self-concept of displaced workers in the United States.

In the ailing Steel Valley of northeast Ohio, the clean-up crews removing equipment from now-silent buildings completed the transformation of the lively mill, once bustling with activity, to a dead one. John

Barbero, one of twenty open-hearth workers asked to mothball and ship out tools from Youngstown's Ohio Works, found that the mill was no longer the same place he had worked for so many years. With the intense heat of the furnaces gone, Barbero's team had to burn benches in order to keep warm: 'The first day back after the last steel was tapped was a shock. Our normally clean locker washroom resembled a garbage landfill. Looters had come in over the weekend and had taken everything that was useful. Everything else ... was strewn about in one hellish mess.' The parallels in John's narrative between the emptying of the plant and the emptying of his own emotional ties to that place were striking. Like the looters, the company owners had stripped the plant and taken away their jobs. To John, both actions amounted to theft. The resulting physical mess had an emotional equivalent. The record of working lives in the mill was systematically erased, and culminated in one final violation. On the last day, after having picked clean the skeletal ruins of the open hearths, a task that reminded him of his days in Hiroshima after that city had been devastated by the atomic bomb, John was asked to obliterate the last remnants of the record of work and labour in the mill by generations of Mahoning Valley steelworkers: 'The last day I burned all the production records – "100,000,000 tons by 1970" – and the attendance and work records of the thousands of people who worked here for over 70 years. We have become non-persons.'[92]

Stripped of their identities, displaced steelworkers like John Barbero feared they were about to become 'the gypsies of the next ten years.'[93] In the wake of mill and factory closings, especially in single-industry towns, workers were separated both from their work and from their working-class communities. Gone were the days when the male breadwinner could provide for his family. Gone, too, was the comforting notion that if people worked hard and did what they were told, they could reasonably expect to retire after thirty years. Like the displaced persons uprooted by the Second World War, these workers became economic refugees within their own country. The heartland had been reduced to 'a region of thwarted dreams – a place where plants shut down and businesses surrender to the economy's structural changes.'[94] This cultural crossing took a tangible form when Youngstown Sheet and Tube workers tossed their hard hats into the Mahoning River as they left the plant for the last time. The fears and anxieties engendered by industrial decline became imaginatively tied to the industrial heartland, turning it into rust and turning displaced workers into metaphorical gypsies, as well as real-life migrant workers.[95]

Given the emotional attachment that working people, especially those with long service, had developed to their mill or factory, it was not surprising that many of those interviewed kept mementoes of their lives working in the plant. Sam Donnorumo got permission to take a slagger shovel as a keepsake of his work in the Brier Hill steel mill in Youngstown; Diane Garner kept her employee badge from the Ford Foundry in Flat Rock in her bag for years afterward; and Willy Eady had a crumpled newspaper clipping about the fire that destroyed Fabricon Products in his wallet.[96] These tangible reminders were clearly insufficient to fill the emotional void of the displaced worker. One former Republic Steel employee in Lackawanna expressed an impossible wish: to return to the demolished mill, where a tomato greenhouse now stands, and to see his old work station again.[97] Speaking for many of the displaced, Youngstown steelworker Sam Donnorumo lamented, 'I miss the guys, I miss the guys ... I miss that place.'[98]

While individual stories vividly illustrate that displaced workers clung to mementoes of their former lives as cherished possessions that would make the coming trials easier to take, keeping in touch with former co-workers presented another means of maintaining a tenuous connection with the past. A chance encounter in the mall, at church, or on the street momentarily reconnected workers. It also reminded them that the plant shutdown had been a collective catastrophe, not just a personal one. Former employees of Republic Steel maintained their bonds through regular monthly meetings of their retirees club. Workers also reconnected with the past at annual reunions. Diane Garner noted that the 'Flat Rock people' reunited every year for ten years. 'It's something they didn't want to let die,' she said.[99] Similarly, Marilyn McCormack noted that twenty former employees of Northland Plastics reunited in Troy nearly fifteen years after that plant closed.[100]

Despite attempts to forge a sense of continuity and the familiar, American workers found their ties to place sundered. Keenly aware of the symbolic meanings of security and rootedness that work had previously denoted, workers inverted these symbols in their narratives in order to illustrate just how much life had changed. This chapter began with a story told by a former employee of Republic Steel in Buffalo in which the pain of job loss found its symbolic expression in a thirty-five-year pin being passed through a chain-link fence. In the telling, the thirty-five year pin – once a sign of loyalty and service – took on a fundamentally different meaning. The pin was recast into an evocative symbol of the instability and unfairness of the changes sweeping the industrial heartland.

Many older men expressed regret at their inability to provide for their families. Used to being breadwinners, these male interviewees still recall painfully how they had to tell their families that they would soon be out of work. A forty-nine-year-old former employee of Republic Steel in Buffalo found himself scrambling to support his wife and four children. After twenty-three years working in the plant, 'You lose money. You lose a little self-esteem too. Especially when you're not the breadwinner. My wife, as soon as I lost my job, she was working a little piddly part-time job and she started swinging right into full-time. But ... There's no money as compared to what we used to get at the plant and benefits.'[101] Similarly, Claire Sferra's husband, a long-term worker at Youngstown Sheet and Tube, found the gender role reversal especially difficult. As Claire recalled: 'Boy it was devastating. I think it was devastating for a woman to watch her husband go down ... To see a grown man lose his job and not be educated ... It's hard to see them so down. They don't know what to do. It's not like a layoff, it was a permanent layoff ... You don't know what's next. It's hard but you go on. You have to go on. It affects the whole family, it really does.'[102] The stigma of being unemployed in a society where work was a source of identity as well as a source of income proved too much for some workers. Many plant shutdown stories are studded with references to marriage break-up, alcohol abuse, and suicide. Dorothy Fisher's fifty-nine-year-old husband attempted suicide three times and stopped eating, before dying of a heart attack six weeks after his Detroit plant closed. In the end, she used her husband's severance pay for his funeral.[103]

A prolonged sense of displacement also proved to be strong among unionized workers who had recall rights with their employers. While this continued contractual obligation ensured that their ties to the employer were not severed straight away, workers often waited months or years to return to work at another factory. The stages of disillusionment are perhaps most vividly depicted by Gabriel Solano, who had worked at General Motors' Fisher Guide plant in southwestern Detroit for eight years when it closed in 1986: 'I bought the GM product: the car, the truck, the house in the suburbs, the new baby, the new furniture and then the dream came crashing down.' Within a year of losing his job, Gabriel had lost his marriage. Eventually, Gabriel watched everything he worked for 'fall away.' His agonizing wait lasted seven years and eight months: 'If a letter came with a [GM] logo on you opened that letter just like you received the lottery ... When the phone rang [shaking his head] "Hello, hi" – it might have been a neighbor calling or a brother or sister. The weirdest thing was for the first year: "I'm going back." "I'm going back." "I'm going somewhere." I'm going somewhere." "They're going to call me back it is a big corporation." Little did we realize at the time this was the start of the paring down.'[104] By the time he was finally recalled, Gabriel's old colleagues at General Motors' closed Fisher Guide plant were scattered across the country.

Incredulously, Gabriel learned soon after being recalled that his new plant was also slated for closure. The same thing happened at his third plant. These repeated sinkings had a profound effect on Gabriel and other survivors of the automotive industry:

> I want to relate this story. It's an interesting one. They shipped me over to the West Plant (which is Plant 5) two weeks before they're shutting it down. So I get there and the foreman gives me this 'you're here to do the job' and I mean he's gung-ho and I'm looking at him like 'I just got a free ticket on the Titanic.' It's already hit the iceberg, its three-quarters sunk and you're telling me 'strike up the band.' And I said 'can life get any worse and then I meet you.' So he read me his riot act about what we have to do for this plant and it is going to shut down in two weeks. Mind you this is at Christmas time. I'm like 'is this real?' It is real. So, 'you're absolutely right, which way is the life boat?' At which point I said, 'you have to have fun with this.' And I made it fun. I was around a bunch of workers who have never been to a plant closing. I had already closed two.

> Q   What was the second one you closed?

> A   It was a Livonia trim shop. I was there briefly. I think it was the *Lusitania* and then I got on the *Titanic* so one got torpedoed and the other hit the iceberg. I was rather enlightened because I had now become so calloused and I understood what was going on. To watch some of these other workers who would threaten to bring guns. The 'I hate everyone' mentality. It was understood. I had seen it. I had felt it. I had done it. Been there. Well it was one hell of an irony because it was Christmas time and I can remember this day so vividly because I was taking notes because I wanted to feel this even further down the road ... I can still remember so vividly: 'Attention. Attention.' Then, they put out flyers and posters: 'Free hot dogs, pops, popcorn in the cafeteria. Please come down.' I said hey, I'll look at the freebies. So I go down there and ... You could see the anger. You could see the hurt. You could see the anxiety. And you could see most of all the fear. They started playing Christmas music over the PA. I think, 'strike

up the band the *Titanic* is going down!' So we get in line and the plant manager and all of his cronies are passing out hot dogs and pop. And they're so damn cheerful and they're taking pictures. So he hands me a hot dog so I dropped it on the floor. He says, 'Here's another one.' So I throw it against the wall.[105]

By the time that he was interviewed in 1998, Gabriel had seen the folly of the widely held belief among industrial workers that their plants were unsinkable. Like the *Titanic*, the Pontiac plant had hit an iceberg. The parallel can also extend to the sense of drowning which permeated Gabriel's narrative of job loss. Only the officers and the captain, it seemed to Gabriel, had reserved seating on the lifeboat. Rank-and-file workers like himself were expected to stay afloat on their own until the next big factory ship came along. While the company had tried to cushion the blow with a Christmas party on the eve of the plant's closing, it did not create the desired effect. Instead, it stirred up the indignation of hardened industrial workers.

Gabriel's story also reveals a sharp distinction between plant shut-down veterans and 'home planters' who were going through their first sinking. Although they took their corporate seniority for pensions and benefits with them, recalled workers had rookie status in their new plant when it came to determine who worked what jobs and shifts, and who would be laid off again in the future. Their sense of ongoing upheaval was such that they began to identify with this displacement. Having experienced several plant shutdowns, these 'trans-plants' came to be known to Gabriel Solano as 'I-75 gypsies,' after the Interstate that runs southward from Flint through Pontiac and Detroit on its way to Toledo and beyond. Many auto plants were located alongside this ribbon of concrete that runs through one of the world's most highly industrialized areas: 'We are the people who shut down plants up and down I-75. That's why we call ourselves the I-75 gypsies. We have no home plants. We are very hardened people. We are very thick-skinned but we are also very good people because we've been at all the battles in the war called the automotive industry ... There's like four or five hundred of us there [Pontiac auto plant] and they stuck us all down near the same building. We're neat because everyone has a story. They're beautiful stories. They're stories of hurt, or fear, of anger, of loss, of gain. The whole roller coaster.'[106] Changed by the experience of job loss, industrial workers like Gabriel Solano developed a new identity as trans-plants amidst the turmoil in the automotive industry during the

1980s. 'You name it we have them there,' Gabriel concludes. These displaced persons had once called home plants such as Fleetwood Cadillac, Fisher Guide, Willow Run, Flint, Grand Blanc as well as closed plants across Ohio and Wisconsin. Regularly comparing notes about how long they had been laid off and how many plants they had been shipped to, I-75 gypsies were a different breed. They had become outsiders looking in, gypsies moving from one place to the next as required for employment.

Their exclusion was confirmed in Gabriel's mind by new rules governing the awarding of the United Auto Workers (UAW) ring at his plant. Given after a quarter century of membership, the UAW ring had once symbolized union solidarity. However, this changed in the 1980s: 'They gave us 1-7-85 plant seniority so a gentleman with corporate seniority of twenty-five years walks in with 1-7-85, January 7, 1985. He can't hold day shift because an in-plant person has more seniority ... You're a UAW member but you're a lower class member. I think about that and it bothers me ... A person can have twenty-five years UAW time but can't receive a ring due to the fact that they've designated in the by-laws of the local agreement that you must have twelve years and one day in that facility ... Something small that means a lot to a lot of the men ... Although we all have fifteen, twenty-five, twenty-eight years, we don't have what is called a home plant.'[107] In ruling that only those union members who worked at least twelve years at the Pontiac plant qualified for the ring, the local union made transplanted workers like Gabriel feel like unwelcome house guests rather than family members. The union ring reinforced the psychological barriers between home plant workers and trans-planted ones. With plant closings and job losses already tearing apart the industrial workforce, the union's actions further contributed to the construction of a new identity derived from worker displacement.

In identifying himself as an I-75 gypsy, a marker of liminality, Gabriel Solano had come to see himself as a displaced person. He was not alone. The identities of several other interviewees also coalesced around their displacement.[108] Diane Garner observed that former employees of Ford's Flat Rock foundry continued to be called 'Flat Rock people' years after the plant had closed: 'We were outsiders so we had to start to cling to each other.'[109] Due to preferential hiring rights negotiated with the union, Diane Garner's name was placed into a hiring pool with tens of thousands of other displaced Ford workers. A year later, Ford recalled Diane to a foundry in Cincinnati. She relocated to that city for a year, leaving her children behind with her sister. Every weekend, she and other displaced Flat Rock people returned home until they could transfer back to the Detroit area. All the plants of the Big Three automakers had displaced persons like Diane and Gabriel.

Bound together by their displacement, Flat Rockers, and I-75 gypsies had seen the devastating impact of plant closings and resigned themselves to the likelihood that their new plants could be shipwrecked any day. Even today, job insecurity reigns supreme, as Diane observes: 'You know what, I believe anything, anything can happen. Nothing is guaranteed. Livonia could close. That whole Rouge complex can close ... All of them could close. You prioritize things.' The sense of ongoing displacement upon which these workers' identities evolved represented a radical departure from the rootedness and security that mill and factory work once accorded them. Asked if the plant shutdown is something that she talks about to others, Diane replied, 'When people are together who have experienced [job loss] we'll talk about it among ourselves. But we don't share it unless someone like you or someone asks about it. We just don't give this information. You're right, that's part of history we are letting down. A very important part of history.' Under the circumstances, workers were left with the choice of 'moving on and surviving or not moving on and dying.'[110] Most displaced workers like Diane Garner moved on. But they were forever changed by the experience.

Displaced workers in Canada, however, did not view themselves in these terms. Many Canadians also found themselves unemployed for extended periods of time, or even permanently. Others were recalled to work at company mills or factories in far away places. The sentiments of Jim Livingstone of Hamilton proved typical: 'I'm here waiting on retirement now. It's a bad thing when you lose your job. As I said you lose your dignity too. I didn't but a lot of people do. It affects them in various ways.'[111] But John was no gypsy. Indeed, none of the Canadians interviewed questioned their old identities as workers or union members. The ties that bound them to people and place, though weakened by layoff and the resulting out migration, remained strong.

What is the explanation for this divergence in the stories told by displaced workers in Canada and the United States? For one, the disparity of experience was due to the fact that no integrated steel mills or auto assembly plants closed in Canada during this time period. The economic situation in Southern Ontario was, on the whole, much better than in Youngstown or Detroit. Despite the high unemployment rate, a much larger proportion of laid-off workers had factories to go back to. Canadian cities did not deindustrialize overnight and, as was shown in the previous chapter, the stigma of the Rust Belt never took hold in Canada.[112] But something more than economics was at work to soften the economic blows in Canada.

While the plant shutdown stories told by American workers described disillusionment and loss, Canadians recalled their own stories in more hopeful terms. Indeed, many took pride in their unions. Ed Lawrenson, for example, claimed that the experience of job loss had made him 'more union now than I have ever been.'[113] Others proudly related how they defied their former employer in the days and weeks following the announcement. In fact, collective resistance represented an important chapter in the plant shutdown stories of Canadian workers. Protest rallies, boycotts, factory occupations, petition campaigns, and political lobbying brought Canadian workers and their union leadership together. After years of health-and-safety concerns about asbestos used in the manufacture of automotive brakes at Bendix Automotive's Windsor plant, union staffer Andy Morocko recalled that the decision to occupy the just-shuttered plant in 1980 was taken in his office: 'We said enough of this shit. These guys have left us with cripples.'[114] Morocko and his co-workers wanted to send the American owners a defiant message that 'you're not just going to leave us.' Ed Lawrenson also recalled with pride his own role in the illegal protest: 'We were the first ones who did it. And it worked out so well for us that there were four or five places that closed down within the next [few] years that took that strategy.'[115] Forced to the negotiating table, Bendix agreed to what Andy called a 'beautiful' close-out agreement.

Seeking greater compensation for their job loss, workers at Beach Foundry in Ottawa also occupied their plant that summer. Brian Hill recalled a spontaneous decision on the part of plant workers: 'A group of the guys started talking amongst ourselves and word went around the plant that – this day we kept watching stuff moving out of the plant – we all decided at 9:30 after break [to] end production until we got what we wanted.'[116] At Beach the company capitulated to workers' demands for more generous severance packages. Even though few plants were reopened, Canadian workers won the right to get 'something more than a pink slip.'[117] In this way, hope was kept alive and new identities based on rootlessness and marginality had difficulty taking hold.

Drawing Conclusions

Important similarities and surprising differences emerge in the stories of job loss on either side of the Canada–United States border. For Americans, the story was one of helplessness and disillusionment in the face of a collective catastrophe, communicated in the recurring metaphors of a sinking ship or floodwaters. When large plants closed, familiar social boundaries dissolved. Workers like Gabriel Solano inverted old markers of class identity and reinvented themselves as the uprooted. Long after workers were recalled back to work by the Big Three automakers, they continued to think of themselves as displaced persons. Their sense of exclusion was confirmed by collective agreements that distinguished between home plant workers and trans-plants. This was no doubt the price of extending company-wide recall rights. While few autoworkers, even transplanted ones, would wish to lose their recall rights, none wanted to lose the perks of seniority. Nor did they want to lose the sense of family that had developed on the factory floor. Under these circumstances, bitterness was probably inevitable. Even so, these workers still had a job to go to. Displaced steelworkers in Buffalo and Youngstown had nowhere to go after their mills went down in the late 1970s and early 1980s. Canadians also felt deeply threatened by plant shutdowns and had a bleak view of present uncertainties and future economic prospects. But while the identities of many of the Americans were irrevocably altered by the experience of the plant closure, Canadians continued to see themselves as workers and as union members. The rusting of hope and self-respect in the United States was less marked in the plant shutdown narratives told in Canada.

3 Back to the Garden: Redesigning the Factory for a Post-industrial Era

'There is an image of the 19th century industrial economy, familiar from a hundred history textbooks: the coal mine and its neighboring iron foundry, belching black smoke into the sky, and illuminating the night heavens with its lurid red glare. There is a corresponding image of the new economy that has taken its place in the last years of the twentieth century, but it is only just imprinting itself on our consciousness. It consists of a series of low, discreet buildings, usually displaying a certain air of quiet good taste, and set amidst impeccable landscaping in that standard real-estate cliché, a campus-like atmosphere.'

Manuel Castells and Peter Hall, *Technopoles of the World*[1]

In their juxtaposition of the old economy against the new, Manuel Castells and Peter Hall clearly prefer the latter. For them, the idyllic surroundings of Silicon Valley exemplify the triumph of post-industrialism over industrialism. The ascent of a new high-technology and service economy, and the simultaneous decline of an older manufacturing one, is widely interpreted to be as inevitable as sunrise and sunset. Left in the shadows, however, has been another dimension of industrial transformation: the emergence of a post-industrial aesthetic.[2]

This post-industrial aesthetic was born out of deeply rooted environmental values and sensibilities. Historian Samuel P. Hayes has termed the post–Second World War period of rising standards of living and levels of education the environmental era.[3] In the decades between 1945 and 1984 planners incorporated environmental values into factory exteriors, by removing the factory from its former industrial landscape and placing it in 'natural' surroundings, either in industrial parks or in the countryside. These greenfield sites – as opposed to older brownfield ones – represented a return to the beginnings of industrialism. Just as rural locations had set apart early North American factory sites from the degrading industrial cities of Great Britain, greenfield sites promised to purge the factory system of its reputation for human and environmental degradation. In effect, this was a return to the pastoral ideals of the factory.

Much like the nineteenth-century tableaux depicting workshops in the wilderness, factories built after the Second World War reflected public concern over the adverse effects of industrialism on the natural and human environment. In order to trace changing concepts of plant design, this chapter delves into the image worlds presented in four trade publications: *Architectural Record*, *Industrial Development*, *Site Selection Handbook*, and *Industrial Canada*. The post-industrial facade did not so much reflect changing corporate attitudes as it did changing societal values about the environment and the nature of progress.[4] In the process, imaginative boundaries between industrial and post-industrial economies, blue-collar and white-collar workers, factory and office, industrial land and park land became blurred.[5] Behind this new facade, however, the old rational factory persisted, smaller, more sanitized, and more disposable than before.

Industrial Pastoralism and the Rational Factory

The ideology of early American industrialism differed sharply from that of Great Britain, the cradle of the industrial revolution. Americans did not want to bring the British factory system – with its reputation for 'human depravity and wretchedness' – to North America.[6] There would be no 'dark satanic mills' in the New World. Indeed, in the early nineteenth century, the image of America as a new Garden of Eden permeated both American and European thought. In an often-cited passage from *Notes on the State of Virginia* (1785), Thomas Jefferson mused that the young Republic would be better served if industry 'let our workshops remain in Europe.'[7] Jefferson nonetheless came to the conclusion that manufacturing could be introduced without disturbing America's rural landscapes and republican ideals.[8]

This ideal was not without its inner contradictions: the garden image was itself a product of the Christian imperative to put the land to work for humanity.[9] Europeans coming to North America did not wish to preserve the wild landscape but rather to create a cultivated one that proclaimed the values of order and taste.[10] The garden would be a controlled environment where nature served people's every need. In his study of early views of the Acadian landscape of maritime Canada, historian Ramsay Cook found that 'when Europeans set about transforming the wilderness into a garden, they were engaged in taking possession of the land.'[11] Thus, the New World's environment would be purified even as it was being taken into possession.

At first, industrialization seemed to conform to the 'machine in the garden' ideal. In Jefferson's time, American factories were powered by water. Long after Great Britain had converted to steam power and developed great industrial cities such as Manchester, mills and factories in North America remained in the countryside, located near falls or rapids. Abundant water-power sites in North America ensured that – at least initially – industrialism was a largely rural phenomenon.[12]

European visitors often recorded their astonishment at seeing New England textile mills. Visiting the mill town of Lowell, Massachusetts, Alexander MacKay 'looked in vain for the usual indications of a manufacturing town ... The tall chimneys and the thick volumes of black smoke.'[13] His surprise was shared by many. Historian Marvin Fisher concluded from an analysis of published travel diaries that 'unlike the factory areas of the Old World, Lowell seemed essentially rural; the most frequent descriptions stressed such words as "clean," "open," "airy," "fresh," "new," "young," and "different."'[14] Even the system of using mill girls from surrounding rural areas as the chief source of labour was widely acclaimed. No less of an authority than Charles Dickens compared these healthy-looking New England women favourably with the 'waifs' who laboured back in England.[15]

It was only the introduction of steam power and the emergence of the urban factory at mid-century that American industrialism began to resemble its European counterpart. For nearly a century – from the 1850s to the 1940s – industrialization and urbanization, and later suburbanization, went hand in hand. The so-called machine age saw the rise of mass production and the idealization of the machine, with industrial engineers and factory owners seeking to construct the ever-elusive rational factory. By the 1920s, new technological advances in material handling, reinforced concrete, and the application of electricity had revolutionized factory design and layout. Electricity in particular permitted far more flexibility in arranging the plant and manufacturing process. As Henry Ford himself pointed out: 'The provision of a whole new system of electric generation emancipated industry from the leather belt and line shaft, for it eventually became possible to provide each tool with its own electric motor ... The motor enabled machinery to be arranged according to the sequence of work, and that alone has probably doubled the efficiency of industry, for it has cut out a tremendous amount of useless handling and hauling. The belt and line shaft were also very wasteful of power – so wasteful, indeed, that no factory could be really large, for even the longest line shaft was small according to modern requirements.' Factories became rationalized and grew to unprecedented size.[16] The new rational factory was realized with the construction of Ford's mammoth River Rouge complex in 1927, where iron ore and other raw materials were shipped to one end of the huge complex and Model A automobiles rolled out the other.[17] The ubiquitous cult of the machine even found artistic expression in the paintings of Charles Sheeler in the 1930s. After spending six weeks at Ford's new factory, Sheeler painted thirty-two views of the complex that would become prime examples of industrial pastoralism.[18] The characteristic American landscape had by this time become an industrial one, and the metaphor of the machine had been imposed on things social, cultural, and religious.

Virtually every major study of factory design ends at River Rouge, enabling scholars such as Manuel Castells and Peter Hall to contrast monolithic industrial complexes with the discreet buildings of the new economy. In doing so, however, they overlook another half-century of change in factory design. Just as suburban homes promised middle-class families clean living in peaceful green surroundings, industrial parks and the countryside promised manufacturers a fresh new start reminiscent of the earliest phase of New World industrialization. This transmutation was made possible by three technological developments: the rapid diffusion of the automobile and increased worker mobility; rural electrification in the 1930s, which allowed the factory to move beyond the industrial suburbs; and the invention of the computer and the resultant feasibility of decentralized production. In addition to these technical considerations, industrialists increasingly wanted to rid themselves of newly unionized workforces in the cities and to cleanse the stain of human and environmental degradation.

Building the Post-industrial Facade

Even though the notion of post-industrialism had surfaced as early as in the 1960s, the term did not become common usage until sociologist Daniel Bell published *The Coming of Post-Industrial Society* in 1973.[19] Bell

Criss-crossed conveyors, River Rouge Plant, Ford Motor Company, 1927.

interpreted the vast changes sweeping the industrialized world as evidence of an emerging knowledge-based economy of computers and telecommunications. While the belief in technology as a key governing force in society was nothing new, technological progress in an environmental age took on a new form.[20] No longer did the billowing black smoke from factory chimneys signal prosperity and progress. Instead, a more suburban landscape of progress resurfaced.[21]

The mills and factories of the industrial age had released a great deal of hazardous waste, causing extensive pollution of air, water, and land.[22] In the course of a century of industrial activity, old greenfield mill or factory towns had turned brown. Assisted in no small part by spectacular ecological disasters such as the Cuyahoga River fire and the poisoning of people's homes in Love Canal, environmentalists and consumer-rights advocates put large corporations on the defensive in the late 1960s and early 1970s. In 1972, the editors of the trade journal *Industrial Development* warned their corporate subscribers to consider 'changing socio-economic priorities' to avoid tarnished corporate images and financial loss. Three years later, the editors claimed that years of 'environmental hysteria' had severely battered the image of large corporations: 'Golden Boy had gone bad and had to be regulated and watched via permits, reports and approvals of his activities.'[23] U.S. senator Daniel Patrick Moynihan credited anti-business and anti-growth attitudes for a policy shift in the early 1970s from a 'war on poverty' to a 'war on dirty air.'[24]

The tarnished image of industrialism was such that local elites did not wait for plants to close to re-engineer their city's image as post-industrial. Hamilton's long-standing association with the steel industry became a matter of intense embarrassment to civic leaders during the 1970s and 1980s. The city's reputation as a 'lunch-bucket town' – a label that had graced David Proulx's 1971 coffee table book, *Pardon My Lunch Bucket: A Look at the New Hamilton* – was downplayed by urban boosters such as Mayor Victor Copps: 'I don't particularly mind Hamilton being called a lunch-bucket city. It's no crime to take your lunch to work. There's nothing indecent in getting your hands dirty in the foundry or rolling mill, making a decent living so you can bring up one of those large families that steelworkers are so fond of.'[25] Yet in due course, Copps claimed, the old lunch bucket was destined to 'become a museum piece, something that us old-timers can take our grandchildren to see one of these days to point out the way it used to be.'[26] In the new Hamilton a set of post-industrial values and images displaced the pride of place that industrialism had once engendered.

The precariousness of life in Canada's industrial towns and cities, combined with an ascendant post-industrial economy worked to undermine people's self-worth. A 1982 survey of three hundred Windsor residents, and a focus group of thirty-five 'opinion leaders,' uncovered many people's embarrassment at living in a blue-collar town. Even though seven thousand area autoworkers had just been laid off, most residents pointed to the working-class image rather than the unemployment problem as the main reason for Windsor's poor image. Fully 67 per cent of respondents believed that the city had developed a negative reputation in the rest of Canada.[27] Blue-collar workers thus faced the problem of diminishing status and prestige. As one scholar observed, a 'factory job is not a station that is often aspired to.'[28]

In responding to the growing force of environmentalism, industrial firms set out to remake their smokestack image. To that end, many development agencies dropped the word industrial from their names in favour of community or economic. During the 1970s and early 1980s, large industries such as U.S. Steel and National Steel eliminated steel from their names or, in the case of the Steel Company of Canada, adopted the less noxious-sounding acronym Stelco. As factory became associated with environmental and human degradation, the word gradually disappeared from the corporate vocabulary. Instead, the environmentally-correct vocabulary included facility, real estate, building, operation, and plant.[29] These words could just as easily have described an office building as a factory.

Evidently, post-industrialism was more than semantics, with flexible production displacing mass production in many manufacturing sectors. In the process, the main centres of technological innovation shifted from industrial cities to post-industrial spaces, from Detroit to the Silicon Valley. Certain critics even likened universities such as Stanford and MIT – the power houses of the new economy – to the coal mines of an older industrial era.

Yet the boundary between the old and new economies remains vague. How different is the manufacture of computer hardware components from the manufacture of appliances? In this sense post-industrialism refers as much to innocuous physical surroundings as it does to the nature of the economic activity. A growing number of enterprises once identified with industrial smokestacks have successfully made the transition to the new economy not by manufacturing different products,

Cartoon by Clarence Eaton.

but by changing factory design, image, and location.[30] As a result, old industrial landscapes such as the Steel Valley of northeast Ohio that once towered over their communities have given way to new post-industrial spaces designed to blend into suburban surroundings. These new spaces are rational factories in all but name.

Factory Design and Location

How were new ideas and values incorporated into factory design and location? Companies have been very conscious of their 'obligation to present an attractive face to the community.'[31] In the late 1940s and early 1950s, an appealing exterior increasingly came to mean pleasant landscaped surroundings, as illustrated in the trade journal *Architectural Record*. General Robert Johnson, head of the Johnson and Johnson Company, declared at the end of the Second World War that the vast majority of American factories were obsolete and ought to be razed to the ground. However, Johnson found that his small factories, located in rural areas, induced pride in work and a sense of loyalty to the company. F.N. Manley, director of construction, described the ideal plant: 'It will be a one-story building ... It will be out away from congested city areas, away from any "industrial slums." Johnson does not want to operate in industrial slum conditions.' In pursuing this goal, the company expected employees to drive to work and walk in, with management, through the front doors: 'The general rule is to enclose everything possible in clean, colorful coverings, hiding all possible working parts and oily bearings. Usually an industrial designer is retained to modify machine designs and work out color schemes, all to the end that girls can operate them safely and simply, without soiling the nurses' uniforms that management provides for them.'[32] As early as 1948, then, Johnson and Johnson employed a mainly female workforce, a source of cheap, non-unionized labour, and had begun the process of redesigning factory work as white-collar.

With larger parcels of land available in the countryside or in industrial parks, post–Second World War designers had a considerable amount of freedom. Writing in 1953, Frank L. Whitney noted that the 'architectural concept of the industrial plant has in the past decade been radically revised.' Once designed to stand fifty years and to possess a dignified institutional quality, factories became increasingly functional.[33] Industrial firms proved more willing to 'enlarge it, change it, sell it, or abandon it entirely, whenever it begins to hamstring the operations. We expect a certain fluidity in manufacturing operations, and we design for it as we can.' In abandoning the masonry that had formerly symbolized distinction and longevity, Whitney encouraged prospective clients 'to think of the industrial plant more as a shell over a mechanical process than as the ancestral home of a corporation, and try to design for fast changing times.'[34] Post-war factory designers discouraged corporate executives from 'institutional monumentality' and instead promoted factories designed for 'flexibility.' Michael F. Roberts, a partner in the Toronto-based architectural firm Wilson Newton Roberts, informed the readership of *Industrial Canada* that 'an industrial building is an envelope wrapped around a manufacturing process.'[35] In light of this new-found concern for flexibility, older factories became inefficient and therefore disposable.

By the 1950s, multi-storey factories had lost out to single-storey ones, in part because vertical material-handling proved to be far less efficient. In the late nineteenth and early twentieth centuries, factory designers had built narrow industrial buildings, then shaped like the letters I, L, E, T, U, H, or F, to allow in natural light and ventilation.[36] Inexpensive electricity not only eliminated the need for natural light, but also made redundant the belts and shafting that had made the multi-storey factory desirable.[37] As a result of technological improvements, a 1954 survey of manufacturers found a strong demand for single-storey buildings.[38] At the same time, the trend was towards constructing smaller plants with less than 50,000 square feet of floor space.

Did anything distinguish Canadian-designed factories from American ones? In a series of articles on 'The Canadian Plant of the 70s,' the editors of *Industrial Canada* admitted there was 'no such animal.'[39] The label proved useful, they suggested, only as it alluded to progress, innovation, and change. The comforting allusion to a Canadian plant at a time of intense economic nationalism in the country was unspoken. Beyond the rhetoric, there was little about the theoretical 1970s plant that could be described as distinctly Canadian. New plants on either side of the border shared many commonalities of design, location, ownership, and post-industrial image.[40]

Even so, the post-industrial facade was further embellished by local association. Most companies named new manufacturing facilities after their locality. When the Acme Cleveland Corporation relocated its Providence plant to nearby Cranston, Rhode Island, in 1978, it initially retained the old name. The corporation later succumbed to the idea that the plant should be re-named. Corporate executive Harry Leckler justified the change with an assurance that the plant's name presented 'a vital link to the community that will provide us with services and political cooperation.'[41] This rhetorical link was particularly important for American multinational corporations operating in Canada. The plant manager of Canadian Mechanical Engineering, an American subsidiary operating in Canada, gave in to demands by workers in Windsor and erected a flag pole to fly a Canadian flag in front of the plant.[42] By adopting local and national symbols, big corporations attempted to blend in to their environment.

The industrial park was another concept that took a firm hold in post-industrial America. Although manufacturers had sought greener pastures in industrial suburbs long before 1945, industrial parks proved different from suburbs in that they promised manufacturers a greenfield site in perpetuity through the strict regulation of aesthetics.[43] As a result, the number of industrial parks multiplied 'as if by magic,' in the words of one American booster.[44] In 1970, the trade journal *Industrial Development* counted 2,400 industrial parks in the United States, a 78 per cent jump from 1965. Many of these new developments were situated along transportation arteries, major highways, and airport hubs, making aesthetics especially important. An author writing in *Industrial Development* claimed: 'Developers, tuned in to the national clamor against environmental quality, are paying increasing attention to controlling the industrial park environment through such requirements as ample setbacks; architectural approval of plant design and construction materials; underground utilities; wide streets and off-street parking; screened outdoor storage.'[45] The trend towards the regulation of industrial landscapes was partly related to the national clamour against industrial pollution.[46] In the case of the Bramalea Industrial Park near Toronto's Pearson Airport, the promise of lower taxes, full-service lots, and a central geographic location attracted investors.[47] In addition, many parks had strict regulations barring obtrusive industry.[48] The industrial park was therefore the destination of choice for light-manufacturing industries ready to reorient their businesses as post-industrial.[49]

The post-industrial facade in plant design, together with the inclination to locate plants in suburban areas, small towns, or rural areas, grew out of changes in corporate thinking since the Second World War. This trend surfaced in 1958 when the magazine *Factory Management and Maintenance* singled out ten plants for special praise, all of which were located in the countryside.[50] Corporate executives readily conceded that the search for pleasant surroundings and cheap labour tended to be one and the same. Pete J. Barber, head of Honeywell's real estate department, noted that real estate was 'a means to an end, that end being specifically sales and profit. Real estate is only a tool to arrive at those ends.'[51] Del Morgano, the manager of facility planning at UARCO, a medium-sized manufacturer of business forms with nine factories, was even more blunt. His company located a new plant in Brockville, Ontario, reflecting UARCO's corporate policy to locate all its production facilities in towns with populations ranging from 5,000 to 10,000. Morgano also noted that small towns had low unionization rates.[52] Numerous studies have called attention to the shift in industrial production from older areas to newer ones that enabled companies to escape unionization and high taxes. While these two factors were undoubtedly major considerations in the corporate boardroom, there was also an awareness that environment played an 'ever-increasing role in facility planning.'[53]

Factory Image

If plant design and location underwent significant revision in the decades following the Second World War, the representation of mill and factory went even further in redefining these as post-industrial spaces.[54] Corporations considering a change in factory location or the building of a new facility were helped in their decision by the *Site Selection Handbook*. Published three times annually, the *Handbook* surveyed state and provincial industrial incentives and plant financing programs, environmental regulations, and rates of unionization. As its readership included many of the corporate real estate executives and facility planners involved in plant location decisions, the *Handbook* was chock-full of advertisements for places for sale in every corner of Canada and the United States. It is thus an ideal resource for examining the changing image of the factory. An analysis of the advertisements appearing in the 1972, 1977, and 1982 *Handbooks* confirms the re-emergence of the 'machine in the garden' ideal.[55]

One of the ways that local or state industrial commissions sold property in their areas was to stress the park-like surroundings. Pastoral landscapes awaited the smart corporate manager. One attractive advertisement in this genre was placed by Canadian National Railways. The CNR's ad featured a briefcase-holding executive gazing in wonder down a picturesque river valley towards the snowcapped mountains in the distance. Amid the brilliant oranges and yellows of the autumn landscape, several factories and a dam blend into the idyllic setting. The same message was delivered – though less colourfully – in an advertisement for the Port of Lake Charles, Louisiana, that displayed a factory surrounded by a field of flowers. The caption was as blunt as the image: 'Plants thrive here ... all year. Give your company roots – here! A growing plant, even a plant branch, needs plenty of fresh water, a healthy warm climate, ample room to grow, and lots of Tender Loving Care!' Both of these advertisements promised firms an industrial location clearly set apart from the traditional industrial landscape.

In other cases, advertisers transformed the relocating factory itself into a plant that formed part of the metaphorical garden. Money may not grow on trees but factories did. San Joaquin County, for example, claimed that, 'We grow all kinds of plants in California where distribution is the key.' This particular variety of vegetation, though, had a cog wheel and an oil barrel as leaves and various transportation networks as its roots.[56] In many advertisements, a natural-looking plant or tree came to represent the factory. Just how hard advertisers worked to cultivate environmentally friendly images is illustrated by captions in the *Site Selection Handbook*: 'We're involved in ecology ... At Raritan Center it is an integral part of our planning. At Raritan Center it is a pleasure to come to work and watch your business grow. We set out to build an environment for business and industry with a true park-like atmosphere ...'[57]; and 'Among the Nation's Finest Parks ... Are some we've Reserved for Industry!'[58] In an environmental age the selling of places to industry meant promising a new life in a fresh, green landscape.[59] But once the idea had been planted, how would it grow?

Changing notions of progress in factory design become readily apparent in the corporate images conveyed in *Industrial Development*'s regular 'Million Dollar Plants' column.[60] The editors showcased single-storey, light manufacturing facilities pictured behind beautifully landscaped lawns. While photographic images may have been the ideal medium of corporate self-representation at the beginning of the twentieth century, it was not particularly well-suited to record the beauty of the new generation of post-industrial factories. As a result, many companies turned towards architectural site renderings.

These architectural sketches often situated pale industrial buildings amid rows of trees and bushes and immaculate lawns.[61] Graphic artists usually located these factories and mills in summer's splendour and, whenever possible, invoked high tech/low wage 'Southernness' by the kind of vegetation shown.[62] The horizontal lines of the factory flowed into the natural landscape around it,[63] and no other industrial buildings were ever in view, to avoid negative associations with other industrial landscapes. Architects proved so successful in their efforts to distance plants from past associations with 'dark satanic mills' that it is virtually impossible to decipher whether the buildings depicted were actually designed for industrial use. Their large windows and other design features made them indistinguishable from office complexes. The boundaries between factory and office became veiled as the post-industrial aesthetic relocated the factory from an urban, industrial landscape to a rural, natural one.[64]

The absence of human activity was another distinguishing feature of the post-industrial factory depicted in architectural drawings. A great stillness pervades the hundreds of drawings surveyed in *Industrial Development*. Apparently, a post-industrial manufacturing firm no longer needed employees as nearly empty parking lots were common.[65] Even though a drawing of a $7.2 million food-processing plant in Vineland, New Jersey, included space for dozens of cars, there are only six automobiles depicted in the employees' parking lot and three others in executive spaces near the front door (the proportion of cars owned by managers was nothing if not miraculous). For obvious reasons, it proved harder to visually reconfigure an assembly plant or a steel mill as an office complex. Yet the natural bearing of these industrial developments did not prevent imaginative graphic artists from trying. Caterpillar's 585,000 square foot Mount Joly, Illinois, plant, for example, was cloaked in tree-lined avenues and landscaped lawns.

The cover of the March 1975 issue of *Industrial Development* dedicated to industrial parks presented a similar picture. In the campus-like setting of the industrial park, industrial buildings were obscured by a tree-lined avenue with attractive street lights at the centre of the drawing. Again, the absence of workers is striking. Other sketches of industrial parks such as the one depicting Lusk Industrial/Business Park in Newport Beach, California, showed orderly rows of square, one-storey buildings with tree-lined streets and a handful of cars.[66] Shown from a bird's-eye view, the Orange County, California, airport-industrial park evoked an image of prairie homesteads, with trees circling each building.[67] Conversely, the proposed Airpark at Dallas/Fort Worth appeared almost stately with its treed avenues and impressive buildings. Industrial land was being reinvented everywhere, at least in the imaginative realm.

Behind the Facade of the Post-industrial Factory

An important internal dialogue of images and text exists in *Industrial Development* that researchers such as David Nye have not considered in their own studies of image world.[68] A close reading of the text that accompanied architectural sketches and photographs reveals a worldview that differed dramatically from the modesty of the images. Much like the booster rhetoric of the 1910s, the written descriptions of the modern 'Million Dollar Plants' stressed their physical grandeur (the bigger the better) and the size of investment (the more the mightier):

> New modular housing production facility at Gulfport, Miss., for Stirling Homex Corp., will have world's largest capacity, producing 100 units daily.

> Progresso Foods has a $7.2 million food processing plant under construction in Vineland, New Jersey.

> Union Bottling Works of Houston recently opened a 197,000-sq. Ft. Plant on a 20-acre tract for bottling Pepsi-Cola products. The $3.8 million facility, largest soft drink bottling plant in the world, will turn out 1.7 million soft drinks per day.

As the sub-text to these images reveals, the editors of *Industrial Development* continued to measure progress in quantifiable terms by showcasing the number of mills or factories, their assessed value, and the value of manufacturing. While the images seemed to illustrate that factories had broken with their past negative associations, the texts continued to emphasize the size of investments. Evidently, the philosophy of growth remained intact behind the facade of the post-industrial factory.

Beneath the mantle of green, the rational factory persisted, save that its ownership was more distant than ever before. In fact, the twentieth-century shift from civic capitalism to national or global capitalism profoundly altered the world-view of corporate executives. In the early-twentieth century, business had been rooted in the local community and looked for status, honour, and brides from that community.[69] While these locally derived and intensely personal relationships had not prevented conflict, 'they bounded and channelled it, humanized it, and obstructed that abstraction and generalization from experience that could constitute class consciousness.'[70] By the 1960s, however, civic capitalism became moribund as the locus of ownership shifted. The result proved disastrous for industrial cities such as Trenton when the entrepreneurial owner of an earlier era was replaced by absentee capitalists.[71] One by one, the Trentons of the world lost control over their economies.

Concurrently, the locus of power and influence within industrial enterprises shifted from operational managers to 'finance men.' These splits are revealed through the business philosophies of W. Lawrence Weeks, who worked his way up the corporate ladder over thirty-one years to become vice president of operations at Republic Steel, and David Roderick, the head of U.S. Steel. In an oral history interview recorded in 1990, Weeks expressed his disillusionment with the upper echelons of Republic that increasingly consisted of 'legal-minded' or 'numbers-minded' individuals rather than persons with steel-making experience. Indeed, he came to use the label 'steelmen' to differentiate those like himself from the new breed of 'top managers' with no operating experience.[72]

The situation obviously appeared altogether different from the perspective of those at the top. Interviewed by Ralph Nader in his spacious office on the sixty-first floor of the U.S. Steel building in Pittsburgh's Golden Triangle, David Roderick freely admitted that he did not consider himself to be a 'steelman.'[73] Instead, he claimed to be in the business of making money. Roderick's distance from the factory floor surfaced repeatedly in the interview. When closing steel mills and terminating tens of thousands of employees, Roderick took into account neither employees' loyalty nor their personal attachment to the company. Instead, he insisted that the interest of 'the steelworker' took a back seat to that of 'the shareholder': 'He's not looking at it from the standpoint of management, which has to manage assets in the best interests of the shareholders, but with total sensitivity to employees. To, in effect, sell them and reinvest them in a business that is earning four percent when I can take them and put them in a business that is earning twelve percent ... I mean, why would I do that? I don't get paid to do that. That's not what shareholders expect.'[74] The differing viewpoints of Weeks and Roderick confirm historian Alfred Chandler's contention that top managers' lack of experience with technological processes such as steel-making contributed to a breakdown in communication between head office and the operating divisions of conglomerates.[75] Sharon Zukin likewise found that the removal or sidelining of steel men from the upper echelons of the big American steel companies cleared the way for radical restructuring and diversification out of steel.[76] Shareholders wanted a bigger return on their investment than traditional steel men could deliver. As a result, the origins of industrial decline lay in the long-term processes of abstraction and internationalization.[77]

The accelerating pace of change and the expanding scope of social relations have transformed how individuals view the world. Anthony Giddens sees social relations being transformed by global interconnectedness and the 'grip of local circumstances' over people's lives being diminished, disembedded through the process he calls social 'distanciation.'[78] Geographer David Harvey and historian Stephen Kern have examined how sweeping changes in technology and culture have resulted in time-space compression and created 'distinctive modes of thinking about and experiencing time and space.'[79] And yet, as British geographer Doreen Massey rightly points out, globalization affects people in unique ways. For corporate executives used to instant communication and jet-setting the world might indeed have become a smaller place. However, those on the factory floor in North America were in no position to benefit from the global changes occurring around them.[80]

By the 1970s, the social divide and physical distance between corporate executives and hourly wage workers had grown as social relations became more distant. The development of industrial capitalism cut the ties between corporations and localities, as managers expanded into new markets and new product lines, making the single-unit manufacturer an oddity in most industries.[81] Behind the more agreeable mask of the post-industrial plant hid a corporation increasingly unwilling to put down roots. Portrayed as a plant or a tree in a suburban garden, the post-industrial factory had in fact become much less rooted than an earlier generation of polluting factories.

Conclusion: Greening the Factory

In the past two centuries, North American industrialism has come full circle, from the garden to the city and back again. This shifting metaphor of production reveals a lingering belief that the factory system can be redeemed through close contact with nature. Manufacturers hoped to regenerate their faded reputations by designing new factories to look like low-lying office buildings. Managers of industrial parks adopted strict environmental regulations requiring that these areas look like suburban landscapes and not industrial ones. In addition, visual images published by industrial firms and development agencies presented the manufacturing plant as part of the natural landscape. Historian Stephen V. Ward observed that this shifting location has been accompanied by a new iconography of industry: 'The factory chimneys have finally gone; the cog wheels very nearly so. A new manufacturing imagery based on the computer and the electronic circuit has taken their place.'[82] Corporations redesigned the public face of the factory in the second half of the twentieth century to conform to an emerging post-industrial aesthetic often associated with the new economy of high technology and service. It may be useful to consider industrial transformataion in terms of a new aesthetic of industry, rather than simply a shift from an old industrial economy to a new post-industrial one. Even though this aesthetic paid tribute to environmental concerns, the subtext continued to emphasize the size of factories and the return on investments. It appears that this image of quiet good taste camouflaged, and perhaps even legitimated, corporate efforts to abandon unionized labour in the cities. Behind the post-industrial facade, the growth ideology maintained its hold on a new generation of corporate managers who had little loyalty to people, place, or product.

4   The Deindustrializing Heartland

Moving from the changing aesthetic of industry to its changing structure, this chapter reconsiders the sharp distinction sometimes drawn
between plant closings and their relocation. While the 'runaway plant'
– a term coined by trade unionists in the 1950s to describe the anti-
union animus leading firms to relocate production – garnered considerable media attention in North America, planned obsolescence quietly
claimed many other mills and factories, displacing millions. These two
major catalysts for plant shutdown in Canada and the United States
were, in fact, two sides of the same coin. In the face of growing global
competition, corporate executives shifted their investments to increase
returns, either by producing the same product in a low-wage area or
diversifying into a more profitable sector of the economy. This shift in
capital was effected through the immediate relocation of factories or
through a more gradual strategy of planned obsolescence.

The global economic dominance enjoyed by the United States at the
end of the Second World War eroded considerably over the decades
that followed. While the United States was home to 111 of the world's
156 largest multinational corporations in 1959, that number had dropped
to just 68 by 1976.[1] In the meantime, the fundamental realignment of
the international division of labour saw rising imports from Japan and
other countries and the shift of labour-intensive but low-skilled work to
newly industrializing countries in Asia and Latin America.[2]

The industrial heartland was also losing ground to a trade and defence perimeter situated east of the Appalachians and west of the
Rocky Mountains.[3] The distorting effects of the Second World War and
the Cold War on the American economy have been well documented.
With the infusion of hundreds of billions of taxpayers' dollars into Cold

War technologies and industries, a high-technology complex – centred on the military-dependent aerospace, communications, and electronics industries – revolutionized the industrial geography of the United States.[4] Instead of locating their operations in the heavily unionized industrial heartland, most defence contractors built their plants on the geographic periphery of the continent. It is little wonder that the once-mighty industrial heartland faced an uncertain future.[5]

The deteriorating position of the industrial Midwest had far-reaching consequences for American industrial workers. Over 100,000 manufacturing plants in all, each employing more than 19 workers, closed their doors between 1963 and 1982 (see Figure 4.1).[6] Fully 20,955 of these closed factories were located in the industrial Midwest, or what the U.S. Census Bureau calls the East North Central district. By using statistical data culled from Dun and Bradstreet, economists Barry Bluestone and Bennett Harrison estimated that 22.3 million Americans lost their jobs to plant closings between 1969 and 1976.[7] Naturally, job losses were greatest in the most-industrialized regions. The brunt of regional deindustrialization fell on five states: Ohio, Michigan, Indiana, Illinois, and Wisconsin. This area saw manufacturing employment drop 19.3 per cent between 1979 and 1986, nearly double the national average. This drop translated into 990,500 fewer full-time manufacturing jobs in the region.[8] Overall job losses in this district peaked between 1967 and 1972 and spiked again between 1977 and 1982 (see Figure 4.2).

More specific statistical data relating to U.S. plant closings are essentially non-existent. The sources typically available to state governments consisted of newspaper accounts and the reports of government field agents. Indeed, so limited was the research capacity of the Connecticut Department of Commerce that it relied on a citizens group, the Committee of Concern for Connecticut Jobs, to provide it with advance warning of plant closings. For his part, Sheldon Friedman, head of research for the United Auto Workers (UAW), admitted that the union had no adequate means of ascertaining the scale and scope of job loss: 'Although few would deny the magnitude and seriousness of this problem, no one knows the exact number of workers unemployed or underemployed as a result of plant closings and other economic displacements.'[9] The full extent of job losses to plant closings can therefore only be guessed at.

Measuring job loss in Canada is nearly as frustrating. Unemployment was on the rise in Canada during the 1970s and 1980s. From a low of 4.4 per cent in 1969, the country's unemployment rate climbed to

Figure 4.1
Manufacturing Plants Opening and Closing in the United States, 1963–82

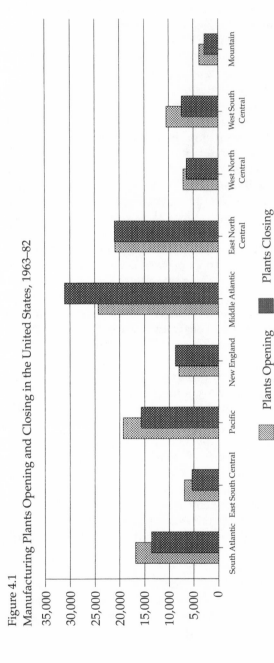

Source: United States, Secretary of Labor, *Economic Adjustment and Worker Dislocation in a Competitive Society: Report to the Secretary of Labor's Task Force on Economic Adjustment and Worker Dislocation* (Washington, DC: December 1986), 19–20.

Figure 4.2
Change in Manufacturing Employment in the East North Central Census District (U.S.)

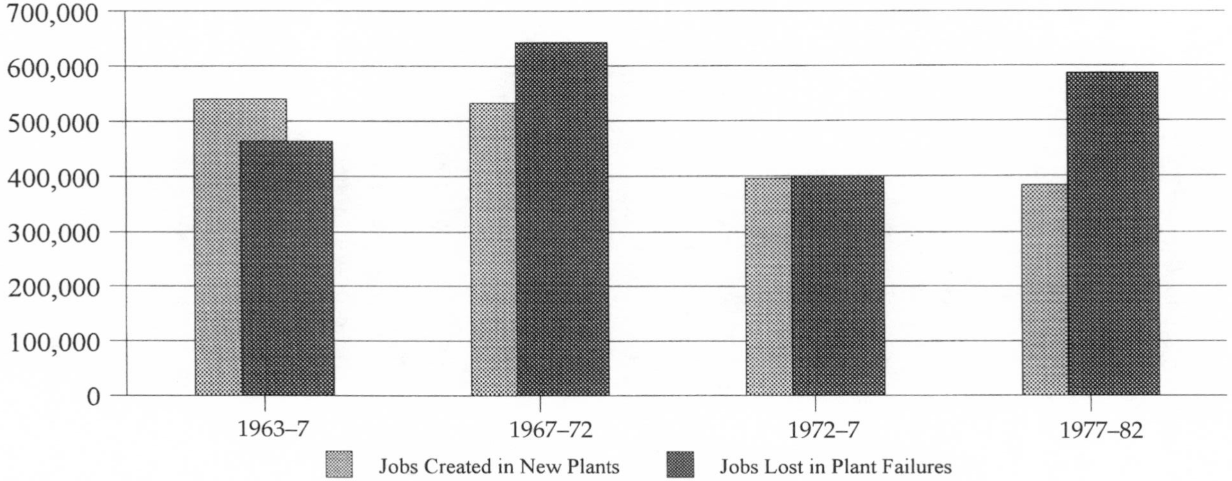

Source: U.S. Secretary of Labor, *Economic Adjustment and Worker Dislocation*, 19–20.

8.3 per cent by 1978, and reached the double digits by 1982.[10] Almost one million Canadians were without work at any given time between 1981 and 1984. In 36 per cent of these cases, job loss owed to plant closure or relocation.[11] Unlike the situation in the United States, the rate of unemployment in Canada's industrial heartland remained consistently lower than the national average. Yet the number of job losers, those Canadians who had involuntarily been laid off or fired from their jobs, climbed steadily as a proportion of the overall number unemployed (see Figure 4.3).

The dearth of hard statistical data, combined with changes in how figures were collected, makes it next to impossible to ascertain precisely how many Canadian workers lost their jobs to plant closings between 1969 and 1984. There was nonetheless a stronger desire on the part of provincial and federal governments than among their U.S. counterparts to track job loss by closing establishment. The Ontario Ministry of Labour, for example, counted 210,726 workers who lost their jobs to plant shutdowns in the province between 1974 and 1983.[12] This incomplete tally could be supplemented by the case files compiled by the federal government's Consultative Manpower Service, created in 1963 to help workers adjust to plant closings, and the manufacturing census compiled by Statistics Canada.[13] These files make it clear that mills and factories closed for any number of reasons: technological change, declining product demand, poor management, bankruptcy, new environmental regulations, consolidation, divestment, high labour costs, and the advancing age of facilities. Plants usually closed because of a combination of these factors.

Analysts examining the make-up of plant shutdowns and the resulting patterns of job loss in Canada and the United States could reasonably assume that national frontiers did not mean much in light of trade liberalization and global economic integration. Yet the border did matter. The geographic concentration of people and industry in the Montreal–Windsor corridor worked against companies that considered relocating to low wage areas in other provinces. In the United States, the earlier development of the industrial Midwest meant mills and factories there began to reach obsolescence between 1969 and 1984. While the overall picture of job loss appeared to be similarly bleak in both countries, there were significant differences between the two economic situations. One important distinction involved job losses resulting from runaway factories.

Figure 4.3
Job Losers as Percentage of Unemployed, Canada and Ontario, 1975–83

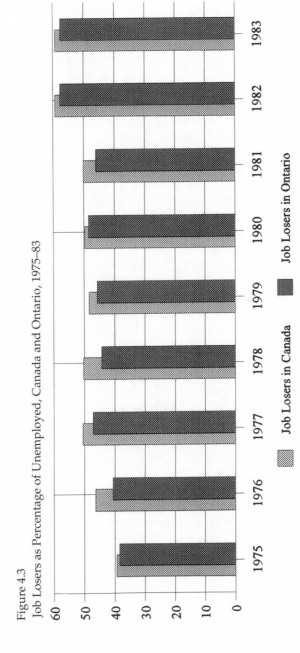

Job Losers in Canada ▨   Job Losers in Ontario ■

Source: Statistics Canada, *Labour Force: Annual Averages, 1975–83* (February 1984), 71, 529.

The Runaway Factory, 1950s–1970s

Nothing raised the ire of trade unionists in Canada and the United States quite as much as the spectre of the runaway plant. Fred Wright's illustrations of the United Electrical Workers provide some sense of union indignation. In both countries, the runaway plant phenomenon was most apparent in the auto parts and electrical industries, although the U.S. textile industry had been the first to move en masse to the low-wage South, abandoning its historical ties to New England and the Northeast.[14] The concentration of industrial production in Ontario, its potential market, and its geographic size did not deter companies in search of cheap labour from relocating to small towns within the province or moving south of the border. Despite a handful of companies that relocated to Quebec and Atlantic Canada with federal government assistance, there was no bidding war in Canada equivalent to the one that raged between political jurisdictions in the United States. There, plant closings in such labour-intensive industries as automotive parts, textiles, and electrical equipment owed, in large part, to employers' desire to escape a high-wage workforce.

Unionized workers enjoyed good wages and benefits but, in some industries at least, they eventually paid for this improved standard of living with their jobs. By the late 1970s, achievements at the bargaining table had pushed the wage gap between union and non-union workers up to 30 per cent from 19 per cent a decade earlier. Those union firms predisposed to shifting production often moved again and again. Numerous cases exist of companies relocating production in the 1950s and again twenty or thirty years later. As a result, workers displaced in these industries rarely had the opportunity to accrue sufficient seniority to retire with a private pension. Trade unions thus became victims of their own success.

Many states actively promoted the promise of being union-free in order to attract footloose employers from the heavily unionized industrial heartland, often using advertisements to entice manufacturers to relocate production. A typical advertisement in the *New York Times* featured a white family arranged around an old jalopy and signalled to readers that the state (in this case, Virginia) had poor white folk willing to work hard for next to nothing. The caption read: 'Working is a privilege. Not a backache. That may be kind of an obvious thing to say. But, what with riots and strikes and all, I wonder about people sometimes. I mean, I've worked in Virginia ever since Anne and I got

Fred Wright, a pre-eminent labour cartoonist for over forty-five years, produced many biting cartoons such as this, which suggests who might be looking after the interests of big business.

married. And I've never been involved in anything like a strike.'[15] The message was black and white: if you moved your mill or factory to Virginia you would have a cheap and docile white workforce and leave behind the race riots and strikes associated with northern U.S. cities.

In fact, twenty states concentrated in the South, in the Plains Midwest, and in the Southwest had right-to-work legislation on the books.[16] Taking advantage of the Taft-Hartley Act of 1947, these formerly non-industrial states overrode federal statutes and outlawed compulsory union membership or closed shops.[17] For companies wishing to reduce their labour costs, a right-to-work paradise appeared to be just around the corner.

Auto parts production, historically concentrated in southeastern Michigan, was among the first industries to shift production southward.[18] In 1950, Borg Warner, a pioneer among large auto parts manufacturers, had twenty-four production facilities in the United States, mostly in the Midwest, as well as two plants located in Windsor. Twenty-five years later, all of Borg Warner's fifty-five U.S. plants were located in the South. The restructuring of corporate operations had begun in 1957 when Borg Warner's Long Manufacturing Division closed two Detroit plants. The following year, the company's Morse Chain Co. subsidiary closed in Detroit. Next, the company moved its refrigeration production from Muskegon, Michigan, to Fort Smith, Arkansas. Finally, the Atkins Saw division shifted production from Indianapolis to Greenville, Mississippi. Simultaneously, Borg Warner's two Windsor plants were relocated to smaller towns in Southern Ontario. The rationale for these moves was only too apparent: unskilled wages in Fort Smith were 40 per cent lower than those at the Muskegon factory.

One auto-parts supplier after another followed suit. In the 1970s, auto-parts giant Rockwell International restructured its operations, closing many factories across North America. Of its 138,000 employees in 1974, the company shed 38,000 by 1982.[19] In the meantime, the Eaton Corporation terminated one-third of its 60,000 employees by ending production at eighteen sites in 1981, followed by the closing of its truck axle plant in Cleveland, a transmission plant in Kalamazoo, Michigan, and a valve-manufacturing plant in Battle Creek, Michigan.[20] Only six truck parts plants – located mainly in the South and built in the 1970s – were spared relocation. As auto parts suppliers such as Dana Corporation, Eaton, Clark Equipment, and TRW shifted production southward, the Midwest's share of auto parts production fell from 74 per cent in

A poster by Fred Wright protesting plant closures.

1972 to 65 per cent in 1982.[21] At the same time, auto-related jobs in North Carolina jumped 72 per cent to 22,000 between 1975 and 1980.

In spite of the transplantation of many auto parts companies to the southern United States, company executives began looking further afield in the early 1980s to escape the clutch of the UAW. The list of companies shifting production to Mexico, Southeast Asia, and Europe from Canada and the United States grew to include many of the big names in the auto parts and machinery business. Allis-Chalmers relocated its farm equipment operations out of Milwaukee to escape the UAW. Company CEO David Scott told the annual meeting of Allis-Chalmers in 1980, that 'We've either got to get away from the UAW ... or get out of the business.'[22] Yet no major relocation surprised the UAW as much as that of Caterpillar, known throughout the world for its earth-moving equipment. Until the big 205-day strike over the winter of 1982–3, Caterpillar management had prided itself on its paternalistic image. Yet the strike, precipitated by the company's demands for wage and benefit concessions, convinced Caterpillar to get tough by shifting production out of the United States.[23] Near the end of the strike, the company informed its 1,700 employees at the Mentor, Ohio, plant that their jobs were being exported to Korea. Soon thereafter, Caterpillar closed four other plants. By 1985, the Financial Times reported that Caterpillar had shifted 'considerable production' to its three European plants. The low Canadian dollar and socialized medicine also convinced some American companies like the Eaton Corporation to relocate production from the industrial Midwest to Southern Ontario.[24]

The situation in Canada differed in other ways too. Instead of calling the relocated mills and factories 'runaway plants,' Canadian trade unionists termed the change 'plant movements' or 'plant migration.' This distinction may have originated from the fact that plant relocations in Canada rarely crossed provincial boundaries. Indeed, no Canadian jurisdiction had right-to-work legislation comparable to that of the United States, making it difficult to escape unionization. Companies either moved to less-unionized small towns or moved out of the country. The different understanding of the problem of plant relocations in Canada also stemmed from the fact that trade union concerns about plant migration originated with the Ford Motor Company's decision in the early 1950s to shift its assembly operations to Oakville from Windsor. As the new plant would be covered by the existing collective agreement with the UAW, there was no indication that the company wished to rid itself of the union.[25] A decade later, trade union concerns about plant closings in the auto-parts sector centred on the dislocation caused by the 1965 Auto Pact between Canada and the United States, and not corporate animosity towards unionized workers.[26] Instead, companies leaving Windsor cited the city's geographic position and high wage rates for their decision to relocate elsewhere in Southern Ontario.[27] Unable to see an anti-union animus behind most shutdown decisions, Windsor trade unionists focused on the negative social consequences of plant relocations: '[UAW] Local 195, which is comprised of feeder plants, has been plagued by callous relocations over the years. In spite of the union's protests, companies have moved out, sometimes with the aid of government subsidies, leaving long-time employees to fend for themselves. And who can forget the magnitude of the blow to this community when Ford moved its assembly operation to Oakville?'[28] While Windsor's reputation as a militant union town contributed to company decisions to relocate elsewhere, migrating companies had little hope of casting off the union altogether.

This pattern could likewise be seen when auto-parts plants closed as a result of lower prevailing wage rates outside of Windsor. A confidential October 1961 report filed by the Greater Windsor Industrial Commission blamed high wages for the economic crisis looming over the city.[29] The report cited the case of Canadian Motor Lamp, which opened a new facility in rural Bracebridge, Ontario, and 'slowly transferred several operations from Windsor.' Even though both plants were organized by the UAW, the wage gap proved significant, especially for women: male production workers at Bracebridge earned $1.15 to $1.25 compared with $1.98 in Windsor; women working in the smaller centre received only $.95 to $1.05 for work paid $1.78 in Windsor. Newly unionized workplaces often took decades to match the wages and benefits negotiated in Windsor.

One of the major economic policy developments of the 1970s was the proliferation of regional development initiatives taken by Canadian politicians to assist poor provinces and regions and to attract industry and employment. The federal government supplied millions of dollars to companies willing to build plants in Atlantic Canada or to relocate production from existing facilities in central Canada. The story of Aerovox Canada, an American multinational that received $236,000 of taxpayers' dollars to relocate from Hamilton to Amherst, Nova Scotia, reveals the uncertain benefits of regional development schemes prevalent in the 1970s and 1980s.[30] The displaced female workforce found relatively few factory jobs available for women in Hamilton. As well,

A cartoon by Fred Wright indicating who gains and who loses from the plant closings.

the higher than average age and above-average salaries of workers at Aerovox made them difficult to place into other jobs. Other companies such as York Lambton, a holding company that had acquired Admiral's appliance manufacturing plants from Rockwell International in 1979, used a Quebec government grant to close down the Beach Foundry in Ottawa and move stove making to Montmorency, Quebec. The Ontario government also joined in the regional development effort, declaring Eastern and Northern Ontario development zones, and making firms that located mills and factories into those regions eligible for financial assistance.

What was the relationship between economic restructuring and the sexual division of labour? At first glance, men seemed to fare the worst: in both Canada and the United States they experienced manufacturing job loss in greater numbers than women. However, women were more likely to lose their jobs, especially in Southern Ontario. Two practices conspired to put women at a distinct disadvantage to their male co-workers. First, separate seniority lists restricted female job mobility within the plant by institutionalizing separate male and female spheres. Secondly, sex labelling of jobs prevented women from bidding for jobs traditionally considered men's work. Most women worked in small- and medium-sized establishments on the margins of industry, whereas men were concentrated in the largest industrial plants. Confined by a rigid sexual division of labour to segments of the auto parts industry (as well as other industries such as textiles and clothing), women were particularly at risk in times of industrial restructuring and disproportionately affected by runaway plants.[31]

When International Harvester terminated several operations in Hamilton in 1969–70, the sex labelling of jobs and separate seniority lists made it virtually impossible for women to transfer to other parts of the plant. Despite the modernization of the twine mill in the mid-1960s, International Harvester had gradually reduced its mill workforce from 300 to just 37 employees. However, no men would lose seniority after the company agreed to transfer 'all of the male employees.' By contrast, female employees had to look for work elsewhere. The gender assumptions in the report that international union representative William F. Scandlon sent to his superiors are telling: 'Our big problem would seem to be with the female employees. There are very few female jobs at Hamilton Works. We have several females with long service (15–23 years) laid-off and they, of course, will have preference. The chances of re-employment are poor for [Local] 2868 laid-off females and for Twine

Mill females even worse. In checking the background of experience of these Twine Mill females it would seem very unlikely that any of them could be retrained for simple or routine office type work – but we will explore every possibility.[32] In March of 1970, Scandlon reported that only three of the displaced women required full-time employment as the 'others are not the sole breadwinners and are in a position to draw UIC [unemployment insurance] for a while and look around for work, either full time or part time.'[33] He later used his influence to get Dorothy Routenberg a job with the City of Hamilton.[34] Scandlon's report nonetheless vividly illustrates how deeply the breadwinner ideology was ingrained in the mindset of both company officials and union representatives. As a result, the partial closure of a large establishment like International Harvester put women at a distinct disadvantage vis-à-vis their male co-workers.[35]

Women working for multinational corporations were expected to be docile and inexpensive. When this attitude ceased to be the norm, employers such as Amplifone Canada, an American multinational with a factory in Belleville, Ontario, simply moved away. The Chicago-based maker of television components had located its Canadian branch plant in this small town because of its low wages for women. Once established, the plant's 120 workers promptly joined the United Steelworkers of America and won a $0.20 raise to $1.25 an hour in 1972.[36] Having closed the gap in wages between Amplifone's Belleville and Chicago operations in their first collective agreement, the union was faced with a dilemma when it came time to negotiate its second agreement: accept the company's demand for a $0.05 roll-back in wages or risk losing the plant. The union refused to buckle, and union member Gladys Wardley discovered that she was without a job when she saw a large van at the local plant and men carrying out machinery.[37] The company moved its production twenty-nine miles north to another small town and the Belleville workers were without jobs.

Annual Manufacturers' Directories identify the sex of all employees, union and non-union, and allow some degree of accuracy in measuring the displacement of men and women after plant shutdowns (see Table 4.1). Windsor was in many ways the quintessential Motor City. It was, with Oshawa, Canada's first major centre of automotive assembly and parts manufacturing. In 1970, there was not a single female employee among the 4,500 UAW members at the Ford engine plant and only 40 women among the 9,625 workers at Chrysler.[38] Women were concentrated in a handful of auto parts factories, many of which closed during

A Fred Wright cartoon suggesting the reasons for U.S. military presence in Southeast Asia.

TABLE 4.1
Plant Shutdowns and Displacement in Windsor, 1970–83

Name of Company (Year of Closure)	Male Workers		Female Workers		Total
	N	%	N	%	
Auto Specialties (1971)	300	100.0	0	0.0	300
Elco Woods (1971)	30	91.0	3	9.0	33
Essco Stamping (1971)	12	70.6	5	29.4	17
Fleetwood Metal (1971)	7	35.0	13	65.0	20
General Fire Extinguisher (1971)	52	74.3	18	25.7	70
Duplate of Canada (1972)	198	97.5	5	2.5	203
Daal Plastics	17	25.4	50	74.6	67
Daal Specialties	110	26.2	310	73.8	420
Sun Tool and Stamping (1974)	175	73.5	63	26.5	238
Dominion Twist Drill (1974–5)	22	84.6	4	15.4	26
MGM Brakes (1974–5)	38	44.7	47	55.3	85
Rockwell Intertnational (1977)	179	81.7	40	18.3	219
Bendix Eclipse (1980)	594	74.0	209	26.0	803
Wheatley Manufacturing (1981)	65	92.9	5	7.1	70
Windsor Packing (1982)	120	64.9	65	35.1	185
Dominion Auto Accessores (1983)	25	19.2	105	80.8	130
Great Lakes Forgings (1983)	125	98.4	2	1.6	127
Wheel Trueing Tool (1983)	12	48.0	13	52.0	25
Mckinnis Equipment (1983)	150	88.8	19	11.2	169
TOTAL	2,231	69.6	976	30.4	3,207

Source: RG 27, Accession 1988–9/007, National Archives of Canada.

the 1970s and 1980s. Woman's work in the automotive sector was by and large an extension of the textile industry, where dexterity and patience were construed as feminine qualities. Sewing machine operators were needed for automotive trim, seats, and some accessories, and other female employees assembled small parts such as wire assembly, brakes, and car radios. As a whole, though women represented only 8 per cent of union members in Windsor in 1970, they constituted a greater proportion of displaced workers than men.

The capital shift model proves particularly useful in looking at light industries such as textiles and auto parts that relied on the low wages paid to women and minorities for competitive advantage. Growing international competition brought on by the dismantling of trade barriers by the General Agreement on Tariffs and Trade (GATT) forced many peripheral employers to find cheaper sources of labour than generally available in older industrial areas. The geographic shift in the textile and clothing industries greatly affected historic production centres in New York and New England. In Canada, job loss in the textile and clothing industries was greatest in the Montreal area as Quebec's share of manufacturing employment in the country fell from 33.8 per cent in 1961 to 30.6 per cent in 1976.[39] The shifting location of the auto parts industry, in turn, caused job loss primarily in Southern Ontario, Michigan, and Ohio. Although plant migration proved to be a key component of job loss in both countries, industrial firms operating in Canada could not escape unionization by running away unless they were prepared to leave the country altogether.

The Obsolete Mill, 1970s – 1980s

Another catalyst that triggered waves of plant closings across North America's industrial heartland is located in the failure of industry to modernize as technological change rendered long-established processes obsolete. In some industries such as auto parts, high wages and obsolescence acted as a one-two punch. In others, huge capital investments made employers unable to relocate overnight. Divestment strategies, though similar, differed on the two sides of the border. Notably, those industries in Canada experiencing the signs of old age did not include the steel and auto assembly industries.

On the face of it, the rash of mill and factory closings that struck the automotive assembly, rubber, and steel industries in the late 1970s and early 1980s constituted death by natural causes. In most cases, these were old and obsolete plants that had become unprofitable over the course of time. Yet the closing of an obsolete mill was often the direct result of management's failure to modernize or their active decision to invest somewhere else. As discussed in chapter 3, plant shape and look had changed too dramatically for an old tire plant in Akron or Kitchener to endure. By the 1960s and 1970s, U.S. rubber producers had embarked on a long-term strategy of opening new tire factories in non-union areas of the South, letting older, unionized plants in Ohio and other Great Lakes states die on the vine.[40]

Generally considered to be the big three employers in the industrial heartland, economic change in the automotive assembly, rubber, and steel industries meant trouble for many of the cities of the region dependent on these large plants that employed thousands of workers. The shutdown of a single mill or factory had the potential to alter the identity of a place and to uproot entire communities.

In adopting a strategy of planned obsolescence, companies shifted the blame for job loss onto aging equipment, unproductive workers, and the apparent unprofitability of the plant. According to one Ohio government study, the 'number one problem of most industries in Ohio [was] the age of the physical plant.' The steel industry, for instance, used obsolete equipment in old buildings located on inadequate parcels of land in urban areas.[41] Similarly, glass manufacturers were becoming marginal producers and the early development of the rubber industry had begun to work against Ohio. In spite of modernization, the working lives of mills and factories proved to be finite.

Economists Wilford L'Esperance and Arthur E. King claimed that corporate relocation decisions often depended on the age of existing plants and equipment. They identified two forms of obsolescence: economic and technological. 'If, for example, the rubber industry in Akron finds that new technologies dictate the use of more capital equipment per worker, arrayed horizontally over large areas in single-story factories, then the existing multiple-story factories located in downtown areas with high land prices and property taxes quickly become obsolete. The time dimension or the age distribution of existing plant and equipment can be regarded as a proxy measure of such obsolescence.'[42] As a result, obsolescence represented a 'dynamic phenomenon, having a distinct time dimension.' Installed over time, equipment rarely became obsolete all at once. As the modernization of plants and equipment was an ongoing process and not a one-shot deal, the decision not to invest in a plant eventually resulted in its closing. The abandonment of millions of American workers in the 1970s and 1980s thus originated in the investment decisions of the 1950s and 1960s.

Industrialization in Canada occurred at a later date, and many American corporations entered the Canadian market only after the Second World War. In consequence, economic obsolescence did not claim as many mills and factories in Canada until the 1990s. Those plants that did close were comparatively small since governments intervened to save larger industrial complexes at risk of closing, such as Cape Breton's steel mill and Canada's aeronautics industry.[43] Ironically, those sectors of the Canadian economy, such as textiles, that had developed indigenously proved far more likely to reach obsolescence by the 1970s. According to a 11 March 1970 confidential memo to the federal cabinet, the minister of industry, trade, and commerce reported that the textile industry faced 'major problems of adaptation to rapid changes in technology, world production and market demands.'[44] Meanwhile, a lack of scale inhibited the electrical and electronics industries. There was widespread agreement that the traditional mission and mandate of Canadian manufacturing subsidiaries had become redundant in an era of global markets. The transformation of the international division of labour forced companies to revise their strategies, thereby making an older generation of purpose-built branch plants effectively obsolete. Typically, Canadian companies in the textile and electrical industries either went through massive restructuring or went bankrupt. Planned obsolescence became, in varying degrees, an integral part of corporate investment strategies in Canada and the United States.

Automotive Assembly

It is difficult to overstate the economic importance of the North American auto industry, consolidated and rationalized in the wake of the 1965 Auto Pact and the 1973 global oil crisis. Among the largest industrial firms operating in the United States, the Big Three auto makers – General Motors, Ford, and Chrysler – and dozens of major parts producers employed 971,000 people in 1978.[45] In the following year, the North American auto industry fell victim to a second oil crisis sparked by the Iranian revolution. Until then, the Big Three had bitterly fought the introduction of new U.S. fuel efficiency requirements, preferring to produce large and extremely profitable cars for the North American market. They were ill-prepared for the sudden shift in consumer demand towards small, fuel-efficient cars. As it took a minimum of two years to retool assembly lines, the Big Three found themselves unable to meet small-car demand until 1981. In the interim, faced with six-month waiting lists for the few small-car makes produced by the Big Three, North Americans bought Japanese automobiles instead.[46] Foreign auto makers' share of the U.S. market rose steadily from 17.7 per cent in 1978 to 26.4 per cent in 1980, contributing to the indefinite layoff of 239,000 American autoworkers, with job losses concentrated in Michigan, Ohio, Missouri, and Indiana.[47]

Times were so uncertain that Chrysler teetered on the brink of bank-

The management leaves in style in this editorial cartoon by Fred Wright.

ruptcy, and was only saved by two government bailouts, major conces-sions from employees, and the leadership of Lee Iacocca. Whereas the U.S. Congress insisted on wage and benefit concessions from Chrysler workers as the price for public assistance, the Canadian government's 1980 bailout loan came with the condition that Chrysler make new investments in its Canadian assembly plants, maintain jobs in Canada, and guarantee that no plants would close without the approval of the federal minister of Industry.[48] These two very different responses to Chrysler's appeal had immediate and long-term consequences for auto workers and their unions.

The restructuring of the Big Three resulted in radical shifts in the spatial location of auto assembly plants in North America. Historically, auto assembly operations had been strategically located near major markets. Ford's Canadian subsidiary once had a decentralized network of assembly plants in Windsor, Toronto, Montreal, Winnipeg, Saint John, and Vancouver/Burnaby.[49] Changing conditions dictated the closing of the company's Montreal plant in 1932 and the remaining assembly operations outside of Ontario closed by 1951. Consolidation proceeded with the move of Ford's Windsor assembly operations to Oakville in 1953.[50] Ford of Canada president R.M. Sale told the *Windsor Daily Star* that Ford transferred its assembly operation to be closer to Canadian consumers. In 1951, the Ford Motor Company had employed 12,000 in Windsor. Ten years later, the production workforce in the city had dropped to 4,000.[51] As a result of this early consolidation, Ford's Canadian subsidiary had newer equipment and fewer workers than its U.S. parent company.[52]

The auto industries in Canada and the United States became integrated in 1965 with the signing of the Auto Pact. According to historian Greg Donaghy, the Auto Pact's origins rested in the Canadian government's desire to 'overcome the limitations imposed on the growth of the automotive industry' by the small domestic market.[53] Although the dislocation in Canada's auto parts industry proved controversial at the time, it turned out to be a boon for both countries. Bilateral trade in auto products jumped from $1.2 billion in 1965 to $6.7 billion in 1969.[54] The pact was particularly beneficial for Canada as the government had convinced the Big Three to sign side agreements that resulted in massive new investments in Canadian assembly operations. General Motors agreed to invest $121 million, Ford another $74.2 million, and Chrysler $33 million.[55] The Auto Pact also established Canadian content rules that effectively prevented these companies from shifting labour-intensive assembly work out of the country. As a result, the agreement gave Canada a disproportionate share of auto assembly and low end auto parts manufacturing, but Canada lost out in research and development and in high value parts manufacturing.[56]

The American auto industry, however, plunged into crisis in 1979. In April 1980, president Carter's Cabinet Economic Policy Group received a memo from its executive director K.C. Kau identifying those auto assembly plants deemed at risk due to 'outdated production methods' and 'changing auto technologies.'[57] Kau identified twenty-four of the most vulnerable Ford plants, employing 89 per cent of Ford's metropolitan Cleveland employees and 23 per cent of Ford's metropolitan Detroit workforce. In addition, he listed seventeen Chrysler plants, comprising 38 per cent of Chrysler's Detroit area workforce. With the exception of six regional assembly operations, all of the Ford plants listed operated in Ohio (seven), Michigan (five), or Ontario (four). At Chrysler, those plants considered the most 'sensitive to change' by the

TABLE 4.2
African Americans as a Percentage of
Chrysler's U.S. Workforce

Year	Total (%)
1977	26.5
1978	25.9
1979	22.1
1980	22.9
1981	21.1

Source: Jane Slaughter and Bill
Parker, 'Black Workers, Detroit Lose
Out in Chrysler Restructuring,' *Labor
Notes* (24 February 1983).

Carter administration were clustered in the Detroit–Windsor area.[58] Only eighteen of the forty-six auto assembly plants in operation in 1980 continued to be active ten years later. During the 1980s, Ford closed plants in Mahwah, New Jersey, and Los Angeles and San Jose, California. Meanwhile, General Motors deactivated plants in Atlanta, Georgia, Framington, Massachusetts, St Louis, Missouri, and Los Angeles. At the same time, Chrysler closed two Detroit assembly plants, a St Louis operation as well as a newly acquired AMC plant in Kenosha, Wisconsin.[59]

African Americans bore the brunt of restructuring. As of January 1980, twenty-two of Chrysler's thirty-eight plants were located in the Detroit area. Their payroll to 25,000 African Americans approximated $800 million annually. Three years later, twelve of these Detroit plants had closed. African Americans suffered a disproportionate share of job losses between 1977 and 1981 as their percentage of Chrysler's overall workforce declined sharply (see Table 4.2). Similarly, across the Big Three, the 'whitening' of the workforce was one by-product of industrial restructuring, undermining the gains made by affirmative action over a twenty-year period, and 'threatening to restore the workforce to its previous, all-white, all-male condition.'[60] Widely considered to have the worst minority hiring record in the auto industry, General Motors saw its proportion of minorities drop from 22.4 per cent of its workforce in 1979 to 18.9 per cent in 1982.[61] As sociologist Gregory D. Squires cogently observed: 'When corporations seek out greener pastures they tend to seek out whiter ones as well.'[62]

At the same time, racial considerations complicated plant relocations and employee mobility. UAW vice president Marc Stepp noted that even though 400 Oakland, California, employees of General Motors had been offered jobs at the new facility in Sparks, Nevada, non-white workers proved to be apprehensive about leaving a bicultural city for one with virtually no minority population.[63] This immobility proved critical as companies increasingly located new plants outside traditional industrial zones in the inner cities, where a majority of African Americans lived. Between 1978 and 1984, Detroit lost a stunning 180,000 manufacturing jobs, most of which had been located in the central city. In 1982, nearly one in five Detroit workers were unemployed. In nearby Flint, that number surpassed one in four.

Changing corporate strategies were vividly demonstrated by the location of new auto assembly plants. Between 1945 and 1960, 96 per cent of new plants built by the Big Three were in the U.S. interior, mostly in the states located between north–south Interstates 75 and 65, the geographic heart of the country. Within this area, auto plant location had shifted southward from southeastern Michigan. According to geographer James M. Rubenstein, the number of assembly plants located outside this strip of land fell from thirty-one in 1979 to fifteen in the early 1990s.[64] Still, companies did not replace old plants to keep existing workforces employed. In almost every instance such as in General Motors' decision to build a new plant in Detroit's Poletown, generous government subsidies played a determining factor.[65] Obsolescence was thus rooted in past corporate decisions to locate new plants outside traditional industrial areas. As a result, corporate investment strategies in the decades after the Second World War led to a gradual aging of plants in industrial cities such as Detroit and Flint. This quiet aging process became dramatically apparent in the 1970s and 1980s when a wave of old obsolete auto assembly plants closed, displacing tens of thousands.

By comparison, Canadian auto industry layoffs and plant closings in the mid-1970s were not as destructive. According to a report by Sam Ginden, the director of research for the Canadian region of the UAW, unemployment figures in Canada were significantly lower than in the United States: only 15 per cent of Chrysler's Canadian workers were on layoff in November 1974 versus 64 per cent of their U.S. counterparts. The corresponding figures for Ford were 14 per cent and 30 per cent respectively. At General Motors, 2.5 per cent of the Canadian workforce was unemployed at the end of 1974, compared with 20 per cent in the United States.[66] A similar pattern resurfaced in 1980. At the height of auto industry layoffs in June 1980, General Motors again let go a far larger proportion of its U.S. workforce.[66] Even more important, the twenty-five thousand Canadian autoworkers on indefinite layoff had plants to return to as no auto assembly plant closed north of the border.

The tendency to consolidate assembly plant operations in the Midwest, the Appalachian states of Tennessee and Kentucky, and in Southern Ontario reconfigured the industrial geography of automaking in North America. Long-established U.S. motor cities such as Detroit and Flint saw their share of auto assembly jobs plummet as obsolete plants closed after newer plants had been built elsewhere. In Canada, this geographic shift had been effected much earlier. Geographer James M. Rubenstein credits this change in industrial location to the fragmentation of the auto market.[68] A growing number of car models, combined with a reduced share of the domestic and international markets, meant that only one or two plants assembled any one model. As a result there was no benefit in locating assembly plants near regional population centres. The inauguration of just-in-time production in the 1980s further reinforced these centralizing tendencies. Hence, branch plants located outside the Great Lakes region closed between 1979 and 1984 as the Big Three consolidated their assembly operations along the two major north–south interstates, and along the east–west Highway 401 in Southern Ontario. Older plants located in the inner cities of the industrial heartland also followed this pattern,[69] and a similar story played itself out in the rubber industry.

The Rubber Industry

The geographic concentration of North America's tire plants in the U.S. Midwest and in Southern Ontario resembled that of the auto industry. Ohio represented the heart of the U.S. rubber industry with eleven plants including five in Akron. Similarly, eight of the fourteen Canadian tire plants were located in Southern Ontario. But with the advent of the radial tire the spatial location of the industry underwent dramatic changes.[70] The radial tire's year-round utility contributed to fuel efficiency in an era of high gasoline prices. By 1976, radials represented 61 per cent of tires being sold in North America. As the production of radial tires required changes in plant design, new facilities were built. All of the plants were built outside of Ohio: three were located in South Carolina, two in Oklahoma, and one each in Texas, Indiana, Tennessee, and North Carolina.[71] Technological change thus combined with management's desire to shift production to the non-union South. Akron no longer could claim to be the 'Rubber Capital of the World.'

The American and British rubber companies operating in Southern Ontario were also challenged by the arrival of French-owned Michelin Tire in the mid–1970s. Michelin built three radial tire plants in Nova Scotia and managed to keep them non-union in spite of repeated organizing drives. Despite this precedent, no existing tire companies shifted production to the Atlantic provinces. Transportation costs and distance to market were prohibitive, with the result that older plants in the cities were gradually closed and new ones built in rural Ontario. But the most wrenching changes in the tire industry once again came in the United States.

By 1980, economic dislocation in the tire industry had resulted in the closure of five of the six plants located in California, and seven of the ten plants in Ohio. Plants also closed in Massachusetts, Pennsylvania, Michigan, Alabama, Arkansas, and Colorado.[71] In total, thirty tire plants closed in North America between 1973 and 1984, displacing almost half of the workers in the industry. By 1987, the number of Americans employed in the tire industry had dropped from over 88,000 to just 52,000.[73] Many of these jobs disappeared in the mid- to late-1970s, when the tire companies slashed tens of thousands of employees from their payrolls.

Akron was hardest hit.[74] J.W. Reynolds, director of industrial relations for B.F. Goodrich, claimed in a May 1971 letter to the union representative on a joint 'Labor-Management Committee for Jobs' that Akron plants were 'not competitive.' It cost more to build a tire in Akron than in competitors' plants located outside the state, he maintained. Reynolds blamed the situation on onerous work rules rather than aging equipment: 'Much has been said to the effect that multistory buildings and obsolete equipment are among the reasons for Akron's non-competitive standing. The fact is that many millions of dollars have been invested to modernize certain Akron facilities. The status of building and equipment are the result of being non-competitive more than they are the cause for it. The labor cost per unit of product is the vital determinant of whether work can be continued in Akron.'[75] Tire production in the city ended in early 1982 when General Tire closed its sixty-seven-year-old, four-storey tire plant, displacing another 1,300 workers.[76] *Newsweek* reporters Richard Manning and John McCormack explored the downward slide of the town's blue-collar workers: 'Today the factory facades along South Main Street are an aging monument to past prosperity.'[76] The loss of these plants cost the Akron area an estimated $2.65 billion in lost income in the ten-year period following 1974.[78]

These local losses had been caused, in part, by corporate decisions taken with the changing global situation in mind. Just as Japan had become a world leader in automotive manufacture and steel-making, it had also built strong tire companies such as Bridgestone. Japanese imports of tires into North America thus chipped away at the market share of American-based companies such as Goodyear and B.F. Goodrich. These companies responded by lowering labour costs.

A closer look at the Firestone Tire Company will demonstrate the enormity of the changes sweeping the rubber industry. Faced with quarterly losses, the board of directors was primed for radical change by 1979.[79] Firestone's decision to restructure its global operations came shortly after it welcomed John J. Nevin into the company. Formerly with Zenith, where he had shifted – albeit reluctantly – production offshore, Nevin had few qualms about closing fourteen of the company's nineteen North American plants. As one director commented, nobody from within the company could have made such difficult decisions. The company announced the first wave of six plant shutdowns in March 1980: production ended that fall in Dayton and Barberton, Ohio, Los Angeles and Salinas, California, Pottstown, Pennsylvania, and in the synthetic plant in Akron.[80] These plants employed 5,000 hourly and 2,000 salaried workers as well as 1,500 already on indefinite layoff. Two weeks later, Firestone Canada, a subsidiary, announced that it would close a plant in Whitby, Ontario, on 18 July leaving 650 workers unemployed.[81] Next, Firestone announced that two unprofitable Welsh plants would cease production, a move that illustrated the growing irrelevance of national frontiers in corporate decision-making. By 1985, Firestone's 1979 workforce of 107,000 had been cut in half.[82] Nevin explained that the 'only way to have kept all those people employed would have been to outlaw radial tires. And if those 52,000 hadn't been cut, there wouldn't be any jobs remaining for anybody else.'

Considering the age of some of these facilities and consumer demand for the radial tire, it would be easy to blame technological change and obsolescence for the plant closings. However, as early as the 1960s, Firestone and other rubber companies had embarked on a divestment strategy designed to avoid the United Rubber Workers. First, the bias-ply truck facility in Akron closed up shop, then the factory in Noblesville,

Indiana. The company transferred the work to its Arkansas plants. On the face of it, the plants had died of old age: Akron Plant #1 had come into production on 8 June 1911 and the Noblesville plant in 1916. By the early 1980s, the United Rubber Workers could not ignore the long-term consequences of not replacing Ohio's old multi-storey plants: 'District #1 has the highest number of people affected. This is probably due to the fact the area, encompassing the "Rubber Capital," most likely has older plants which have been organized for a longer period of time (or the average) than the other districts. Much of the effect in District 1 is the result of the gradual curtailment of production among Goodyear, Goodrich and Firestone in Akron itself. The production left because it could be done more cheaply in modern one-story structures which were not organized, especially in the South and Southwest. This process has been going on for many years.'[83] Even though the strategy of union avoidance failed – the new plants became unionized – all but one of the seventeen tire plants constructed between 1967 and 1984 were located in the South, thus foreshadowing economic dislocation in Ohio.[84]

Yet the apparent obsolescence of Ohio plants deflected public criticism by providing a convenient justification for plant closing decisions. In public debates over the future of the industry, Ohio's rubber factories were regularly dismissed as 'archaic' or 'ancient.'[85] The comments in the *Akron Beacon Journal* upon the closing of the multi-storey, red brick Mohawk Tire factory, built in Akron in 1913, proved typical: 'The wonder of the Mohawk story is that the company was able to continue operations here as long as it did. Its dirty, tired-looking turn-of-the-century building on Second Avenue placed both management and workers alike at a disadvantage in their attempt to stay competitive.'[86] Playing on this public perception, company president and CEO Henry M. Fawcett called the plant the 'Achilles heel of the company.'[87] Tellingly, nobody raised the question of why Mohawk and other rubber companies did not provide for their employees when closing obsolete plants.[88] Failing rubber companies such as Firestone abandoned their unionized employees as surely as any ruthless runaway in the auto parts or textile sectors. While some workers were bound to be let go in light of technological change, job loss was inevitable only insofar as Firestone and other tire companies decided to build their newest plants elsewhere. It was not the natural aging process of plants that ultimately caused unemployment for longtime unionized workers but rather corporate decisions to abandon unionized employees in the spatial restructuring of the rubber industry.

The Steel Industry

The steel industry was not dominated by transnational corporations, but instead had a strongly national orientation.[89] U.S. Steel, Bethlehem Steel, Republic Steel, and Jones and Laughlin were among the largest corporations in the United States. Likewise, the Steel Company of Canada and Dofasco were among the largest Canadian-owned firms. All of these companies faced outside challengers, however, as an increasing proportion of the world's steel production became destined for foreign markets. Peter Dicken notes that whereas only 10 per cent of the world's steel production was exported in 1950, that number had risen to 25 per cent in the 1970s.[90] Further, Japan's share of world production went from 8.5 per cent in 1960 to 31 per cent in 1978. Growing international competition from imports, in turn, greatly reduced North American shareholders' return on investments.

Unlike the belated modernization of the auto and rubber industries, the American steel industry failed to modernize anywhere after sinking large sums of money into already-obsolete steel-making processes during the 1950s.[91] Even then, the basic oxygen furnace (BOF) proved to be faster and cheaper than the open hearth furnaces still being built. As a result, U.S. steel companies trailed their Japanese and Western European competitors in adopting this new technology.[92] North American steel companies also lagged behind in the adoption of continuous casting, a technological innovation that reduced the number of stages in the steel-making process.[93] By 1978, the global comparison was stark (see Figure 4.4).

Yet the U.S. government stood aloof from the developing steel crisis.[94] The Carter White House rejected the steel makers' contention that their problems originated from cheap imports.[95] Instead, presidential advisers Stu Eizenstat and Bob Ginsburg pointed to large increases in wages and other costs, low productivity, and 'outmoded' plants.[96] They cited the recent closure of the Youngstown Sheet and Tube's Campbell works as evidence that the U.S. steel industry had failed to modernize. In his comprehensive review of the industry, Anthony M. Solomon reported to the president that, 'In the steel industry, the variance in plant age and efficiency is sizable, with many facilities only approaching a break even point even at high operating rates. Not all of these plants can be modernized economically because of their location and existing facilities ... The domestic market for steel has shifted from the East to the Midwest, and new technologies have not been easily adapted

Figure 4.4
Basic Oxygen Furnace Technology in Steel Production (%)

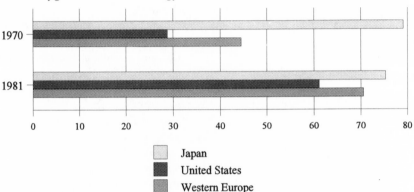

Source: Peter Dicken, *Global Shift: Industrial Change in a Turbulent World* (London: Harper and Row, 1986).

to some Eastern plants which face problems of crowding, small-scale blast furnaces, out of balance finishing facilities, and environmental constraints.'[97] The geographic shift in production to the Chicago area was, to some extent, already underway. The decision of Youngstown Sheet and Tube to expand its mill at Indiana Harbor and Bethlehem's decision to build a new mill at Burns Harbor doomed older mills in Youngstown and Lackawanna.[98] As economist Alfred E. Kahn noted: 'It appears that the steel industry is in the process of improving its efficiency, not so much by capital investment and modernization as by the elimination of relatively inefficient plants.'[99] Charles Bradford, research vice president for Merrill Lynch, put it more bluntly: 'Junking older steel mills is one way they stay competitive.'[100]

Other steel companies stayed competitive by getting out of the steel-making business altogether. U.S. Steel diversified into more profitable sectors of the economy. In the company's 1979 annual report, management regretted the necessity of closing 'marginal' plants and promised to work with affected communities.[101] The following year, the company told shareholders that these tough decisions had enabled U.S. Steel to channel available capital 'into activities generating a competitive return.' The nature of this so-called redeployment became apparent in 1982 when U.S. Steel acquired Marathon Oil for $5.2 billion. For its part, National Steel got out of the steel-making business altogether.

In sharp contrast to the deteriorating situation in the United States, Canada's steel industry was in solid shape.[101] Industrial geographer W. P. Anderson credited the steady moderate growth of the Canadian steel industry throughout the 1960s, 1970s, and 1980s, and the generous tax incentives to modernize, for keeping Hamilton's steel mills highly productive.[102] Ultimately, the structure of Canada's steel industry, which consisted of four single-site steelmakers, Stelco and Dofasco in Hamilton, Algoma Steel in Sault Ste Marie, and Sysco in Sydney, Nova Scotia, prevented the milking of profits by conglomerates thirsty for higher returns on investment.[103] Existing mills were modernized, not abandoned. When the steel mill in Sydney got into trouble in 1967–8, the provincial and federal governments interceded in the public interest and operated the mill for another thirty years.

Unlike the mill towns of Pennsylvania or Ohio, the population of Hamilton continued to grow during the 1970s, albeit at only two-thirds of the rate of population growth in Ontario.[104] The number of production workers in Hamilton actually expanded by 12.4 per cent during that decade, as shutdowns were confined to small- and medium-sized plants employing fewer than five hundred workers, most having less than one hundred. Modernization caused much of the job loss of the early 1980s as labour-saving devices were introduced into the mills. Indeed, one in four manufacturing jobs disappeared, pushing the Hamilton unemployment rate up briefly to 16.7 per cent.[105] Although growing uncertainty in the steel industry led Stelco to phase out its aging Canada Works finishing mill in 1984, employees were transferred elsewhere in the company's vast Hamilton operations. Hence, Canada's steel industry did not experience obsolescence between 1969–84.

In the United States, 'an intergenerational way of life that provided a sense of continuity, security, family cohesion, and communality' was swept away with the demise of dozens of integrated steel mills.[106] Over a ten-year period, 269,000 U.S. steelworkers lost their well-paid unionized jobs. Plant closings displaced 40,000 steelworkers in 1977 alone.[107] Many of the plants were located in the steel valleys of western Pennsylvania, where one integrated steel mill after another fell silent: U.S. Steel closed its Donora (1966), Rankin (1982), Duquesne (1984), Clairton (1984), Homestead (1986), and McKeesport (1987) works; Jones & Laughlin (now LTV Steel) closed its South Side (1985), Hazelwood (1985), and Aliquippa (1985) works; and in 1986, Wheeling-Pittsburgh closed the Monessen West mill.

Figure 4.5
Employment in the U.S. Steel Industry, 1973–83

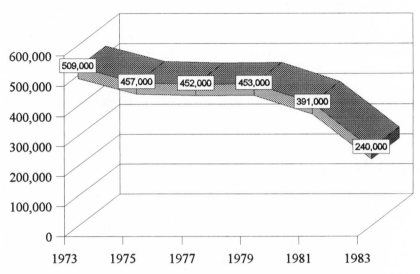

Source: Daniel Rosenheim and James Warren, 'Why South Works Declined,' *Chicago Sun Times*, 30 October 1983.

For many, Youngstown was representative of the problems plaguing older industrial towns and cities. Observers pointed to the gradual westward movement of steel production from Youngstown to the Chicago area as an example of a larger trend to relocate production. What little modernization Youngstown Sheet and Tube completed at its two Youngstown plants came to a halt in 1969 when the Lykes steamship conglomerate, a company a fraction of its size purchased the company. Even though it promised to modernize the Campbell works by building a new BOF facility, the company admitted the project had lower corporate priority than other projects.[109] During the uncertain 1970s, Lykes-Youngstown even delayed installing pollution-control equipment and waited for better times.[110] Those times never came, and in 1977 the Campbell works closed, followed two years later by the Brier Hill works. By then, few questioned that Youngstown steel mills had become antiquated: their blast furnaces were small, all of them used the obsolete open-hearth method, and ancient steam engines continued to run steel-making operations.[111] While the company promised that construction would begin once 'internally generated or other funds are available to support the project,' those funds never became available.[112]

'Smart management' in the steel industry operated marginal mills until they were no longer profitable and then closed them down. For Youngstown State University economist J.J. Koss, the Lykes corporation acted just as it should: 'They didn't reinvest back in that facility. When it was about ready to collapse they shut it down ... if LTV did milk that facility dry, that's exactly what an intelligent management should have done. What do you do when you have various facilities and one of them is almost marginal? You work it as long as you can, and make the repairs that you need in order to keep it going. Since you know you're not going to reinvest there, you are reinvesting somewhere else. They were reinvesting out in Indiana Harbor in a plant where they had more economic advantages. When it is just about ready to collapse, you shut it down.'[113] Yet there was nothing inevitable about the aging process. This apparent death by natural causes resulted from a conscious decision on the part of corporate managers to use up older facilities. In so doing, management actively abandoned workers in the former industrial heartland, laying waste to the Steel Valley in the process.

Industrial firms generally operated older auto, rubber, and steel facilities in the United States until they were no longer needed. This management strategy of planned obsolescence led the Youngstown Sheet and Tube Company to abandon its namesake in favour of modernizing a more centrally located mill at Indiana Harbor, near Chicago. Similarly, the big U.S. rubber companies turned their backs on Akron, the signature city for that industry. Detroit may have been saved a similar fate by the willingness of local political leaders to subsidize the construction of two new assembly operations in the city. Yet the toll of job loss can plainly be seen in the scarred and pockmarked urban landscape of Detroit and in the faces of the city's poor. Corporate strategies to prevent the unionization of new plants paved the way for the mass dislocation of industrial workers. Only rarely did unions succeed in convincing companies to build anew in proximity to soon-to-be-closed factories or mills. The investment decisions made by corporations during the 1950s and 1960s, seen in the location of new mills and factories, led inexorably to the mass closings of older American plants that took place mainly in the late 1970s and early 1980s.[114]

Canadian Branch Plants and Marginal Manufacturers

Obsolescence did not claim a single major auto assembly plant or integrated steel mill in Canada during the 1970s and 1980s. Nor did the handful of rubber factories that closed constitute the wholesale abandonment of Canada's heavily unionized industrial heartland. While Canadian auto and steel industries proved to be far more resilient than those south of the border, obsolescence displaced large numbers of workers in other industries. Hardest hit were Canadians who worked in the electrical, electronics, textile, clothing, and footwear industries. Trade liberalization, in combination with the advancing age of Canadian factories in these sectors, had a two-fold effect. First, branch plants established by foreign multinational corporations closed. Second, Canadian-based firms found they could not compete with imports from low-wage areas in Asia or Latin America.

Canada was an importer of capital throughout the twentieth century.[115] Many American companies established branch plants in Canada early in the twentieth century in order to supply the Canadian market. As historian Michael Bliss has pointed out, the tariff wall erected by Canada's first prime minister, John A. Macdonald, was never intended to keep the Americans out,[115] it was built to be hurdled. As hoped, foreign-controlled companies, an estimated four hundred and fifty by 1913, established manufacturing facilities in Canada to supply the relatively small domestic market with a range of products. As a result, Canada's manufacturing sector has been largely foreign controlled (see Table 4.3). The statistics demonstrate the extent to which Canada had become a branch of the American industrial heartland.

The expanding level of American direct investment in the Canadian economy was met with unease. In her 1970 work, *Silent Surrender*, political economist Kari Levitt argued that the subsidiaries and branch plants of American-based multinational corporations 'replaced the operations of the earlier European-based mercantile venture companies in extracting the staple and organizing the supply of goods.'[116] This nationalist argument maintained that as new technologies were imported instead of being developed domestically, Canada became dependent on American technological know-how. Research and development as well as economic decision making were all concentrated outside the country. As in an often-repeated expression, Canadians were reduced to being 'hewers of wood' and 'drawers of water.'

TABLE 4.3
Foreign Control of Selected Canadian Industries (percentage of capital foreign-controlled, 1954–73)

Industry	1954	1963	1970	1973
Agricultural machinery	35	49	39	55
Rubber	93	96	99	99
Textile	16	21	22	26
Auto assembly and parts	95	95	96	97
Other transportation equipment	36	79	76	70
Electrical apparatus	77	76	77	73
Iron and steel	—	14	9	—
Pulp and paper	56	48	50	53

Source: Ontario, Office of Economic Policy, Ministry of Treasury, Foreign Investment in Canada: Ontario Background Paper for 15th Annual Premiers' Conference, 12–13 September 1974, Committee for an Independent Canada, Box 23, File 1000-3-1, Foreign Ownership Article, Queen's University Archives.

Critics of this nationalist line dissected the myths surrounding foreign ownership. Economist A.E. Safarian, for example, argued that American investment had contributed greatly to the development of Canada's manufacturing and resource sectors, creating jobs for hundreds of thousands of Canadians.[118] Regardless, the level of direct foreign investment in Canada had levelled off by the 1970s.[119]

With the downturn in the economy during the 1970s, Canadian economic nationalists shifted their attention from foreign direct investment to divestment. Canadian employees of foreign firms, they argued, were subject to the whim of corporate headquarters. As will be seen in chapter 6, it was widely believed that American companies closed branch plants operating in Canada in order to keep plants humming south of the border. Various studies have tried to determine whether this was in fact true. Fred Caloren concluded in 1974 that closings were 'inevitably' of branch plants or subsidiaries of large corporations.[120] Yet Caloren found no direct link between foreign ownership and dislocation. By contrast, J. Paul Grayson's study of the closure of SKF's plant in Scarborough, Ontario, concluded otherwise.[121] In the most careful study to date, Ian Robertson MacLachlan found that foreign multinationals did not account for a disproportionate number of jobs lost to plant closings between 1981 and 1986.[122] When MacLachlan's findings are examined more closely there is evidence that foreign companies were more willing to shut down and relocate production. First, most of the Canadian-owned firms that closed plants were bankrupt. This was not true of foreign-owned firms operating in Canada. Second, foreign companies closed a disproportionate number of plants. MacLachlan conceded that foreign ownership was significant for small branch plants operating in Canada because the traditional mission and mandate of Canadian manufacturing subsidiaries was rendered obsolete by falling trade barriers.[123] Four successive rounds of multilateral trade negotiations made redundant many branch plants in Canada. By 1987, two-thirds of all imports from the United States were crossing the border duty-free.[124]

American branch plants operating in Canada proved to be a mixed blessing. While these factories created work for Canadians, they were terribly inefficient. Economists estimate that productivity in Canada lagged 25 to 30 per cent behind the United States during the 1960s and 1970s. One of the chief reasons for this result was the inability of branch plants to take advantage of the economies of scale and produced instead a wide range of products for the domestic market.[125] This situation was exacerbated, the Science Council of Canada reported in 1972, by the fact that branch plants operating in Canada were often not allowed to export outside the country, making these inefficient plants highly vulnerable to imports.[126]

Taking advantage of the emerging global market and economies of scale, multinational corporations moved quickly to rationalize their production. Integration allowed companies like Westinghouse to dedicate factories to the building of a single product. At Canadian-controlled Massey-Harris, makers of farm combines and balers, the company moved to replace twenty-two different combine models produced at twelve locations around the world with three standard models in 1973. The company wanted to produce the guts of the machine in Canada but found itself saddled with two decrepit multi-storey factories.[127]

The need for change in the face of trade liberalization was not lost on world leaders.[128] The Canadian government, for its part, set out to promote 'organization changes' within selected industries.[129] The 'lack of scale' in the electrical and electronics industries, in particular, 'inhibited' their full potential. The general policy goal of the federal government was to encourage the consolidation of these two industries through mergers and acquisitions. In an influential 1978 study, *For a Common*

Future, the Economic Council of Canada concluded that some heavily protected sectors would inevitably 'disappear.'[130]

No industry was as hard hit as Canada's textile industry, but the problems in this sector could not be blamed on branch plants. With trade barriers falling, home-grown Canadian textile manufacturers found themselves in an impossible situation. Built to satisfy the Canadian market, these labour-intensive plants now had to compete with companies based in low-wage areas. The age of the plants was also a concern. The case of Glendale Spinning Mills in Hamilton exposes the extent of the problems facing many marginal Canadian operations.

Glendale Spinning Mills was one of the oldest and best-known spinners of cotton, worsted, and synthetic yarns in Canada. Nestled in a residential area of Hamilton's east end, the company was clearly in financial trouble by the mid-1970s. In fact, it had not prospered for years.[131] Trouble in the textile industry had already resulted in the closure of most of the other cotton mills in the city: Cosmos Imperial Mills, Kaylee Textiles, and the Hamilton Cotton Company had all disappeared. To avoid this eventuality, company management asked the assistance of the federal government to improve productivity in the mill. The resulting study conducted by C.B. Landstreet, president of the Testing and Research Laboratory in Knoxville, Tennessee, revealed remarkable inefficiencies.

Landstreet found that in seventeen years of operation over four thousand people had passed through this troubled plant. What made this figure noteworthy was that the plant employed only three hundred and fifty at any one time. The constant turnover of personnel cost Glendale an estimated $200,000 annually in wasted salaries and slowed production. The report blamed this astronomical rate of turnover on a combination of high unemployment benefits and the low wages paid in the textile industry. Competition from overseas and the American South, Landstreet believed, prevented the company from offering its employees a higher wage.

If Glendale Spinning Mills management was largely helpless to stem the rate of employee turnover, Landstreet indicated that much could still be done to improve efficiency. For starters, he recommended a thorough cleaning of the plant. During his inspection, he found the cotton warehouse cluttered with old boxes, machinery parts, waste carts, unused cans, old ducts, and pieces of sheet metal. Within the plant itself, all of the dust fans and hoppers were out of operation due to missing drive belts. Elsewhere, missing lights and leaks in the roof made it difficult for workers to do their jobs. Machinery was also found to be damaged and lacking adequate maintenance. At any given moment, one-third of the carding machines were out of operation. 'Good yarn quality and high production depends upon efficient carding,' Landstreet reported. Also, because the plant was old, its layout was not conducive to optimal work flow. Even though Glendale's management responded energetically to the report, the company sank into receivership in 1981 after losing $1 million over a decade of marginal operations. In summarizing the situation, the Ontario Ministry of Labour reported that the plant was 'antiquated' and would need $2.5 million in new investment to make a go of it.[132]

Given this changing international context, job loss in Canada proved to be greatest in industries where the majority of workers were employed in small plants. Although firms with less than twenty employees had represented 20 per cent of total employment in Canada, they accounted for 41 per cent of permanent layoffs by the end of the 1980s.[133] By contrast, large industrial establishments with more than five hundred workers, representing 40 per cent of all employees in the country, incurred only 17 per cent of layoffs. The likelihood of being displaced from a large firm operating in Canada during the worst period of the recession in the early 1980s did not approach the probability of being laid off from a small firm in better times. Clearly, the pattern of industrial transformation differed between Canada and the United States.

Conclusion

Primed by their physical and psychological detachment from the factory floor and their disengagement from the products being produced, corporate executives wanting to reduce labour costs executed a strategy of union avoidance that left millions unemployed. Some companies, concentrated in the textile and auto-parts sectors, relocated production in dramatic fashion by moving from one site to another in the blink of an eye. These runaway plants attracted the attention of trade unionists and symbolized the apparent social irresponsibility of some employers. Other companies, concentrated in the rubber and auto assembly industries, chose to divest themselves of high-cost workers in the Midwest quietly over two decades. These industries located new plants far from their historic heartland. Unburdened by any emotional attachment to employees, corporate executives judged individual plants 'against cost-profiles of rival American regions and international sites and against technological and market opportunities.'[134] When obsolescence made the operation of older plants unprofitable, the transplantation of production had been completed. Runaway plants and obsolete mills were two sides of the same coin.

What chiefly distinguished the pattern of plant closings in the United States from that of Canada was the obsolescence of towering steel mills and sprawling auto assembly plants. While dozens of these mills and factories closed in the United States displacing hundreds of thousands of American workers, not one integrated steel mill or auto assembly plant closed in Canada between 1969 and 1984. The continued vitality of steel-making and auto assembly in Canada, thanks in part to newer technology and the generous financial assistance of the Canadian government, ensured that residents of Southern Ontario did not wake up one morning to find that an era had passed. Even so, Canada's branch-plant economy put it at risk for industrial restructuring as a new international division of labour took hold with fewer barriers to trade and investment.[135] In the end, the deindustrialization of parts of the industrial heartland in general, and American inner cities in particular, came about through corporate strategies to run away from high wages and rigid work practices and to phase out older, less profitable facilities that employed costly, older unionized workforces.

5   In Defence of Local Community

A great debate has raged over the apparent passivity of American workers and their unions in the face of plant shutdowns and job loss. Many historians in the United States blame the business-as-usual attitude of trade union leaders[1] while others point to the 'dejected acceptance' that typified worker responses to plant closings.[2] Few would disagree with David Bensman and Roberta Lynch's assertion that a 'sense of the inevitable cloud[ed] all discussions about the industrial crisis' that confronted the United States.[3] Discourses of decline conveyed messages of 'collective powerlessness,' and their apparent inevitability acted to undermine a sense of collective moral responsibility. Michigan state senator John Kelly accounted for the political paralysis this way: 'Everyone knows Michigan is hurting. That is familiar news ... Like the surrealistic TV clips from Vietnam in the '60's we see three dimension[al] images of a padlocked factory gate, a long unemployment line and worried faces of throngs of jobless workers ... No probing at the themes. No rage. No visionary response. We are expected to recover, naturally. We have before. Lull yourself off to a warm hibernation, everything will be alright. Not this time.'[4] It is far too easy, however, to blame lacklustre union leadership or public opinion for worker acquiescence. It is important to consider where the possibilities for identification and collective action came from.

The dampening effect of the Cold War on militant trade unionism in the United States, combined with the radicalizing effect of the Vietnam War on American college students, influenced how Americans responded to industrial transformation. In the early years of the Cold War, the American labour movement purged thousands of activist members from their ranks and expelled left-wing unions such as the United

Electrical Workers.[5] As a result, by the late 1960s, American unions were highly nationalistic and politically moderate. Indeed, the bellicose patriotism of union leaders such as George Meaney, president of the AFL-CIO from 1955 to 1979, confirmed how conservative much of the union movement had become during the Vietnam War. Organized labour's strong support for military intervention drove an ideological wedge between economic liberals in the trade union movement and the tens of thousands of affluent college students who were being radicalized by the escalating and increasingly unpopular war.

The anti-government animus of these youthful protesters distinguished them from both the statist Old Left and the patriotic labour movement. In effect, the Cold War militarized American nationalism, making it distasteful to many young people. In response, the New Left developed a strategy of decentralization and an aversion for bureaucracy. Given their anti-nationalism and their troubled relationship with organized labour, these young, middle-class activists embraced localism as well as the politics of identity. As historian Christopher Lasch has persuasively argued, communitarianism was an important ingredient in the political discourse of the New Left.[6] Accordingly, the 1970s witnessed the proliferation of local community and neighbourhood organizations.[7]

The ideological ambiguity of community and its association with radical students made it suspect among trade union leaders, who assumed that local identifications undermined union solidarity. In order to defeat companies that whipsawed one union local against another, trade unionists were strongly encouraged to work together. Even so, the social upheaval of the late 1960s and early 1970s spilled into the union hall. In some unions, dissident rank-and-file activists challenged their unions' more patriotic leadership in hotly contested elections. Although for the most part unsuccessful, these efforts contributed to the unwillingness of union leaders to build coalitions with other social movements.[8] The growing chasm between American workers and students was acted out each week between Archie Bunker and his son-in-law, Michael, aka Meathead, on the popular television show All in the Family.

Within this charged political climate, then, American workers and others responded to plant shutdowns. While rank-and-file insurgents in the union movement joined with local ecumenical coalitions and public-interest groups in the name of defending community against capital disinvestment, union leaders stressed American nationalism in their contention that imports were largely to blame for industrial re-trenchment. Unlike the situation in Canada, where the political left embraced nationalism, American nationalism had been tarnished by the Vietnam War and McCarthyism, making it unattractive as a symbolic weapon to fight plant shutdowns. Needing a rhetorical lever to politicize what was generally considered to be a private contractual matter between employer and employees, opponents of plant closings fell upon local community. This chapter will show the relationship between the struggle to define and use community and the miserable failure of plant closing opponents in the United States during the 1970s and early 1980s.

Patriotic Trade Unions and Procedural Due Process

A great deal of recent scholarship in labour studies has focused on how legal developments have shaped and reshaped trade unionism in the United States. Christopher L. Tomlins, William Forbath, and Victoria Hattam have argued that the National Labor Relations Act (NLRA) of 1935, more commonly known as the Wagner Act, produced a legal regime governing industrial relations that worked against trade union militancy.[9] Unions gained compulsory bargaining rights and recognition from employers only in exchange for their agreement to act responsibly and within the law. The law, as always, shaped trade unionists' calculation of what was possible and desirable.[10]

In part, the Wagner Act established that 'wages, hours and other conditions of employment' were subject to mandatory collective bargaining.[11] What constituted those other conditions of employment was left undefined and in dispute. Early rulings of the National Labor Relations Board (NLRB) during the 1940s and 1950s established that unionized employers wishing to shut plants, in whole or in part, had to meet with the union to discuss the decision and its effects on the bargaining unit.

Management's legal obligation to collectively bargain with unionized employees over plant closings has been undermined by a series of court decisions that began in 1964. The *Fibreboard* ruling of that year held that an employer need not bargain over a decision to subcontract bargaining unit work to a third party. Managerial prerogatives were further bolstered by the Supreme Court's 1965 ruling in *Darlington* v. *NLRB* that limited the scope of collective bargaining to the effects that might result from an entire plant being slated for closure. Prior to 1981, the courts and the NLRB were divided as to the employer's obligation to consult unionized employees over the decision to partially close a mill or factory.[12] The Supreme Court's *First National Maintenance* decision of that year put the matter to rest.[13] Thereafter, as long as the company was not motivated by anti-union animus, it could do as it pleased. It was only required to bargain in good faith over the *effects* of the decision.

Union activists nonetheless used every legal means at their disposal to help their members. In the words of attorney Peter Pitegoff, the NLRA 'provided the basis for a variety of plant closing responses.' It was common practice for unions to file a complaint to the NLRB once a plant shutdown had been announced. These complaints usually involved two clauses of the NLRA, section 8(a)(3) which prohibited the employer from discriminating against an employee on the basis of union membership, and section 8(a)(5) which required both parties to bargain over matters involving 'wages, hour, and other terms and conditions.' Legal challenges to plant closings, however, proved a disappointment for the labour movement, even in those cases when judges were openly sympathetic to the workers' plight.[14]

Plant closing agreements also proved to be exercises in frustration for displaced union members and their representatives. Without any bargaining power to speak of, workers won little above and beyond what was guaranteed in their collective agreements. For a contractual promise not to interfere with the close-down of the plant, they might receive nominal extensions of health and life insurance and pension guarantees. Detroit union activist Bernice Adams recalled that 'you don't have much leverage. You take what they're going to give you.'[15] Another trade unionist with considerable experience negotiating plant closing agreements for the United Auto Workers, Marilyn McCormack, agreed:

Q   What was it like sitting across the table from management during a close out agreement?

A   You' re begging is what you' re doing because you don't have a leg to stand on. You don't have contract language. You don't have law. You have nothing.

Q   How do you negotiate then?

A   You just try to go on the fact that you got people out there with twenty, thirty years seniority. They devoted their life to this plant. They need something.

Q   Do those arguments work with management?

A   I don't think so. They just gave us the two weeks just to get rid of us.[16]

These agreements were typically negotiated after the announcement had been made and the plant summarily closed. By then, the union had no leverage with which to bargain. But it never had much to begin with as the company did not have to come to an agreement with the union. It only had to bargain in good faith. Afraid that public protests against shutdowns would jeopardize even these small tokens of corporate goodwill, unions tended to stifle protest.

Even though the right of the employer to terminate individual employees had been constrained by the Fourteenth Amendment, managerial prerogative to terminate groups of employees went largely unchecked. The at-will doctrine, which has framed legal decisions in the United States, allowed employers to terminate without notice or justification. Pointing to the fact that the effects of plant closings were a matter of mandatory collective bargaining, industry spokespersons claimed that plant shutdowns were a contractual matter between themselves and their employees. Given this existing legal framework, legislative proposals that would have softened the blow of displacement were opposed in the name of 'free collective bargaining' and 'due process.' Industry thus proved highly successful in turning a familiar union position against working people, and American labour law worked against a militant political response to plant closings.[17]

The Trade Adjustments Act (TAA) of 1963 also worked against labour militancy in the 1970s and 1980s. During the boom years after the Second World War it was understood that a displaced worker could always find employment elsewhere and draw on unemployment insurance in the interim. This supposition began to break down in the early 1960s as trade liberalization brought with it massive dislocation that often involved older workers with few other job prospects. The TAA was designed to cushion the effects of trade liberalization after the Kennedy round of the General Agreement on Tariffs and Trade (GATT). Typically, an application was made by a local union to a Trade Adjustment Board, which then investigated the claim. If the job loss was found to have been due to cheap imports caused by tariff reduction, the displaced workers would be awarded extra benefits.

Anti-imports signs at the entrance to the parking lot at Solidarity House, the headquarters of the United Auto Workers, Detroit, May 1982.

Once workers began to be awarded compensation in large numbers in 1969, the TAA provided unions with a powerful incentive to blame plant closings on imports since to suggest otherwise would have undermined their bid to win extra benefits for displaced members. Under the TAA, Meyer Bernstein, a senior representative of the United Steelworkers of America (USWA), coached locals on how to put together a convincing package to back their claims.[18] Bernstein's techniques helped Youngstown Sheet and Tube workers to be certified by the government for extra assistance even though oral history interviews reveal that the workers blamed the American-owned parent company for the closing.[19] In consequence, debates surrounding plant shutdowns were channelled into a patriotic critique of imports that let American corporations off the hook.

Historian Dana Frank has shown that the waves of plant closings that struck the northern United States during the 1970s and 1980s was accompanied by a Buy American movement – the longest and deepest wave of economic nationalist sentiment in United States history. Unions such as the International Ladies Garment Workers' Union (ILGWU) and the United Auto Workers (UAW) did everything possible to wrap the union label in the Stars and Stripes. Unions faced companies relocating production and jobs outside the United States with a revamped strategy to attack imports and to urge American consumers to buy American-made products.[20] Beginning in the early 1970s, the union movement abandoned its previous support for trade liberalization and lobbied politicians for import restrictions to protect American jobs.

The Buy American campaign peaked in the early 1980s with the downturn in the automotive industry. Many American workers expressed their anger at imports and job loss through bumper stickers, t-shirts, posters, and public signage that proclaimed: 'Buy American: The Job You Save May Be Your Own.' At union halls across the Industrial Midwest, signs were posted warning drivers not to park their foreign-made cars there. Dana Frank argues that the strategy failed because it set up the wrong us versus them contrast: 'On the one side were domestic employers, domestic workers, and unionized shops. On the other were "imports," made by "foreign workers" in nonunion shops owned by "foreigners."'[21] The protectionist thrust of American economic nationalism actually distracted trade unionists from the American companies that were shutting the plants and laying off workers.

Advocates of a more aggressive government role in regulating plant shutdowns tried unsuccessfully to advance legislation through Congress that would require compensation for displaced workers and local communities for reasons other than trade. From 1974 to 1984 a bill was introduced annually that would ensure that workers and their communities had advance warning, severance pay, assistance in job placement, and short-term compensation, for lost tax revenue.[22] None of these bills made it out of committee until a scaled-back version was introduced in 1985. That bill, shorn of any reference to severance pay, transfer rights, community compensation and employee ownership was narrowly defeated, 208 to 203, on the floor of the House of Representatives.[23] Ultimately, federal politicians refused to regulate plant shutdowns until the watered-down Worker Adjustment and Notification Act (WARN) was passed in 1988.[24]

Prior to 1988, the only national legislative victory for trade union opponents of plant closings came with the adoption of the Employee

Retirement Income Security Act (ERISA) in 1974. Legislative reform of the private pension system, begun under John F. Kennedy in the early 1960s, had a tortured journey. The termination of Studebaker automotive operations in the United States, and the closing of its massive South Bend, Indiana, plant in 1964, highlighted the need for reform. The company's private pension fund was millions of dollars short of its obligations to its aging workforce. As a result, thousands of employees (who were on average fifty-two years of age with twenty-three years of service) with vested pension rights received only fourteen cents on the dollar.[25] Demands for pension reform grew louder. Unions such as the USWA and the UAW urged the federal government to ensure the adequate funding of private pension funds and provide for a re-insurance scheme to further protect workers.[26] The cause of pension reform was advanced by the resignation of Richard Nixon: wanting to show the American public positive congressional leadership, the House of Representatives voted overwhelmingly for ERISA, 375 to 4.

Pension reforms had unintended consequences. The stepped-up funding requirements soon resulted in huge surpluses in many private pension funds. More than one cash-hungry company closed its plant in the early 1980s in order to discontinue these pension plans and recover the surpluses. A congressional committee discovered that 114 plans with surpluses exceeding $1 million each, were terminated in 1980–2.[27] By 1988, 1,600 pension plans had been terminated 'in order to recoup overfunded plan assets,' amounting to $18 billion.[28] ERISA was a hollow victory for trade unionists; it protected them from one risk only to create another.

Why did federal politicians fail to go much beyond pension reform in order to assist displaced American workers? Three factors worked against government intervention. Clearly, a legal framework already existed that regulated, albeit nominally, plant closings under the NLRA. Second, the TAA encouraged trade unionists to channel their opposition to plant closings into an ineffective anti-imports or anti-Japanese political discourse. Just as important, particularly in federal politics, was the perception that plant closings were confined to the once-mighty industrial heartland. Closings could therefore be dismissed as a regional crisis, not a national one. Exacerbating matters further, regional chauvinism within the Republican and Democratic parties in Washington ensured the immobility of the federal government. Southern Democrats and western Republicans opposed attempts to regulate plant shutdowns on the premise that these efforts favoured one region over another. Republicans and Democrats from right-to-work states under-

Labor Day parade, Detroit, 1982.

stood that Michigan's loss was often their gain. With political power already shifting to the South and West, and the Republicans adopting an aggressive Southern Strategy, the Democratic party proved unwilling to take the political risk involved in regulating plant shutdowns.

The past failure of government to improve demonstrably the situation in the inner cities despite pouring massive amounts of federal money into the problem undoubtedly acted against federal intervention in industrial decline.[29] This inaction was made easier by the knowledge that the union movement, a key constituency of the Democratic party, was not of one mind on the issue. In the absence of federal plant shutdown legislation, the U.S. government used import restrictions, additional adjustment assistance programs, retraining schemes, tax relief to companies, non-enforcement of environmental and safety regulations, employee stock ownership loan guarantees, and unemployment insurance to placate plant closing opponents.[30]

Advocates of plant shutdown legislation fared little better at the state level. In the hypercompetitive atmosphere of the 1970s and early 1980s, state governments feared that shutdown legislation or its enforcement would hasten the departure of capital. Companies used this fear to wring tax concessions and subsidies from the state. The most energetic campaigns to introduce state regulation of plant closings occurred naturally enough in the industrial Northeast and industrial Midwest.[31] These areas had the most to lose from plant relocations and closings, but often legislative action only followed the closing of a large and symbolically important mill or factory. This type of closure also motivated non-industrial states such as Montana. The idea of interfering with managerial prerogatives was political poison in that state until Anaconda Ltd. closed its huge smelter and refinery operations in the late 1970s, laying off 1,500 workers. Thereafter, calls for state intervention gained new credibility. Yet public support for plant closing legislation was deemed – in a survey of state AFL-CIOs in 1981 – to be minimal or non-existent in every state except Iowa, New York, and Ohio. And even in those states, there was no serious hope of legislation.

To ascertain the likelihood of legislative action, United Rubber Workers' Director of Research Carl Dimengo distributed a series of questionnaires to Ohio lawmakers and union affiliates in 1981. Eight state legislators who had co-sponsored a previous attempt to legislate plant shutdowns in Ohio responded to the questionnaire. Their responses revealed the deep pessimism that gripped the anti-plant-shutdown movement in the early 1980s. In explaining why the Ohio bill had failed, they pointed to the 'unified' and 'vehement' opposition of manufacturers in the state and acknowledged that the opponents of the bill had done a better job of explaining their position to the public.[32] Opposition, they added, hinged on the fear that passage of the bill would irrevocably harm Ohio's 'business climate' and result in additional plant shutdowns. Even in deindustrializing Youngstown, where steel mill closings were displacing thousands of workers, the union movement could claim only 'some' support for plant-closing legislation.[33] When asked if they intended to co-sponsor another bill, five of the eight Ohio state legislators said they would not, claiming that such an effort was doomed to fail.

Only a handful of the estimated 125 plant-closing bills introduced in state legislatures during the 1970s and early 1980s were ever ratified.[34] Prior to 1988, only Maine (1971), Wisconsin (1975), and Hawaii (1985) passed legislation requiring mandatory advance notice of shutdowns (usually thirty days) or severance pay to long-service employees. Other states (among them Massachusetts, Maryland, and Michigan) legislated indirect programs to encourage businesses to provide advance warning of job loss. Displaced workers in Massachusetts, for example, could draw on state-funded supplemental unemployment benefits for a ninety-day period if a company did not provide advance notice of shutdown. This legislation predictably worked against companies actually providing advance notice of any kind.[35]

The existence of mandatory legislation did not necessarily mean that advance notice was actually given. In practice, neither Wisconsin nor Maine enforced the legislation.[36] For example, a study by the Legislative Audit Bureau found that only 21 of 255 Wisconsin businesses gave advance warning of their decision to close a plant between January 1985 and September 1987. Another government source estimated that no more than 27 per cent of Maine-based companies and 10 per cent of Wisconsin-based ones actually gave the legally required notice to their terminated employees.[37] Enforcement of Maine's severance pay requirements reached 56 per cent due to the vigilance of the workers themselves, as most of the payments occurred 'after successful litigation by the state or by individual claimants.'[38] The influence of Southern right-to-work states in support of non-compliance was unmistakeable. Michigan director of commerce, Norton L. Berman, advised the governor in December 1981 that General Electric had given 'us the ultimate compliment' by saying that 'Michigan has gone South-

Girl holding protest sign at a demonstration by UAW members opposing contract concessions at Ford, 1982.

ern.'[39] Sporadic attempts to regulate plant shutdowns at the state level were dashed on the rocks of interstate competition.

In the absence of political leadership at the federal or state levels, Americans facing job loss or community dislocation increasingly turned to their civic leaders for guidance. As the editor of the Detroit News conceded in 1981, 'the public desire for leadership, active leadership, to guide Michigan out of the economic morass is loud and clear.'[40] In an ironic twist, civic elites in many de-industrializing towns actually celebrated the loss of mills and factories. Pittsburgh's newspaper editors, for example, were 'eager to write an obituary for steel production within the city's limits.'[41] The impatience to throw smokestack industries into the dustbin of history was based on assumptions about a post-industrial future. Typically, leadership responded in time-honoured fashion by boosting post-industrial schemes.[42] A study of the declining auto town of Flint concluded that civic leaders turned to boosterism in times of deindustrialization.[43] Millions of Flint taxpayers' dollars went into the building of a Hyatt hotel, an indoor amusement park celebrating the automobile, and a major retail complex, all of which failed miserably.

Frustrated by the inaction of state governments, several municipal governments adopted city ordinances requiring pre-notification of mass layoffs or plant shutdowns. Philadelphia was the first city to regulate plant closures with a 1982 by-law that empowered the courts to force a company to remain open for the sixty-day notice period. This law does not appear to have been enforced, however. Next, Pittsburgh city council, politicized by the fight to keep the Nabisco plant open, overrode the mayor's veto in 1983 and adopted a three-month minimum pre-notification period for plants shutting down within city limits. The Pittsburgh ordinance also called for the establishment of a city office to investigate possible closings and develop economic alternatives.[44] The ordinance was quashed as *ultra vires* of the state's home-rule law by the District Court in 1984, a ruling that was sustained by the Court of Common Pleas in *Smaller Manufacturers* v. *Pittsburgh*.[45] Unable to win legislative protection, it was little wonder that trade unionists turned to collective bargaining in order to provide a measure of job security for their members.

Having been defeated in the political arena, the union movement resorted to an over-riding legalistic response. The UAW, for example, designated its legal department as 'primary contact' for union locals going through a plant shutdown. Lawyers rather than political strategists coordinated the union's response to plant closings.[46] An effective union negotiator in the rough-and-tumble world of the early 1980s had to be a 'legal innovator' and a 'bargaining tactician.'[47] Yet unless the existing agreement with the union provided for severance pay, prenotification, preferred hiring rights, early retirement, or health care extension, even the most creative and innovative union negotiator had little bargaining power. In good times, workers wanted wages and benefits. But in bad times it was often too late to negotiate a job security provision, or agreement came at the price of major wage and benefit concessions.

Failure to convince politicians to intervene on their behalf with companies, coupled with the string of unfavourable court decisions, forced unions into concession bargaining. The 1979 Chrysler bailout acted as the catalyst, setting a pattern duplicated by other smokestack industries, as well as by General Motors and Ford and their auto parts suppliers. Nearly all of the major trade unions were wholly unprepared for the sharp downturn in the economy. Having failed to negotiate job security provisions, many unions now agreed to exchange existing wages and benefits for them. In 1980, advance notice, preferred hiring, and severance pay provisions were included only in 10, 11, and 34 per cent of American collective agreements, respectively.[48] In the six-year period between 1979 and 1985, the number of contracts that included the first two provisions doubled and the number of collective agreements with severance clauses increased seven-fold.[49] Among the 203 concessionary agreements analyzed, the Bureau of National Affairs found that one quarter of these agreements included explicit job guarantees.

Notwithstanding these union inroads into the job security issue, only 20 per cent of companies gave notice of more than thirty days, due in large part to existing collective agreements. This trend is confirmed by a 1983–4 survey of business executives that found that the median notice given of layoff was just 7 days. One-third of American employers gave no notice whatsoever.

By the early 1980s, the fear of job loss had primed the membership of the big industrial unions for concessions. Indeed, plant closings hung over their heads like the sword of Damocles.[50] After two tentative concession agreements with the big steel companies were defeated, an embarrassed USWA leadership amended its ratification procedure to limit voting eligibility, clearing the way for final approval of a 9 per cent roll-back in wages.[51] Despite this obvious case of elite manipulation, it would be wrong to conclude that ordinary union members were more willing to resist concessions than their leadership.[52] For one thing, local union minute books revealed a great deal of resignation in the face of plant shutdowns. Locals formed in the heady days of the Steel Workers Organizing Committee (SWOC) in the 1930s often died with a whimper. As the recording secretary of Local 4384 in Monessen, Pennsylvania, noted on 20 January 1972, 'people are leaving now.'[53] Even more importantly, a majority of union members continued to vote for the status quo in union elections and consistently ratified concessionary agreements – albeit narrowly in some cases – across the United States. Apparently, the mainstream of the union movement accepted the logic that the 'misfortunes of US industry' were caused by high wages.[54]

To a great extent, plant closing agreements were treated like any other collective agreement. International unions usually considered shutdowns a local responsibility. One senior union official, for example, recalled that, 'In all my experience dealing with plant closings and economic dislocation in my state, I have never had an occasion to involve any international [central union]. Most of our involvement comes after the fact, after the closing with local unions if applicable.'[55] Moreover, unions generally responded to plant shutdowns in a highly bureaucratic fashion. In the USWA, for example, once a plant shutdown had been announced, the international headquarters of the union placed the local union into trusteeship to protect union funds. The trustee, usually the local's business agent, then proceeded to liquidate local property and send the proceeds to USWA international headquarters.

Even though there were valid reasons for winding up local business in an orderly manner, the rapid disappearance of the union embittered many workers, with far-reaching consequences for American trade unionism. According to one UAW official, 'Where there is no hall available to the members of the closed plant, very little of the foregoing is available and separation and isolation quickly develops. It's in situations like these that workers end up with the view that the Union has done nothing for them, or has looked after itself rather than after the members.'[56]

In the wake of the closing of mills and factories across the industrial heartland, thousands of local unions were declared defunct or cancelled, with local union halls sold and office equipment auctioned to the highest bidder. Hundreds of steelworker locals, representing over one hundred thousand members, folded between 1979 and 1983 (see Table 5.1). Other union locals merged in order to stave off extinction. In

Table 5.1
Discontinued Local Unions and Displaced Members in North America,
United Steelworkers of America

Dates	Discontinued locals	Displaced members
1979–82	448	60,895
1983	649	44,273
TOTAL	1,097	105,168

Source: Hearing on Plant Closing Legislation, Hearing Before the Subcommittee
on Employment Opportunities of the Committee on Education and Labour, House
of Representatives, 98th Congress, Second Session, Washington, 1984.

Detroit, for instance, inner-city amalgamated locals like UAW Local 205 in River Rouge (organized in 1937) merged with their suburban counterparts – a change that union members such as Bernice Adams recalled as difficult: 'It's kind of hard to let that heritage go.'[57] Bernice noted that the union had no choice but to follow relocating industries to the northern suburbs. In the Mahoning Valley, where USWA District 26 had once represented tens of thousands of steelworkers, an entire administrative district was erased in 1980 and divvied up between its neighbours.[58]

By 1983, field organizers in the UAW were telling their superiors that former union members who had experienced plant shutdowns in Michigan and who now worked in non-union shops were among the most resistant to signing a union card.[59] Union organizers repeatedly heard complaints about union inaction the last time these workers had been employed in an organized plant. At around the same time, steelworkers warned their union leadership that laid-off members who lost their union recognition after one year, even though their recall rights remained active, naturally concluded that the company 'cares more about them' than their union.[60]

The union movement's bureaucratic handling of plant closings disillusioned members who expected their union to fight for them. In consequence, from 1967 to 1985, the UAW lost 32.6 per cent of its overall membership (representing 489,000 members), while the USWA lost 40.6 per cent of its membership (392,000 members).[61] The overall decline in the percentage of all private non-agricultural and non-construction employees who belonged to a union was just as dramatic: from 34.4 per cent in the early 1950s to 23.8 per cent in the late 1970s.[62]

Membership has dropped much further since then. Deserted by federal and state agencies and confronted with union failure to challenge seriously corporate restructuring, workers turned to their own local communities for support.

Appealing to Community

Idealized local communities lay at the heart of the deindustrialization thesis developed by plant shutdown opponents who were outside the mainstream of the trade union movement. Barry Bluestone and Bennett Harrison, in their landmark 1982 study, *The Deindustrialization of America*, argued that at the root of deindustrialization was a 'fundamental struggle' between capital and community.[63] They observed that workers in Youngstown saw the steel mill closings as the potential destruction of 'their community.'[64] Once the mills closed, these 'victims of deindustrialization' felt disoriented and isolated, which led to a kind of 'community anomie.' To counteract this reaction, Bluestone and Harrison proposed a series of measures designed to soften the blow of displacement.

In the context of the Cold War, where any talk of nationalization was considered dangerously radical, community strategies represented an acceptable middle road between laissez-faire capitalism and socialism. But communal solidarities resulted in local responses to plant closings and in pockets of determined resistance. Sometimes, as was the case when National Steel decided to close its Weirton, West Virginia, mill in 1982, resistance efforts proved successful.[65] Successes were few, however, in the aging industrial heartland. The pattern of protest there followed a predictable path: 'first, overflow public meetings and a brief season of unfocussed militancy, an ebbing of group support as each displaced worker concludes that the plant will probably not reopen and begins to devise a private strategy for survival.'[66] This repeated dissipation of protest energy reflected the institutional incapacity of the community-based movement as well as the unwillingness of politicians to react swiftly to popular pressure. The failure of the community strategy will be examined through two Ohio case studies: the manipulation of community identity in Dayton in the early 1970s and the most visible pocket of resistance to mill closings in the United States, Youngstown, which symbolizes the limits of the community discourse.

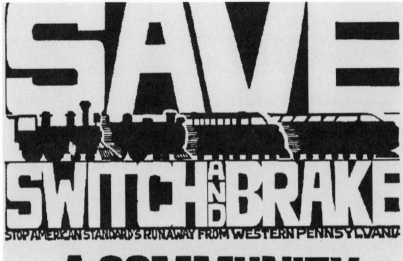

Community poster announcing a meeting to save the local company Switch and Brake.

Dayton's Pride

One of the clearest examples of corporate manipulation of community identification was Frigidaire's behind-the-scenes effort to wring concessions from the union at its home plant in Dayton in 1971.[67] A subsidiary of General Motors, the largest multinational corporation in the world, Frigidaire pioneered the trend towards corporate demands to reopen existing collective agreements in order to roll back wages and benefits. The company was motivated by Frigidaire's deteriorating share of the home-appliance market, and by the wages paid to its Dayton employees, the highest in the industry. To push union members into voting to reopen their collective agreement, which had been signed only six months previously, Frigidaire director of public relations, Rex Smith, spread the rumour that the plant would close and urged the formation of the 'Save Our Frigidaire for the Community Committee' by the Chamber of Commerce, designed to whip up anti-union sentiment in the area.

In his plan of action, Smith saw the Community Committee placing newspaper advertisements, distributing leaflets at the plant gate, and even overseeing a secret ballot among employees: '"Save Frigidaire Committee" letter and questionnaire to hourly employes, urging a vote to mandate union leadership to expand the offer. This could be presented to the community very dramatically with Frank Anger conducting a press conference, involving all media. Would have blowup of newspaper ad, announcing the membership letter and questionnaire, advising the ad would appear in next day's Journal and News. Also announce that letters and questionnaires will be handed out at factory gates to union membership. Have self-address envelope forwarded to a local accounting firm so that the balloting can be secret. Return ballot within five days.'[68] Smith then planned to leak a story that White Consolidated would purchase the Frigidaire name, adding that, 'we would give a "no comment" when queried to further amplify the issue. Infer layoffs bound to follow.' Clearly, the company's community strategy had union concessions as its goal, through the creation of a crisis atmosphere.

General Motor's manipulation of Dayton's pride began with a 12 June 1971 speech by Harold W. Campbell, Frigidaire's general manager, who claimed that the company was at a distinct disadvantage due to its relatively high wages. Campbell announced that as a result, 'We have investigated having another manufacturer build our appliances. We have investigated the possibility of plants located in the area outside of Dayton. We have talked with one of the largest manufacturers in Japan concerning the possibility of building our appliances. These investigations have not been resolved at this time and no decisions have been made.'[69] This speech fell like a ton of bricks in Dayton, a city long identified with Frigidaire. Within five days the 'Save Our Frigidaire' committee had been formed, composed of eleven representatives drawn from business, labour, academia, and the community. Yet as journalists immediately recognized, the committee was primarily the vehicle of Frank G. Anger and the Dayton Chamber of Commerce.[70]

On 29 June the committee asked local residents to write to both the company and the union expressing their desire to keep Frigidaire in Dayton. In an open letter addressed to 'All Interested Citizens,' Anger urged Frigidaire and International Union of Electrical Workers local 801 to 'work together' in order 'to keep appliance manufacturing here in this community ... If heads need to be knocked together or compromise is necessary, then let's do it. Full employment and a living wage is far more important than insisting on travelling down a one-way street to destruction.'[71] Throughout the crisis, Anger presumed to speak on behalf of all local residents.

For the hundreds of local citizens who responded to the call, Frigidaire was Dayton's pride. For George T. Lytle, the Frigidaire name had become synonymous with Dayton: 'I have lived in Dayton and used Frigidaire products since 1926. I don't say "refrigerator." To me the refrigerator is the Frigidaire. NCR, Wright-Patterson and Frigidaire mean Dayton. Save Frigidaire and you save Dayton.'[72] The attachment to Frigidaire was particularly strong for Martha Murphy: 'I am writing on behalf of keeping the Frigidaire plant in our Dayton community. Do hope the management will see fit to keep it here, it means so much to all the people and the many different businesses here. I work in a Restaurant and needless to say I have to depend on my "tips" to make my living. I am a widow and need to work very badly and without the "customer" I can't make it so therefore when people are working here- they use the Restaurant – I say if it means Frigidaire get rid of Mr. Campbell and the present management – then do it – or maybe the union could get a new negotiator and try and work something out. Am praying "Frigidaire" stays with us here in Dayton, Ohio. Thank you.'[73] A letter signed C. Thomas summed up the anxiety many Daytonians felt during the summer of 1971: 'Talk in terms, to the FRIGIDAIRE EXECUTIVES and UNION OFFICERS, that this is THEIR COMMU-

NITY, not only the employees, and they should definitely feel that it is THEIR RESPONSIBILITY to keep FRIGIDAIRE HERE and be willing to use a solution for the good of all.'[74] As hoped, the fate of Frigidaire had become emotionally entangled with the fate of the city as a whole.

Not everyone bought the company's line. Women took a leading role in turning the rhetorical weapon of the local community against the company. Women letter writers often spoke with authority, boldly castigating politicians and businessmen alike in the name of family, community, and the consumer. Most writers were not directly dependent on Frigidaire for employment, so the voice of the family often gave way to the voice of the consumer. One woman after another defiantly warned the company that it would pay a heavy price indeed if it abandoned Dayton. Several women tallied the number of Frigidaire appliances in their homes and vowed never again to purchase the company's products.[75] Others urged the company to make design alterations to their appliances to bolster sales.[76] Still others took considerable pride in the apparent superior quality of Frigidaire products and claimed it unthinkable that the company should ever leave Dayton.

In the days and weeks that followed, Frigidaire worked closely with the Dayton Chamber of Commerce and local media to turn up the heat on the union. To that end, General Motors intimated it was actively looking for a new factory to house Frigidaire production. A 16 July 1971 statement by GM noted that it had 'several study teams go through the surplus RCA plant in Memphis, Tennessee' but had no plans 'at this time' to purchase it.[77] In the wake of this press release, petitions were circulated and Sunday sermons were conducted on the issue. By mid-June, the story dominated the talk shows with most callers believing that Frigidaire workers would gladly accept concessions to keep the plant in Dayton.[78]

Throughout the 'Frigidaire situation,' Smith reported the latest news clippings daily to his superior, Thomas E. Groehn, director of news relations at General Motors world headquarters in Detroit. On 13 July he reported that Frigidaire answered queries about the rumours 'in the same manner, only admitting as our earlier statement indicated, that "the company is continuing to investigate all possible solutions to our difficulties. One of the avenues selected was to investigate having another manufacturer build our appliances. Another was to investigate sites outside of Dayton. Beyond that we have no comment."'[79] Smith also met with reporters, like Don Bauder of *Business Week*, to ensure that 'he heads down the right track.'[80] On 13 July, Smith noted the escalating media frenzy consuming the city: 'Obviously this morning's Journal Herald front page story stimulated the Dayton Daily News to further action; hence another front page story this afternoon. The small story also appeared on the front page of the Cincinnati Enquirer this morning. Common sense writing seems to have been replaced by some rather wild speculation, but then under the circumstances I suppose that this is to be expected. When queried, we' re sticking to our original declarations which were contained in our June 12 statement. Also, a wild rumor swept the city this afternoon that "Frigidaire had been sold." This came to me from both newspapers, radio and one of the television stations. This concludes today's report.'[81] So great was the uncertainty in Dayton that voters defeated new school bond issues and the city government pared down services in anticipation of the closure.

From the outset, Frigidaire was careful not to ask employees explicitly to reopen their collective agreement. This would have been politically inastute and legally dubious. As expected, the company's silence only served to fan public hysteria about the future of the plant. All summer long Smith reported that he was 'getting plenty of help from all quarters, now that we're in the public arena.'[82] When asked to comment personally, Smith called the potential plant closing 'rumour' and 'innuendo.' He happily reported that the 'local community is really putting on the heat with all kinds of offers of help, for the employes, depending, of course, on the decision of the union membership at Sunday's meeting. With TV and Radio stations following up full blast today, I think you can see the community is now putting on the heat.'[83] The local Committee, then, swung into action with a full page open letter outlining the 'Community's Position' on the outside back page of the *Journal Herald*. It sustained the company's position in every way. Three days later Smith reported that the Frigidaire 'situation' was about to 'run its course' with press activity building to a climax just before the union's meeting.

By the time workers cast their ballots on 12 September on whether or not to reopen their contract, Smith was convinced that they would bow to the will of the community. He was shocked to find that union members 'turned their backs on the community'[84] when workers overwhelmingly voted neither to reopen the contract nor to roll back wages by the desired $1.00 an hour. In response, Frigidaire issued a brutally terse statement to the media in which it warned that the union's unwillingness to meet the problem 'halfway' forced it to investigate 'possible alternatives.'[85] Taking the perspective of a community bystander, the editor of the *Journal Herald* acknowledged that union members voted against wage rollbacks because they were sceptical, rightly or wrongly, about the company's claim of financial trouble.[86]

Despite this setback for Frigidaire, communal pressure generated through the Chamber of Commerce's committee was such that the local union reversed its decision two months later, voting for concessions in exchange for a new guarantee to callback 850 laid-off employees and a renewed commitment by General Motors to make a go of its Frigidaire division. By agreeing to forego raises for the next two years, the company saved $18 a week on every Dayton worker. The local daily newspaper naturally heralded the agreement as 'a boon to the community.' As the editors of the *Journal Herald* noted, 'Intense community pressure was brought to bear on the workers in the first go-round. It was pressure generated by the fear that Frigidaire would leave Dayton and take 5,000 jobs with it unless the workers agreed to wage adjustments. But the workers refused to be stampeded. Their deliberateness, and that of their leaders particularly, was probably best in the long run.'[87] To maximize favourable press coverage, Frigidaire spaced the call-back of employees. Not without justification, Rex Smith claimed that no recent business story had garnered as much national media attention as the Frigidaire situation.[88]

Was the permanent closure of the plant a possibility? Clearly, Smith believed so. A Dayton resident himself, he argued forcefully within Frigidaire for keeping production in Dayton: 'To summarize, the pressures of business failure and closure of such a Division as Frigidaire would result in extremely serious public relations problems for the Corporation, especially in social, civic and economic fields. In these days of demonstration and protest, undoubtedly GM would be questioned publicly on its social obligations and responsibilities by pressure groups headed by the Naders, the Moores and many others ... All factors considered, without any question of doubt, the Corporation's public posture would be extremely difficult to defend, if not untenable.'[89] Although Frigidaire refused the union's request to examine its books, the records held at Kettering University in Flint suggest that the company was at a disadvantage because its wage levels far surpassed those of its competitors.[90] As a General Motors subsidiary, Frigidaire employees benefitted from the master agreement, making them the highest-paid appliance makers in North America. Declining market share since Frigidaire's heyday during the 1920s, 1930s and 1940s, when one in four major home appliances sold in the United States was a Frigidaire, had left the company with only eleven per cent of the market by 1970.[91] Although older customers remained loyal to Frigidaire, the company had not attracted younger consumers. Still, the paradox of giving concessions to one of the richest corporations on the planet outweighed the problems of the Frigidaire division in the minds of most local union members. This balance shifted after the company offered to exchange wage concessions for a renewed commitment to the community in the form of a greater obligation to the Frigidaire division and the recall of laid-off workers.

In the end, the concession agreement received considerable nation-wide attention as it dovetailed with Nixon's fight against inflation. It was widely acclaimed as a bow to 'realism' and a blow against infla-tion. Akron's political leadership was particularly impressed by 'Dayton's example.'[92] Still others predicted Dayton was where the pen-dulum began to swing from labour towards management.[93] Jim Good, the daily business news editor for the *Dayton Daily News* called it a 'poker game' won by Frigidaire. In fact, after Dayton, there was a rush of companies demanding concessions and forming citizens committees to bring 'civic pressure' to bear on the unions.[94] Unions steadfastly refused to reopen existing contracts in the early 1970s, and the dam holding back concessionary demands, albeit weakened, held another eight years until the bailout of ailing Chrysler. General Motors quietly sold its Frigidaire name in 1979 to White Consolidated and converted the facility to automotive parts production. Dayton's pride was no more. Yet the Frigidaire situation revealed in corporate records and local news reports indicated how the notion of local community be-came a rhetorical weapon for an employer keen to roll back union wages and benefits. Community had proven to be a feeble weapon in the industrial relations arsenal of opponents of plant closings.

Defending Youngstown

Youngstown first garnered international media attention when the Youngstown Sheet and Tube Company announced the closing of its Campbell Steel Works on 19 September 1977, a day that quickly earned the epithet Black Monday. This closure represented one of the largest displacements of American workers since the Second World War. In all, upwards of 5,000 workers lost their jobs in the following weeks.[95] As one local reporter wrote: 'The community's identity is up for grabs. People are confused, frustrated and bitter.'[96]

Procession leaving Stop 14 Gate at Youngstown Steel. At right are attorney Staughton Lynd and Reverend C. Edward Weisheimer.

The story would have ended there, as it did in so many other hard-hit Rust Belt towns and cities, had a vocal minority of Youngstown area residents not decided to fight the closing.[97] Yet the locus of resistance did not come from elected local politicians. No coordinated response to the closing proved possible as the valley consisted of a patchwork of political jurisdictions, each with its own personalities, partisan affiliations, and agendas.[98] Civic leaders in the Mahoning Valley mounted their horse and rode madly off in all directions. Concrete results were so meagre that Anthony C. Centofanti spoke for many area residents when he recalled: 'I can't really think of any political figure who distinguished himself by his services during that time.'[99]

Given this political vacuum, it took someone with the stature of Bishop James W. Malone to launch a fight-back campaign that would garner widespread community support and international attention. Religious leaders, joined by a motley group of union dissidents, political radicals, public interest advocates, and displaced workers seemed uniquely qualified to speak on behalf of area residents. Their determined efforts under the banner of the Ecumenical Coalition to Save the Mahoning Valley kept the city in the national spotlight for two more years. In fact, they came closest to resolving the dilemma raised by regional lobbyist William Sullivan: 'The community, in the fullest sense of that, has no lobby. There is no lobby that is broad enough to cover that kind of lobby together and you need more time than we had to get it in place.'[100]

The Ecumenical Coalition proposed to reopen the Campbell works under community ownership and convinced the United States Department of Housing and Urban Development to fund a technical feasibility study. This report was contracted to the National Center for Economic Alternatives in Washington and was written in large part by Gar Alperovitz, a left-wing economist. Alperovitz concluded that the reopening of a newly modernized mill was feasible with a $15 million federal grant and $394 million in federal loan guarantees.[101]

With this objective in mind the Ecumenical Coalition entered the national political arena under the community banner.[102] A pastoral letter circulated to valley church goers vividly illustrates that the Ecumenical Coalition viewed the closing of the Campbell Works through the lens of community.[103] In seeking to understand what Black Monday meant 'for us and our community,' Bishop James Malone evoked community no less than thirty-eight times. By speaking of 'Our Valley,' 'neighbors,' and 'Youngstown,' the pastoral letter implied that the clos-

Gerald Dickey speaking to protesters on the first anniversary of Black Monday, 1978.

ing involved everyone in the Mahoning Valley. Believing it to be their Christian duty to 'serve our community,' the religious leaders appealed for 'unity, common purpose and coordinated action for the good of the community.' They stressed the moral dimension of the crisis and rejected claims that this decision was a 'private, purely economic judgement.' Rather, it was a matter of public concern. Corporations, these spiritual leaders agreed, have a social and moral responsibility towards local communities.

Thus, the Ecumenical Coalition became the de facto voice of community shortly after Black Monday. This same community-oriented discourse permeated all subsequent public statements of the Ecumenical Coalition and its allies. Within the Mahoning Valley this appeal to place resonated. Thousands of Youngstown area residents deposited millions of dollars into special 'Save Our Valley' accounts to provide support for the plan.[104]

Just how important the community discourse in Youngstown had become can be illustated by the lyrics of a song by a little-known San

Francisco singer-songwriter named Tom Hunter. Hunter wrote 'Back to Work in Youngstown' in 1978 after being inspired by the local struggle to reopen the steel mill. Each of the four verses deals with an element of the local economic situation. As Hunter noted: 'When I'm performing the song in coffee houses or church meetings I can see the indignation rise in people as I sing the first verse. It's good to know you can affect people that way with your music.' Hunter begins with Black Monday and identifies the chief villain: the Lykes Corporation, the parent company of Sheet and Tube. But the song is really about the community's defiant response to this crisis, as Hunter recounts:

> Then some church leaders started talking, like church leaders always do.
> But this time they had something to say, and a plan for something to do.
> The community could buy the steel mill, with the people owning shares.
> And then the profits could stay right here, instead of way off somewhere.
> So they set out to find the money, and they set out to let folks know. That
> the steel mill could open its doors, worker run and community owned.

He goes on to claim that Youngstown represents the 'same old story' of conglomerates and communities in conflict. Hunter ends the song with the defiant shouts of 'save our valley' that could be heard 'all around town.' Tapping into the spirit of resistance, 'Back to Work in Youngstown' quickly became the Ecumenical Coalition's anthem, sung repeatedly at meetings and protest rallies in the Mahoning Valley.

Yet unbeknownst to outside observers, the movement itself was torn over whether it should be a national or local struggle.[105] Oral history interviews with key members of the Ecumenical Coalition reveal this tension. Father Edward Stanton of the Roman Catholic diocese recalled his frustration with the 'crazies from the outside,' a clear reference to political radicals, and concluded that he thought that 'the good of the valley' could best 'be determined by the people in the valley.'[106] Like many others in the Coalition, he liked the local control aspect of the plan to save the Campbell Works. Bishop Malone nonetheless maintained that a strategy that universalized Youngstown's plight should be adopted.[107] Although the advocates of local strategy predominated, the plight of Youngstown's residents soon spilled over into the national arena.

Due to the extraordinary media attention in the years between 1977 and 1980, the city's name became synonymous with the crisis sweeping the industrial heartland of the United States. In a special report on

Flyer protesting plant closings in the Youngstown area.

Youngstown in 1978, ABC News noted that the community's refusal to die was something new.[108] Journalists sensed a story of national dimension, and descended upon the valley. They were like ants at a summer picnic, 'lugging typewriters, tape recorders, and camera equipment to steelyards, mill bars, and ethnic neighborhoods. From Tokyo and Topeka, they came to report the saga of Steeltown.'[109] The resulting Youngstown story consisted of a basic formula: an interview with the mayor, an interview with a spokesperson for the Ecumenical Coalition, and video footage of the closed mills. Soon, other industrial states began to point to Youngstowns of their own.[110] In due course, Youngstown became the site of numerous congressional hearings investigating the issue of factory closures. At one such hearing, congressman Clarence Brown of Ohio summarized the opinion of many: 'What happened in northeastern Ohio is a sad symbol of our total national decline.'[111]

Union leaders did not join in this pilgrimage to Youngstown, in part because they did not want a reopened plant, even under union stewardship, that might undercut union wages and benefits elsewhere, and because their top economic advisor considered the plan unworkable.[112] Like many of the Youngstown workers interviewed, Sam Donnorummo felt betrayed by the USWA: 'Our International didn't care. Pittsburgh never came down. Them guys never came around. They didn't care about us.'[113] The social and physical distance between union members and the union leadership seemed to have grown immeasurably.

At its 1978 biannual convention, the USWA refused to endorse the Ecumenical Coalition's drive to reopen the mill. The convention proceedings reveal a union leadership unmoved by the spectre of plant shutdowns and displacement. Blaming imports, president McBride told delegate in an otherwise upbeat state-of-the-union address that the year had been 'one of significant transition.'[114] Following his lead, delegates adopted two resolutions to that effect, including Resolution 18, which dealt with the shutdown of steel plants. Conspicuously absent from the resolution drafted by the union leadership was any mention of community or employee ownership in general and the Ecumenical Coalition's bid to reopen the Campbell Works in particular. This omission is telling, as at least one resolution from Youngstown Local 1462 had called on the union to endorse the local drive. Instead, unions remained wedded to traditional industrial capitalism.

Two years later, another bureaucratic-sounding resolution blaming steel imports for the shutdown of American mills was adopted in Los Angeles. Union dissident Ron Wiesen from the Homestead Works of

U.S. Steel called on delegates to support communities resisting shutdowns: 'That our International join with other unions, religious groups, community organizations, etc to put a stop to this rape and abandonment of our communities by the giant steel corporations.'[115] Wiesen urged delegates to support the efforts of the Ecumenical Coalition in Youngstown: 'They had no moral help, no financial help from the International. We had two plant gate collections for Youngstown. That's more than I can say for the Executive Board from the International.' Others joined Wiesen in calling on union leaders to act decisively in response to the 'radical steel executives.' With the failure of these resolutions, community largely failed to act as a catalyst for cooperation between unions and public interest groups or local ecumenical coalitions.

Calls for communal solidarity held little promise for centralized trade unions with members in dozens of towns and cities across the United States. Instead, union leaders stressed group solidarity among their members. The closure of Youngstown Sheet and Tube's Campbell Works in 1977 could be reformulated by the USWA as a necessary evil in order to reduce overcapacity in the domestic steel industry and add a measure of security for the rest of the membership. In the face of plant shutdowns and union ambivalence, union rank-and-file dissidents like Ron Wiesen, and Ed Mann, union local president at the Brier Hill Works in Youngstown, were drawn to communal solidarity. Yet the community banner acted to confirm state and regional difference in national politics.

Politics figured highly in the Carter administration's measured response to the crisis in the steel industry.[116] Jimmy Carter, a Southerner, had little sympathy for the deindustrializing cities of the North. In November 1977, just two months after Black Monday, he turned down several recommendations from an inter-departmental task force that would have increased eligibility and benefit levels for displaced workers. More radical ideas proposed by the Department of Labor such as extended health care coverage, community assistance, and mandatory advance notification of plant shutdowns had already been rejected by the task force.[117] Carter's point of view perhaps was best articulated by a 1980 report on cities that urged the relocation of inner-city populations in the North to the South.[118]

The steel industry's dismal pollution record in an age of environmental concerns, also coloured the Carter administration's response to 'the steel problem.' Shortly after Black Monday, Douglas M. Costle, director of the Environmental Protection Agency, advised the president that the steel industry was one of the worst polluters in the nation. Steel mills affected public health by releasing sulphur oxides and various hydro-carbons into the air and discharging solids, acids, heavy metals, ar-senic, cyanide, phenols, ammonia, oil, grease, and heat into the water.[119] Costle further noted that 7.3 million Americans were exposed to carci-nogenic coke-oven emissions, and that air pollution contributed to asthma, bronchitis, emphysema, and cancer. Even though the potential political fallout of closing marginal mills worried the administration, the closure of the Youngstown mill erased a lingering public embarrass-ment for the Carter administration.[120]

It is clear that the government never seriously considered giving the loan guarantees necessary to reopen an old polluting mill, but it kept its decision secret until after the congressional elections of 1978. A visibly upset Bishop James Malone wrote to Carter: 'Mr. President, for this community the incumbency of Jimmy Carter has not been an experi-ence of compassion. Rather, you are associated with cruel indiffer-ence.'[121] This judgment, one shared by many in the Mahoning Valley, would haunt Carter during his re-election bid in 1980.

The failure to save the Campbell works profoundly influenced how Youngstown residents responded to the news that three more steel mills were slated for closure in the coming year. Unlike the sudden shutdown of the Campbell Works, the closing of Lyke's Brier Hill Works in December 1979 and U.S. Steel's closure of the Ohio and McDonald Works in 1980 came months after the decisions were made public. The time lag gave community activists and union members a window of opportunity to resist the closing. This time they took their fight directly to the steel company, occupying U.S. Steel offices in Youngstown and Pittsburgh and bringing the company to court.[122]

This change in emphasis was reflected in the political slogans scrawled on home-made placards during the occupation of U.S. Steel's sky-scraper in 1980: 'US Steel Kills Communities' and 'Steel Companies Kill Communities.' Most of the twenty slogans that appeared in photo-graphs of the direct action demonstrated strong place attachment: pro-testers frequently evoked 'community' and 'our valley.' A growing sense of abandonment crept into messages such as 'Cobweb City' and 'Ghosttown USA' and revealed an edge of desperation and hopeless-ness not seen earlier.

Although efforts once again failed to stop the mills from being closed, some good came out of the court fight. The genesis of the idea of the community right to industrial property represented nothing less than an 'ideological breakthrough' to historian-turned-attorney Staughton Lynd. In court, Lynd claimed that the company had broken a contractual agreement based on an oral promise not to close the plant if it remained profitable. Overtly sympathetic to the Youngstown workers, Judge Thomas D. Lambrose introduced the notion of community property rights, or 'eminent domain,' in the mill. Although eminent domain had been regularly used by municipalities to expropriate private dwellings in slum clearances or highway expansions, this was the first time the concept was applied to industrial property. Lynd subsequently won a temporary injunction against U.S. Steel in December 1979. Even though the lawsuit ultimately failed, the notion of eminent domain had the capacity to counter capital's summoning of private property rights. In Lynd's words, 'eminent domain offered the movement against plant shutdowns a version of constitutional rhetoric as ancient and deeply rooted as the appeal to due process in defense of private property.'[123]

From now on, companies that refused to sell closed plants would face the prospect of local governments expropriating the private land for a public purpose.[124] In 1984, the threatened use of eminent domain proved sufficient in New Bedford, Massachusetts, to convince Gulf & Western to sell its unwanted factory to employees. Elsewhere, nine municipalities in the Monongahela Valley of western Pennsylvania granted the power of eminent domain to the Steel Valley Authority.[125] Although rarely used, the threat of eminent domain to expropriate closed mills and factories became a potentially powerful legal weapon in the arsenal of communities. This legal innovation was but small consolation to laid-off Youngstown steelworkers.

As long as the fight continued, Youngstown remained a symbol of hope in the Rust Belt. Three mill closings later, however, it had come to exemplify the inevitability of industrial decline.[126] The community strategy employed by opponents of plant shutdowns failed to rally the American public to its cause. As the former mayor of Youngstown, J. Philip Richley, bluntly stated: 'What we were trying to deal with was a national problem. Youngstown was simply one piece of that national problem and there was no way that Youngstown could solve this problem alone.'[127] Many outspoken plant closing opponents agreed. Mary Lynne Cappelletti, legislative director of the Ohio Public Interest Campaign, told state politicians that, in spite of national media attention and the energetic efforts of some members of the Youngstown community, 'it wasn't enough.'[128] Defending community therefore remained a local affair of little concern to state or federal politicians, or to trade union leaders who represented members in many – often competing – towns, cities, and states.

Conclusion

The opponents of plant closings who met in January 1981 to discuss the prospects of the movement wondered whether 'local citizens' had any 'realistic hope that their actions will make a difference?'[129] It may be a harsh verdict, but it seems that as long as protestors continued to think of themselves as local citizens they had little chance of besting corporations operating over vast geographic areas. The anti-plant shutdown movement, such as it was, did not fail due to a lack of community identity. Rather, it faltered because the kind of community it repeatedly invoked did not sway legislators and businessmen who lived far away from affected towns and cities. Despite the best efforts of Bishop Malone, Barry Bluestone, and Bennett Harrison to nationalize the sense of community responsibility, community identification within the movement remained place-bound. Hence, community identity acted to confirm state and regional difference and did little to dampen the hyper-competitive atmosphere that existed among the fifty states within the breadth of America.

And yet, the protectionist strategy adopted by the AFL-CIO and many of its major affiliates also failed to mobilize public opinion against American companies that closed plants. Historian Dana Frank has persuasively argued that what was 'good for General Motors' was, in fact, not good for the autoworkers.[130] By focusing their attention on imports, trade unionists shifted the blame for mass layoffs from American multinational companies to foreign countries. Given the divisive legacy of the war in Vietnam, economic nationalism in the United States proved incapable of uniting trade unionists with the younger generation of political liberals in common cause. Frank's suspicion that economic nationalism was, and is, racist, proved typical.[131]

The confusion of the times became most striking when Detroit mayor Coleman Young and the UAW teamed up in the early 1980s to find millions of dollars to subsidize the construction of a new GM assembly plant in the downtown core. To make room, the cities of Detroit and Hamtramck used their powers of eminent domain to demolish the surrounding Poletown neighbourhood. In responding to the demolition order, many of the same social forces defending community against capital elsewhere found themselves in opposition to this effort to save

Demolition of Dodge Main with a wrecking ball in the winter of 1981.

thousands of industrial jobs. Given the choice between jobs and community they chose rhetoric over substance. The Poletown story is a reminder that there are different levels of community comprising an urban neighbourhood, city, region, or country. To constrain the destructive tendencies of capitalism between 1969 and 1984, protestors needed to rise in defence of a community based on nation. Failing that, the anti-shutdown movement in the United States floundered.

6 'I'll Wrap the F*#@ Canadian Flag around Me': A Nationalist Response to Plant Shutdowns

Recent studies of trade union responses to plant closings and industrial restructuring during the 1970s and early 1980s have juxtaposed Canadian militancy against American passivity. The contrasting fortunes of the labour movements in Canada and the United States are perhaps best represented in the changing rates of unionization in the manufacturing sector. While the rates of unionization were comparable in the two countries during the 1950s and 1960s, this was no longer the case by the 1980s.[1] In 1986, Canada's 41.6 per cent rate of unionization was nearly double that of the United States. The divergent paths taken by the two labour movements is particularly surprising given that workers in both countries usually belonged to the same unions and faced the same multinational corporations across the bargaining table.

The debate over the divergent trajectories of the Canadian and American union movements has revolved around two competing explanations. First, scholars such as John Holmes and A. Rusonik have provided an economic basis for the different responses.[2] The union movement in Canada benefited from the low Canadian dollar and the fact that the gales of creative destruction did not gain the same force in Canada prior to the signing of the Free Trade Agreement in 1988. While dozens of massive steel mills and sprawling auto assembly plants closed permanently in the United States, none closed north of the border during this time period; mainly small and medium-sized mills and factories closed in Canada. These vastly different economic contexts gave Canadian trade unionists more room to manoeuvre.

The second major explanation comes from scholars who have studied the institutional structures and cultures of various trade unions. Several scholars have juxtaposed Canadian 'social unionism' and American 'business unionism.' In this rather facile bipolar opposition, the blame for the debacle in the United States is placed squarely on the shoulders of union elites who chose to sell concessions to their members instead of resisting them.[3] Rank-and-file trade unionists in the United States, it seems, had no choice but to acquiesce. A related, but far more satisfying, explanation has been provided by those influenced by social movement theory in the social sciences. As will be discussed later, Charlotte Yates points to the greater capacity of the United Auto Workers (UAW) in Canada to resist plant closings and concessions.

Institutional and economic theories, however, do not explain why Canadian politicians required companies to provide advance notification of plant closings, or why they made severance pay and preferential hiring rights mandatory in Ontario. These legislative actions were remarkable given that, with the exception of border-hugging Maine, no political jurisdiction in the United States effectively regulated plant closings before 1988. Explanations for the legislative victories of plant closing opponents in Canada must be sought beyond the internal dynamics of militant trade unions such as the UAW, in the tactics and rhetoric of the wider anti-plant closing movement that emerged in Southern Ontario at the height of nationalist anxiety over American influence in Canada.

Opponents of plant closings in Ontario drew inspiration and legitimacy from the new nationalism, a term first used in the late 1960s to describe this growing unease. Historian Stephen Azzi has noted that while this nationalism took many forms, its main focus was Canada's 'economic reliance' on the United States.[4] By the mid-1960s, a growing number of English-speaking Canadians believed that their country was in imminent danger of becoming an American colony.[5] The stark choice facing Canada, said former federal minister of finance Walter L. Gordon, was between 'independence' and 'colonial status.'[6] In the broadest sense, an emerging economic nationalist discourse incorporated plant closings into its anti-imperialist critique of direct foreign investment and later, deindustrialization. As a result, it is virtually impossible to disentangle concern over plant shutdowns from anxiety over foreign direct investment and the presumed threat to Canadian sovereignty presented by American multinational corporations.[7]

At first, the new nationalism focused on rising levels of American direct investment in Canada. Foreign ownership in the manufacturing sector, for example, rose to 54 per cent in 1963 from 38 per cent in 1926.[8] In seeking a means of escaping the potential dangers of such a close and dependent relationship with American capital, the 1957 report by the Royal Commission on Canada's Economic Prospects, chaired by Walter Gordon, and subsequent reports filed by Mel Watkins in 1968 and Herb Gray in 1972, confirmed many Canadians' worst fears.[9] New nationalists in the Liberal and New Democratic parties repeatedly pointed out that American multinationals were 'dedicated to their own survival' rather than to the 'national interests' of Canada.[10]

With the downturn in the North American economy in 1969–70 and the continued uncertainty thereafter, the anti-American discourse within new nationalism shifted from a lament about too much foreign investment to dire warnings of disinvestment. U.S.-controlled companies, it would seem, closed branch plants in Canada in order to keep Americans employed back home. The protectionist measures introduced by U.S. president Richard Nixon under his Domestic International Sales Corporation (DISC) worked to generalize this suspicion.[11] New nationalists argued that in providing generous corporate tax credits for corporations that shifted branch plant production back to the United States, Nixon's New Economic Policy of 1971 aimed to deindustrialize Canada. In his foreword to *(Canada) Ltd.*, Robert Laxer proposed the idea of deindustrialization within the broader context of a developed anti-imperialist analysis of dependency.[12] For the book's contributors, deindustrialization did not simply refer to the reduction of the work force employed in manufacturing, 'but to the special distorting effects of US ownership of Canadian manufacturing, in particular, US attempts to enhance American employment at home at the expense of Canada.'[13] Nearly a decade before its adoption by plant closing opponents in the United States, the deindustrialization thesis had thus been put to use by the left-wing Waffle faction of the New Democratic Party.[14]

While few Canadians agreed with the Waffle's plan to nationalize parts of the economy, by 1972 two-thirds of the population had 'accepted its diagnosis of the disease.'[15] Far from being a tool employed exclusively by Canada's economic and political elites, the new nationalism became a powerful rhetorical weapon in the hands of working people to be used against companies that closed plants.[16] Trade unionists, along with left-wing students, increasingly relied on nationalist oratory and the deindustrialization thesis to legitimate their demands for increased legislative protection for Canadian workers. This chapter begins with a brief examination of how Canada's labour law opened the door to a political response to plant closings. It then shows how the

Fred Wright cartoon supporting United Electrical, Radio and Machine Workers of America (UE) in Canada against the multinationals.

closing of Dunlop Tire's Toronto plant in 1970 established a pattern of nationalist defiance. New nationalism was put to work by trade unionists and other opponents of American multi-national corporations, a process that culminated in a wave of plant occupations in the early 1980s. Canada's nascent anti-plant shutdown movement had a ready villain in the foreign multinational corporation, usually American, that allowed it to stoke the fires of national outrage and advance public demands for corporate social responsibility.

The Regime of Industrial Legality

When it comes to the post–Second World War social compromise between labour and capital, Canadian labour historians are in general agreement with their American counterparts. Jane Jenson, Rianne Mahon, Don Wells, and, most recently, Judy Fudge and Eric Tucker have argued that the labour struggles of the 1930s and 1940s produced a regime of industrial legality that defused trade union militancy.[17] As a result, the collective actions of trade unionists are, as Fudge and Tucker rightly observe, 'irretrievably enmeshed' with the law and the state.[18] In Canada, strikes during the life of the collective agreement were rendered illegal and unions were legally required to police their own members. This regime of industrial legality, dubbed industrial pluralism on both sides of the border, left managerial prerogatives not only intact but reinforced.

Unlike the Wagner Act in the United States, the scope of compulsory collective bargaining in Canada never included an obligation to negotiate a close-out agreement with the local union over the effects of a plant closing decision.[19] No legal framework existed for dealing with plant closings and the resulting dislocation of workers. Plant closings remained outside the post-war social compromise, and Canadian trade unionists were free to find a political solution to the plant closing problem.

Prior to 1969, few constraints were placed on managerial prerogative to close plants at-will in Canada. Only common law and collective agreements gave workers a modicum of job security. In the case of common law, it was customary for employers to provide reasonable notice to workers of their termination, usually fixed at one pay period.[20] Labour law in turn held that employers could legally terminate their operations so long as they were not motivated by anti-union animus.[21] Few collective agreements of the time went beyond seniority rights in providing job security for union members. A 1967 study identified only eighty-seven collective agreements in Canada, representing 38,000 workers, with advance notice or consultation clauses.[22]

Beginning in the early 1960s, however, Canada's federal and provincial governments began to play a more active role in mitigating the impact of job loss. In 1963, the federal government formed the Consultative Manpower Service to assist workers in finding new employment in anticipation of economic dislocation from international trade liberalization. The following year, Justice Samuel Friedman filed his report on Canada's railroad labour problems in which he recommended that employers provide advance notice of all major changes to workplace relations.[23] In 1967, Canada's centennial year, an energetic campaign to save the Dominion Steel Company's (DOSCO) steel mill in Sydney, Nova Scotia, resulted in its reopening under the public ownership of the province. The successful Save Our Steel (SOS) campaign showed that a determined local campaign with national trade union and political support could in fact work. Two years later the province of Quebec became the first jurisdiction in North America to require mandatory advance notice of mass layoffs.[24] Many provincial jurisdictions and the federal government immediately considered following suit. A January 1970 meeting of the Ontario Committee on Labour Relations, for example, expressed its intention to codify present common law principles, possibly extend their provisions, and to legislate modest severance pay.[25]

Dunlop Sets the Pattern

Political events soon pushed the Ontario government to go well beyond its original intention. The first sign of trouble came in March 1970 when British-owned Dunlop Tire announced its intention to close its east-end Toronto factory employing 597 people.[26] Almost overnight, Dunlop developed – in the context of Great Britain's diminishing influence – into a concrete example of Canada's growing dependency on the United States. 'Doing a Dunlop,' became a derogatory term applied to foreign-owned companies that abruptly laid off their Canadian workers.[27]

Despite the best efforts of Canadian subsidiary president Neville Proctor to manage the closing announcement, nothing could have prepared him for the political firestorm it unleashed.[28] Popular protest took the form of rallies at Queen's Park, all-night vigils, a street benefit dance, picketing, and a court challenge. When workers, under the leadership of United Rubber Workers local president Phil Japp, tried to purchase the plant, Dunlop refused to sell the factory or to open the company's financial records for an independent audit.[29] The NDP canvassed much of Toronto's east end in the course of collecting thousands of signatures on a petition. In the meantime, nationalist students marched from the University of Toronto campus to the rubber plant and a special edition of the student newspaper, the *Varsity*, savaged Dunlop.[30] These events signalled to the public that the fight against plant shutdowns had become a nationalist cause célèbre and the Dunlop workers had become the first martyrs. Coming as it did at the height of economic nationalist agitation, Dunlop's decision to give its workers only six-weeks' notice struck many as a 'stark injustice.'[31] It only underlined for the public the negative effects of foreign companies operating in Canada.

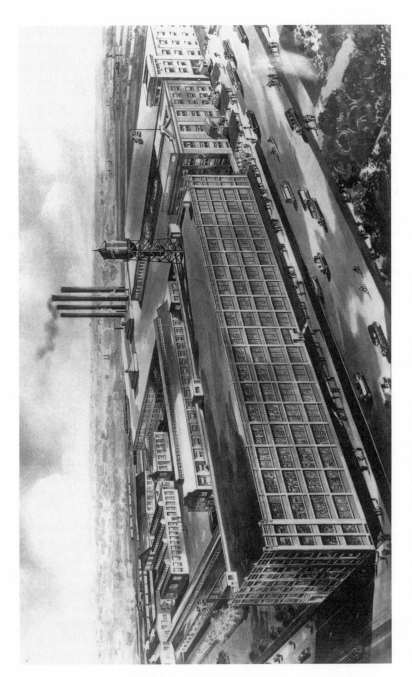

Illustration of Dunlop Tire and Rubber Goods Company in Toronto, 1930.

Newspaper editors expressed sympathy for the displaced workers and wholeheartedly supported the introduction of new government regulations. It seems that the size of the factory, its prominent location in downtown Toronto, and its seventy-one years of operation set Dunlop apart from previous plant closings. In painting their sympathetic portrait of Dunlop workers, editors emphasized the workers' advancing age, their long service with the company, and their Canadian citizenship. Editors also stressed that Dunlop Tire was a huge foreign-controlled company and that the decision to close the Toronto plant probably originated outside Canada. 'The suspicion is widespread that the decision was made somewhere in the higher reaches of the huge multinational concern that more profit could be made by transferring the production,' the *Toronto Star* held. Such 'tragedies' would happen time and again, it continued, until adequate legislation was adopted. The interests of a multinational like Dunlop did not coincide with the 'best interests of the Canadian people.'[32]

The editors of Canada's major establishment newspapers wanted the federal and provincial governments to at least regulate how foreign companies would close plants in Canada. The Dunlop shutdown had 'put a big question mark over the hallowed rights of company management to do as it pleases.'[33] The *Globe and Mail* contended that the Ontario government had a duty to respond to the Dunlop shutdown. By claiming that companies should demonstrate to the public that the closing was unavoidable, editors revealed that they did not believe in the inevitability of industrial decline.[34] Even a reporter for the pro-business *Financial Post* thought a company should be required 'to show at least some cause to somebody.'[35] These reactions were brought about by a torrent of economic nationalism, reflected in protests on the streets of Toronto and the unprecedented politicization of mill and factory closings. Local protests entered national public discourse through the media and prompted legislative action.

The federal government was under intense pressure to nationalize the Dunlop Tire plant. Politically, the issue dominated question period as the Conservatives and the New Democrats battered the government.[36] Discontent over the Dunlop closing spread to the ranks of the Liberals, whose Standing Committee on Policy and Research urged Prime Minister Pierre Trudeau 'to take all measures necessary to keep the Toronto plant of Dunlop Rubber operating.' For committee chairperson Stephen Clarkson, a prominent economic nationalist, the Dunlop situation represented 'a critical example of a general national problem –

multi-national corporations taking steps that may be in their world interests without regard to the best interests of the host country.'[37] He also stressed that requiring companies to provide advance notice of mass terminations would give workers a chance to adjust to job loss. Both internal party pressures and external popular protests urged the government to do something dramatic about the Dunlop situation.

Trudeau declined to intervene directly. The government instead required that pre-notification and mandatory severance pay be fixed at the relatively low rate of two days per year employed (to a maximum of forty days wages) for displaced workers with a minimum of five years continuous service. The government also released a White Paper on Unemployment Insurance (UI) that recommended a major overhaul of the program, nearly doubling the maximum UI benefits, making all workers contribute to the plan, and penalizing companies that regularly laid off employees. In the charged atmosphere after the Dunlop closure, the government even pitched the changes to UI as a part of its larger legislative package to assist displaced workers.[38] A.G.W. Sinclair, president of the Canadian Manufacturers' Association (CMA), hoped that these changes would deter more radical proposals to regulate the problem of plant closings. To his chagrin, the closing of Dunlop set in motion a chain of events that led to the adoption of the Foreign Investment Review Act (FIRA) two years later. By enabling the federal cabinet to disallow those foreign takeovers deemed not of 'substantial public good,' FIRA gave the anti-shutdown movement the legal basis to fight shutdowns.[39]

In the face of this opposition, provincial politicians also scrambled to legislate pre-notification. Ontario premier John Robarts had initially declared in the legislature that the government 'was not going to tell an industry what to do.' His 21 April reversal of position was largely attributable to public outrage directed at Dunlop.[40] To assuage these concerns, the Ontario government proposed amending the Employment Standards Act to compel companies to provide advance notice of mass terminations. The bill was first brought to cabinet on 28 April and approved at its 12 May meeting.[41] The Ontario legislature adopted the measure despite opposition demands for a longer notice period.[42] Dismissing the legislation as 'woefully inadequate,' critics on the Left pointed to its many inadequacies including the fifty person or 10 per cent (of the workforce) minimum thresholds, the absence of a severance pay provision, and the many loopholes available to employers.[43] Even so, most companies operating in Ontario now had to provide eight to sixteen weeks of advance warning to terminated employees (the extent of notice required was dependant on the number being let go).[44]

These provincial and federal government initiatives provoked only muted public criticism from business leaders. In private, the CMA tried unsuccessfully to convince the Ontario government to limit its advance notice requirements to cases of partial or complete plant closures and not all mass lay-offs workers. However, when the government went ahead and stipulated minimum thresholds for lay-off notice, the lobby group nonetheless thanked Premier Robarts for his rational response 'when this emotional subject brought the Government under severe attack,' adding that 'manufacturers could not fail to appreciate' the government's position.[45] As one business journalist explained, it was 'hard for employers to oppose advance notice, unless they are prepared to be regarded as reactionaries.'[46] Politically, employers understood that the government had little choice but to respond strongly to plant closure.

The fight against the Dunlop Tire closing culminated in amendments to the Ontario Employment Standards Act and the Canada Labour Code, which required advance notice of mass terminations and, in the case of the latter, provided for mandatory severance pay. Equally important, the fight to keep the plant operating had brought together youthful economic nationalists and internationally organized trade unionists in an unlikely coalition. After Dunlop, the fate of the nation and the fate of industrial workers would become conflated in the popular imagination and would reinforce public demands that the state regulate the plant shutdown process. Despite their failure to reopen the plant, the strength of the anti-shutdown movement convinced Ontario cabinet minister Stanley J. Randall to write to his colleague Dalton Bales, the Ontario minister of labour: 'We should, however, learn a lesson from the Dunlop Corporation ... so that we don't receive another barrage from the NDP permitting them to make a mountain out of a mole hill.'[47] Be it mountain or mole hill, the anti-shutdown movement found itself with its first, albeit partial, legislative victory.

Putting Nationalism to Work

In the years that followed, the Ontario ministry of labour received a flood of private complaints from Ontario businessmen and moved to review the efficacy of the province's advance notice regulations. In order to placate business supporters of the Progressive Conservative government, ministry official Ian Welton met with company executives across the province to discuss the application of the province's advance notice regulations. He found that some companies operating in the province had already found loopholes in the legislation, and others simply ignored it. Most alarming was Welton's discovery that the managers at Stelco's Page-Hersey works in Welland, Ontario, dodged the advance warning regulation by keeping 150 workers on continual notice. He reported that company managers spent 'a fair amount of time and effort in arranging layoffs so as to take advantage of the "10% Rule"' and, in so doing, made 'a complete farce' of the legislation.[48]

Adding to the confusion, the province's advance notice regulation was often rendered meaningless by collective agreements. In March 1974, the minister of labour met with the Big Four auto makers to discuss the disturbing fact that only a 'relatively small proportion' of auto layoffs came to the minister's attention.[49] In response, the managers of Chrysler Canada pointed out that it was impossible to satisfy the requirements of the legislation. While the collective agreement with the UAW held that laid-off workers enjoyed recall rights for three years, the government considered them 'terminated' after only twelve weeks. As a result, Chrysler found itself engaging in the 'fairly meaningless ritual of [regularly] issuing the necessary notice in advance of the layoffs' to escape paying substantial sums of money in lieu of notice.[50] In consequence, senior officials in the ministry of labour remained uncertain over the legislation's 'effectiveness in achieving its stated aims' of providing workers with clear and ample warning of impending job loss. [51]

The shortcomings of Ontario's new pre-notification regulations were not lost on academics such as Fred Caloren at the University of Ottawa. In his exhaustive study of layoffs, shutdowns, and closures in Ontario from January 1971 to June 1972, Caloren found that employers routinely evaded provincial minimum pre-notification requirements through graduated layoffs.[52] To that end, one company managed to lay off 1,300 workers in four locations during 1971–2 without giving notice because each termination affected less than 10 per cent of the employees.[53]

As business opposition to the new legislation mounted, ministry officials secretly recommended that the government replace the province's advance notice requirements with a severance pay program. Economically, this modification of the law would have limited the substantial financial obligations incurred by employers who found themselves paying in lieu of advance notice, something Ontario employers continued to complain bitterly about. However, the political cost of rolling back employment standards regulations worried civil servants and provincial politicians alike. 'Removing a benefit once bestowed may be politically difficult. Consequently, the separate schedule [advance notice of mass termination] may have to be kept unless an adequate sweetener were found.'[54] A March 1975 letter from the Ontario Federation of Labour to the deputy minister of labour called for the adoption of a pension plan termination-insurance program. In their private deliberations, the ministry considered instituting such a program in exchange for 'less popular changes to the notice of termination section of the Act.'[55] While 'tactically attractive,' this plan of action proved too risky in the years following the Dunlop shutdown.

Significantly, legislation in the wake of the Dunlop closing left unresolved the larger issue of how foreign companies should close their Canadian plants. This question was taken up by trade unionists and their political allies in the NDP.[56] Despite tensions between the sometimes-dogmatic left-nationalists in the NDP and internationalist-minded trade union leaders, both groups eventually came to draw upon Robert Laxer's concept of deindustrialization.[57] Laxer had offered a compelling explanation of plant closures across Southern Ontario by blaming deindustrialization on Canada's dependent relationship on the United States. Thus, years before the deindustrialization thesis was taken up in the United States, Canadian trade unionist Stewart Cooke would refer to the 'crime of de-industrialization' when pointing to the wave of plant closings in Ontario's industrial heartland.[58]

Laxer's notion of deindustrialization resonated with economic nationalists as it tapped into the common belief that American multinationals operating in Canada were closing branch plants in order to protect jobs in the United States. As journalist Robert Perry reported in his book, *GALT, USA*: 'Several times in the Grand River Valley I heard about layoffs in subsidiaries implemented to keep the payrolls fat in Pittsburgh and Akron, and I have no reason to disbelieve the accounts.'[59] The convergence of economic nationalism and the anti-shutdown movement resulted in a fundamentally different understanding of the issue in Canada; every time a mill or factory closed, it signalled the negative effects of American economic domination over Canada. Even when the factory was British-owned, as in the case of Dunlop's industrial rubber products factory in Toronto, it became intertwined with the role of foreign multinationals in Canada and, by extension, American economic domination.

Importantly, the new nationalism did not go unchallenged on the political left. In early 1972, *Canadian Forum* published an essay by George Woodcock that suggested that economic nationalists on the one hand and left-wingers preaching local control on the other were working at cross purposes.[60] To be sure, these two approaches, representing the major political movements in Canada, invoked two very different communities of identification.

In 'The Perils of Patriotism,' an essay in response to Woodcock's, Christian Bay warned Canadians that they were being taught a 'we-feeling' that exploited 'negative feelings' towards outsiders. For him, this 'make-believe' or 'false' community of the nation-state diverted Canadians from 'two kinds of real community': the neighbourhood community and the international community.[61] Apparently, there was no room in between for group solidarity. Canadians were told to 'think globally but act locally' but advocates of the new nationalism, such as historian Bruce Hodgins, wondered how local communities could hold large corporations accountable: 'How can Sudbury take on INCO, or New Brunswick even a home-grown (if non-resident) K.C. Irving?'[62] Others simply dismissed the turn to the local as yet another imported idea from the United States.

For their part, Marxist opponents of economic nationalism took issue with the characterization of Canada as a colony of the United States. In a world divided between third world victims and first world oppressors, Canada was an imperial power, albeit one of secondary importance. Steve Moore and Debi Wells argued in the mid–1970s that the deindustrialization thesis was a myth, symbolic of the 'theoretical poverty of left-nationalism.'[63] For them, international patterns of economic dislocation proved that American workers did not gain jobs at the expense of Canadian workers. Rather, plant closings and job loss were part of a worldwide trend in capitalism that had little or nothing to do with nationality. Nationalist talk of American domination distracted Canadians from the true source of disruption in their lives, international capitalism.

The admittedly simplified perception of American bosses versus Canadian workers nonetheless proved to be an empowering myth for organized labour. Just how powerful it continued to be became clear when Columbus McKinnon, a manufacturer of chains and hoists, closed its St Catharines, Ontario, plant seven months after a strike had been called in late October 1977.[64] The company chose instead to supply the Canadian market from the United States. For local UAW president John Washuta, the shutdown proved that foreign ownership was 'detrimental to the welfare of Canadian workers.'[65] In response, the Canadian region of the UAW launched an aggressive boycott against Columbus McKinnon products. UAW staffers drew up a list of alternative suppliers of hoists and chains and canvassed virtually every company with whom they had collective agreements to press them to change suppliers. Their efforts met with surprising success. At Northern Telecom, where the UAW represented office staff, the change was made quietly without bothering to consult upper management.[66] The managers of the GM diesel plant, Massey Ferguson in Toronto, and Pullman Trailmobile in Brantford also agreed immediately to the request.

The 'buy-Canadian aspect of our argument,' the UAW noted, compelled many businessmen to agree to the boycott even when they worked for American-owned companies.[67] Favourable responses were elicited from companies such as American Motors, Bundy Tubing, Sheller-Globe, and Long Manufacturing. The local UAW president at Daal Specialties in Collingwood, Ontario, urged the plant manager 'to cease dealing with such a company, that obviously regards the Canadian people as nothing more than pawns on a chess board, that can be moved and removed at will.'[68] Ironically, the company's affirmative response came from corporate headquarters in Mt Clements, Michigan.

Not surprisingly, some Canadian managers did not appreciate the UAW's brazen advice. Union organizer Pat Clancy reported from Sarnia that three small companies met his request with stony silence and a curt '"we'll buy from whoever we like."'[69] In St Catharines, home of the closed Columbus McKinnon plant, the president of Kelsey-Hayes initially refused to 'acquiesce' even though he acknowledged the 'seriousness' of the situation. UAW plant chairman Bill Dow 'laid it right on the line to him saying if the Company [was] going to use Columbus-McKinnon products that he had better be prepared for lots of shutdowns and sit-downs. In addition, Brother Dow pointed out we have approximately 40 laid off Columbus McKinnon workers in this area and if they heard we were using Columbus McKinnon products made in the United States, undoubtedly there would be an informational picket line go up.'[70] To avoid a confrontation, Kelsey Hayes ordered the cancellation of all future orders with Columbus McKinnon. Although these efforts failed to compel Columbus McKinnon to reopen its St Catharines plant, the boycott campaign reassured workers that their union could do something meaningful in the face of a plant closure and that its actions might have contributed to Columbus McKinnon's 1979 decision to return the production of chains and hoists to Southern Ontario.

Standing Up by Sitting Down

The legislative successes of 1970–1 and the broad public appeal of the UAW fight-back campaign against Columbus McKinnon left union leaders and economic nationalists hungry for more. In 1980, job loss was pushed once again to the political forefront. The enraged mood in Ontario could be attributed to the cumulative impact of a wave of plant closings that had struck the province. As stockman George Thorne filed out of Bendix Automotives' Windsor plant for the last time, he angrily told a reporter that the government should 'throw all the Americans out of Canada,' adding that they 'rape the country dry, make big profits here, then they pull out.'[71] It was in these tumultuous times that workers across Ontario took direct action against their American employers and returned to the famed sit-ins conducted in the formative days of industrial unionism.

The Canadian UAW was primed to escalate its resistance to plant closings when 350 delegates gathered in Port Elgin for their regular council meeting in June 1980. Instead of the usual low key affair, delegate after delegate from doomed plants rose to say their good-byes. Local 195 delegate Rick Byrne was one of those losing their jobs, as Bendix Automotive had abruptly closed his plant just prior to the council meeting. At that meeting, the 'horror of what was happening was focused as never before.'[72] In response, Canadian UAW director Bob White told delegates that something 'dramatic' needed to be done to focus public attention on the crisis facing industrial workers.[73] Years later White claimed that it was his decision to 'fight back': 'We needed a tactic. There was no point putting pickets in front of a deserted plant. I remembered the days when the Reuthers occupied plants so that scabs couldn't get in ... The only weapon we had against plant closures was to occupy the plants so the company couldn't get its equipment out.'[74] White recalls that his proposal to occupy plants slated for closure was made on the spur of the moment.

There was nothing impulsive in how White and the Canadian UAW implemented its new strategy. Plant occupations were illegal actions and the union risked being sued by companies. Police could also be called in to make arrests. White struggled to rein in rank-and-file activism but the new tactic got off to a rocky start. Immediately following the meeting, Rick Byrne returned to Windsor to lead a hastily organized sit-in of the now-closed Bendix plant. During the six hour occupation, workers lowered the plant's Canadian flag to half mast, sending a message of national mourning.[75] In his memoirs, White criticized this unauthorized action: '"That's exactly the wrong thing to do," I told my staff. "We've got to think this through before we act and make ourselves vulnerable."'[76] In oral history interviews Andy Morocko and Ed Lawrenson took pride in the fact that they had been the first ones to defy their American bosses. They both noted that their actions had forced Bendix to provide its dismissed Windsor employees with larger severance packages than initially offered.[77]

Despite this early victory, the Bendix sit-down strike was soon eclipsed by the two-week occupation of the Houdaille Bumper plant in Oshawa. Bob White and the Canadian UAW chose to make their stand at Houdaille because it was an American-owned company, and the workers were older ('many of them veterans' of the Second World War), and far from 'the stereotype of labour radicals.'[78] Virtually all 200 employees of Houdaille occupied the plant on 8 August 1980. They prepared themselves for a long siege by bringing in all of the essentials: sleeping bags, food, a television set, a dart board, and dozens of decks of cards. Frank Byra notified UAW readers of *Solidarity* that the sit-down strikers at Houdaille were acting on behalf of workers across Canada: 'I could be home sleeping in a soft bed. But I've made up my mind to stay here because it's time we showed the plant owners across the country that they have to start treating their employees with respect ... We're standing up by sitting down.'[79] Economic nationalism loaned a sense of urgency to the occupation as well as an added perception of national purpose.

In the days that followed, the protesters received hundreds of telegrams of support and a steady stream of politicians and union leaders. Houdaille's decision to close the plant was particularly galling as FIRA had approved the purchase of the company by an American conglomerate in December 1979. At the time, workers feared that the new owner would close down production in Oshawa. As a result, a sign displayed prominently during the occupation read 'Another FIRA Giveaway' and Canadian flags billowed from every window.[80] A *Financial Times* editorial wrote that Houdaille Bumper provided the ultimate economic nationalist passion play: 'The company behavior that provoked the sit-in of 200 workers at Houdaille Industries Ltd of Oshawa has been

Bob White (left) visiting occupied Houdaille Factory in Oshawa.

roundly condemned by all the professional nationalists and political axe-grinders of the land. That was to be expected. It provided an almost perfect text of their oft-repeated sermons.'[81] Television viewers across the country took pride in seeing Canadian workers mowing the lawn and trimming the hedges and leading their families through the immaculately clean plant. 'It's our plant now,' declared occupier Bob Valliers, a thirty-seven-year man.

At its most basic level, the fight at Houdaille stemmed from miserly pension eligibility and severance pay offered by the departing American company. If left unchallenged, thirty-eight of the plant's two hundred workers under fifty-five years of age with more than thirty years service would have been ineligible to collect a pension until age sixty-five. By the end of the two-week occupation, 'the thirty-eight,' as they became known, won the right to retire early with full pension rights. In addition, the company reluctantly agreed to augment severance payments from one week's pay for every eight years worked to $200 or more for each year of service. As a result, one worker with twenty-nine years service received a lump sum payment of $7,250 instead of the initial $1,332 offered by the company.

The Canadian UAW acknowledged the strike's importance and accorded strike pay to an illegal strike for the first time in its history. Buzz Hargrove called the Houdaille occupation a historic victory for labour: 'You've not only shown that workers can go out and win a better settlement. You've served notice to every politician in this country that workers are not going to go on taking it and that they are going to have to bring legislation restricting company's rights to close plants and protecting people from the terrible effects of these closings.'[82] This view was shared by many Canadians outside the union. Film-maker Laura Sky called the showdown 'enormously significant' as it provided a 'model of militant and dignified action' for Canadian workers defying an American multinational.[83]

For Canadian workers, it seemed that economic nationalism and worker militancy paid off. Seeking greater compensation for their job loss, workers at Beach Foundry in Ottawa also occupied their plant in the summer of 1980. The spontaneous action by the members of the UAW, done without prior approval from the union, nonetheless got the leadership's approval. This evidence of trade union solidarity was sufficient to convince the company to capitulate to demands for more generous severance packages.

Was labour militancy confined to Canada's autoworkers? Charlotte Yates has argued convincingly that the 'militant strategy' adopted by the UAW stemmed from a strong sense of collective identity. The capacity of the Canadian UAW to resist plant closings and demands for concessions rested on its ability to mobilize rank-and-file members through its democratically elected district council.[84] The American UAW, by contrast, had disbanded its district councils in 1945 as part of the push to drive out suspected communists. American trade unionists, Yates argues, therefore had a 'weak' and 'conservative' collective identity in the Cold War era.

While the Canadian UAW was at the forefront of resistance to plant closings, the union was not alone in its militant strategy. By the mid–1970s, the Canadian Labour Congress and the Ontario Federation of Labour both had abandoned their previous support for continentalism in favour of economic nationalism.[85] Many other national and international unions operating in Canada followed suit, but none with more energy than the Canadian section of the left-wing United Electrical Workers (UE).[86] A reading of the UE News published during this period reveals a union quick to wield the stick of Canadian nationalism to bludgeon American corporations operating in this country. These per-

Protesting the closing of Houdaille Bumper, Ontario Legislature, October 1980.

ceptions came sharply into focus when members of the UE occupied the Tung-Sol factory in Bramalea, in Ontario premier Bill Davis's own constituency. Having won a six-fold increase in severance pay, these still-defiant workers filed out of the building in the summer of 1980 singing 'O Canada' and 'Solidarity Forever.'[87] Much as the Canadian flag had done at other occupations, the choice of protest anthems summed up the distinctive nationalism of plant closing opponents in Canada.

In the wake of the sit-ins, the Ontario government announced amendments to the Employment Standards Act in the fall of 1980 to encourage the portability of pensions, to compel employers to participate in adjustment committees, and to ensure that they continued to pay their employees benefits throughout the pre-notification period. Organized labour once again dismissed these proposals as insufficient.

To maintain the pressure on the provincial government, the Ontario Federation of Labour mounted an aggressive political action campaign, 'Ontario Can Work,' which culminated in an October 1980 rally of nearly 10,000 trade unionists at the provincial legislature. In preparation for the rally, the Niagara Peninsula's UAW Local 199 gathered three hundred signs, a large banner, three coffins (each representing a recent plant closing), and three Canadian flags, one of which featured a 'big wedge through the Maple leaf indicating Plant Closures and Unemployment.'[88] Once again the symbolic power of nationalism was put to use by opponents of plant closings in Canada. But nationalist sentiment at the protest took many forms: 'Heading up UE's contingent was a visual display on runaway plants that elicited an enthusiastic response ... The display featured a costumed Uncle Sam with a placard reading "For Higher Profits," and he carried a long chain that had attached to it brightly painted mock-ups of six UE plants or operations that have closed. There were also two TV sets which depicted the loss of Canada's home entertainment industry to the United States and other off-shore countries.'[89] Those in attendance cheered wildly when Bob White said that the worker occupation of the Houdaille, Beach, Bendix and Tung-Sol plants showed the country that 'we can do something' in the face of shutdowns.[90]

Forced to go further, the Ontario government formed a Select Committee of the legislature in the fall of 1980 to investigate plant shutdowns. Committee transcripts reveal that members from all three political parties associated mill and factory closings with concerns over American control and repeatedly inquired about the ratio of foreign-owned and domestically-owned plants that underwent closure. Top managers of several American-owned companies were compelled to justify their decisions to close plants in Ontario. The ensuing dialogue with corporate leaders rattled elected members regardless of political party and politicians plaintively reminded the managers who had made major disinvestment decisions that there was 'a little something like a border.'[91] A spokesperson for the Canadian Federation of Independent Business complained: 'Reading the Committee testimony and discussion, one gets the distinct impression that the Committee is looking for a villain – a villain who can be forced to pay the price of his own malfeasance. Members must ask themselves, which corporation is responsible for high interest rates? Whose fault is foreign ownership? Who is responsible for the saturation of the Ontario market by imports? Whose fault is poor management of a business and how do you force the individual to pay? This business of assigning fault for layoffs and shut-downs is a fruitless exercise.'[92] Industry minister Larry Grossman likewise told committee members in no uncertain terms that firms

Protesting Ontario plant closures in 1980.

closed plants for economic reasons, 'not reasons of patriotism.'[93] But the committee, no doubt reflecting the public's mood at the time, was not yet receptive to this line of argument.

Citing the more aggressive stance ostensibly taken in Europe, the Select Committee released its interim report on 12 December 1980, which called on the government to go beyond its pending legislation and make severance pay a requirement. It justified the measure politically by invoking the spectre of the American multinational corporation: 'The decision is not only a head office decision but in branch plants one which is made with little input from Canadian management.'[94] Despite being disbanded after an election, the Select Committee compelled the Conservative government of William Davis to legislate severance pay regulations, making Ontario the second jurisdiction in Canada, after the federal government, to do so.

Although the adoption of severance pay softened the blow of displacement for some workers, many did not benefit from the legislation. Women tended to work in smaller plants than men and were far less likely to benefit from the statutory regulations introduced to protect employees in plant shutdowns. This differential impact became abundantly clear when Dominion Auto Accessories closed its doors on 20 May 1983, putting forty-six Windsor autoworkers out of work. Despite its modest size, the maker of protective lighting equipment and car mirrors sparked a major political controversy. As the number of employees dismissed fell just under the fifty person threshold set by the 1981 severance-pay law, none of the long-service employees qualified for the mandatory payments of one week's pay for every year worked. Even though the company had employed 150 workers only a few years previously, the U.S.-controlled company managed to duck its obligations through gradual layoffs. In fact, each employee with at least ten years' service would have qualified for an average lump-sum payment of $4,700 had there had been four additional people to lay off.[95] Since the employer was not legally obligated to offer a penny, the union managed to negotiate only a paltry $150 for each employee.

Dominion Auto Accessories was remarkable if only for the publicity it engendered. A memo prepared for the Ontario minister of labour estimated that only one-third of terminated employees in Ontario actually received severance pay.[96] Small workplaces, bankrupt companies, and employees with less than ten years' seniority fell outside the legislation. Severance pay would have made an enormous difference for the employees of Dominion Auto Accessories, many of whom were 'women in their 40s and 50s' who had 'roots, a home.'[97] In an extraordinary move, the joint labour-management manpower adjustment committee formed at the plant called it quits after just three meetings, deciding unanimously to use the money saved by suspending job placement efforts in order to purchase extended medical benefits coverage for the displaced workers. As committee chairperson T.L. Wickett explained: 'It was felt that in a city with 26% unemployment the money would be better spent' this way. As a result, the committee notified the federal government that not one of the twenty-nine Dominion Auto Accessories employees who had requested assistance was to be placed in a new job.

Despite the inadequacies of the legislation, economic nationalism in Canada had begun to influence decisions made in the corporate boardroom. A 1986 U.S. Office of Technology Assessment study of plant shutdowns compared how three American-controlled forestry companies operating in Canada and the United States dealt with layoffs. While the unnamed executives of the Canadian subsidiaries believed they had a moral obligation above and beyond the statutory minimum to their employees, top managers at the headquarters of the American parent companies expressed their opposition to all constraints on management's right to terminate employees at will.[98] In fact, two of the U.S. parent companies reportedly dismissed employees without any advance notice whatsoever. The fundamental philosophical differences between American and Canadian managers within the same multinational corporation were striking.

Although Canadian nationalists succeeded in politicizing plant shutdowns, their success was only partial, as the labour movement and its allies failed by and large either to reopen plants or to reverse publicly announced decisions. As one senior trade unionist observed: 'The Houdaille example, where the membership was solid, the union unambiguously supportive, and the public sympathetic shows that we can protest and even win some concessions, but even here we still lost the jobs and lost pension monies [in] the absence of pension portability.'[99] And sit-ins sometimes backfired. For example, Wheatley Manufacturing abruptly closed its Windsor plant in December 1981 after managers heard rumours of a potential plant occupation.[100]

To avoid triggering the early closure of their plant, Canadian workers adopted new forms of resistance. American-owned Allen Industry's east end Hamilton plant announced its plans to relocate production to Mexico in 1984. Instead of occupying the plant, workers turned to a psychological game of cat and mouse aimed at harassing management and slowing production. According to local UAW president David Christopherson,

The main strategy inside the plant was to drive them absolutely crazy. Every time you didn't have to work, you didn't but this wasn't an acknowledged slow down, it was an individual thing ... All day long all you had was all these whistles going off all over the place. Day after day after day and they couldn't stop it. We had the public behind us. There was just enough going on, and enough trouble, it was interfering with their ability to get their product out ... We drove the supervisors crazy with these bloody whistles. It was driving our people nuts too but not in the same way because it was [our] fight. Our people felt good because through it all we all felt so hopeless ... We had to do something. By engaging our people, without realizing it at the time, but in hindsight I know now, we were also giving people hope. They were fighting and at least doing something ... at the end of the day we did get a settlement.[101]

The company agreed to a six-month extension of health benefits and a 25 per cent increase in severance pay worth $500,000. David Christopherson counted the fight against Allen Industries as yet another 'huge victory' for Canadian trade unionists in so far as they won the right to get 'something more than a pink slip.'

Continued labour unrest in the early 1980s, including a successful eight-day occupation of Windsor Bumper that won the plant a reprieve, prompted the minister of labour to demand preferential hiring rights for all workers in the province. To make his point, the minister argued that the 'refusal of some employers to give serious consideration to such problems' had 'generated a degree of acrimony and labour-management tension in specific instances which has heightened public concern on this issue.'[102] By 1983, the most extensive plant shutdown legislation in North America had been enacted by a government far more 'progressive' than 'conservative' in its approach to plant closings.

This string of legislative victories relieved Ontario trade unionists of the burden of negotiating job placement, advance notice of plant closings, severance pay, and preferential hiring rights. At a time when American unions were having to exchange wage and benefit concessions for these same protective measures, Canada's unions could afford to take a tough, no concessions stance. Many unions, including the Canadian Labour Congress at its May 1982 convention, adopted defiant resolutions. To bolster local union resolve, the Canadian Region of the UAW created a 'No Concession Fund' to supplement normal strike pay for workers who were resisting demands for wage and benefit concessions. Union records suggest that rank-and-file workers broadly supported this principled stance, at the risk of losing their own jobs. Andy Morocko recalled: 'We were the sacrificial lambs. The labour movement in Canada, the whole society, owes these guys a great debt.'[103] When faced with the threat of plant closure unless workers agreed to concessions, many union locals voted to take their chances on the picket line. In an optimistic moment, Bob White wrote, 'we not only won the battle [at Houdaille], we won the war, too.'[104]

The secession of the Canadian region from the UAW in December 1984 was filmed by the National Film Board in its award-winning documentary, *Final Offer*, a behind-the-scenes look at high-stakes collective bargaining between the Canadian UAW and General Motors.[105] Over the course of these negotiations, the camera caught the mounting war of words between Canadian Region director Bob White and UAW international president Owen Bieber. In one famous scene, the camera recorded a telephone conversation between the two men in which Bieber threatened to withhold the union's strike fund in a hapless attempt to undermine the Canadians' firm no-concession position. A defiant Bob White warned Bieber: 'I'll wrap the fucking Canadian flag around me ... I will tell them all that. When I get through, the membership will sit.' After years of struggle within the international union, it appeared that Canadian UAW members could no longer see much mutuality of interest with their counterparts in the United States.[106]

Conclusion

Where did the possibilities for community identification and collective action arise? In making her case for larger communities of identification, historian Christine Stansell cited the ability of the nineteenth-century women's rights movement to override 'deep structures of class and racial arrogance' by using 'ideas of shared humanity.'[107] It was only their ability to see likeness – and to overlook difference – that made collective action possible.

The identification of the inhabitants of industrial Ontario with a national community provided the unity of interest necessary to resist plant closings. If there was any message in the string of legislative and plant victories for the anti-shutdown movement in Canada, it was the usefulness of economic nationalism for their cause. Canadian trade unionists literally wrapped themselves in the flag in order to defy foreign-owned companies that wished to abandon workers with little or no compensation. Their efforts were not in vain, as the flag softened the blow of economic displacement during the 1970s and early 1980s. But the gains made by worker protests proved to be only a partial victory. Despite frequent appeals for a public review process, opponents of plant closings did not seriously impinge on management's legal right to close plants. Mills and factories were closed and hundreds of thousands of Canadian workers lost their jobs. Yet foreign companies operating in Canada were keenly aware of the growing public unease and these political constraints may have slowed the pace of creative destruction and job loss. At the very least, the closing of Dunlop's Toronto plant in May 1970 established a pattern of nationalist resistance that we continue to see today.

Conclusion

American theologian Reinhold Niebuhr once stated that only myths had the motive power to effect political change.[1] For Niebuhr, hope was the product of emotion, not cold calculation. It was only natural, then, that opponents of plant closings appealed to the emotional bonds of local and national communities of identification as a political strategy designed to elicit cross-class identification and cooperation. Although a discourse of inevitability surrounded the process of industrial transformation, resistance was not futile. There were, however, definite limits to what people could hope to achieve.

The emptying of the mythical heart of the United States – and the birth of the Rust Bowl and Rust Belt labels – signalled the decrepitude of the heavily industrialized states of Pennsylvania, Ohio, Michigan, Indiana, Illinois, and Wisconsin. As the Great Lakes states metamorphosed into the Rust Belt, the problem became imaginatively contained, tied to one place. Having interpreted industrial decline through the filter of popular regional identities, Americans settled on a new regional hierarchy of have and have-not regions. In the public's mind, the industrial Midwest became a no man's land between the fading smokestack industries and the ascendant post-industrial economy. It was as though the giant hand that had plucked Youngstown from the industrial heartland also had removed other industrial centres such as Pittsburgh, Akron, Dayton, and Detroit. What remained was a jigsaw puzzle of the industrial heartland made unrecognizable by the empty spaces in between.

In the wake of the Vietnam War, opponents of plant closings in the United States proved incapable of coming together. This bitter conflict pitted patriotic trade unionists against leftist anti-war activists and

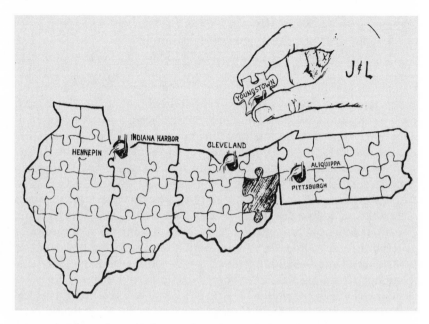

Editorial cartoon from the *Brier Hill Unionist*, 1979.

profoundly altered the political landscape. As the New Deal coalition of liberals, trade unionists, Southerners, and African Americans crumbled, soon to be supplanted by a new coalition of the political right, any hope of a unified response to the emerging plant closing problem faded. While unions directed their patriotic response at Japanese imports and a buy American campaign, young activists conducted a guerilla war against capital in hard-hit industrial cities across the country. These divergent responses within the United States fatally weakened the nascent anti-plant shutdown movement.

Further, by invoking a notion of community tied to place, the bulk of the movement contributed to its own demise. The miniaturized notion of community proved to be a feeble weapon for workers facing job loss, in part because the nation's political and business elite felt little attachment to communities other than their own. The antipathy of union leaders towards a discourse of community stemmed from their fear that local solidarities would drain union strength. As a result, the community strategy, predicated on emotional appeals to people and place, failed to politicize plant closings. To constrain the destructive tendencies of capitalism between 1969 and 1984, a larger solidarity was needed, namely the ideal of a national community.

The motive power of community to validate and legitimate resistance to plant shutdowns by enlarging the radius of trust was greatest in Canada. Beginning with the closing of Dunlop Tire in 1970, the convergence of economic nationalism and a mainly international (U.S. based) trade union movement in Southern Ontario resulted in a fundamentally different understanding of plant shutdowns. Instead of symbolizing the last rites of local community, or a rite of passage into a new post-industrial world, plant shutdowns in Canada seemed to threaten national sovereignty. By literally wrapping themselves in the Canadian flag, industrial workers won important legislative victories that forced companies to soften the blow of displacement. Given the fact that Canadian economic nationalism was imbued with the working-class agenda, it follows that the Canadian public viewed the resistance to plant shutdowns – including illegal plant occupations in 1980 – as meaningful and legitimate. Economic nationalist resistance to plant shutdowns thus softened the blow to industrial workers and their local and national communities. It also appears that by inflating the political and economic cost of terminating employees, Canadian nationalism slowed the pace of creative destruction. American companies operating in a hypersensitive political environment could be forgiven for thinking twice before closing Canadian plants, enforcing what could be called a moral economy on companies operating in Canada. The possibility for identification and collective action thus came from the universalizing impulse of nationalism that allowed Canadians to overlook class, regional, or gender differences in order to identify with the cause of trade unionists fighting American companies that shut plants. The labour-based New Democratic Party's 1984 election slogan of 'ordinary Canadians' encapsulates this strategic coupling of class and national identifications.

The divergent responses to plant shutdowns in Canada and the United States were not lost on trade unionists. A conference convened in Detroit in 1983 by the alternative newspaper *Labor Notes* brought together seven hundred union dissidents to discuss 'how American workers can adopt the Canadian approach.'[2] The keynote speech, given by Canadian postal union president Jean-Claude Parrot, called on American trade unions to resist concessions. Parrot told delegates that workers deserved 'to have institutions that they can trust, that will defend their interests, that will lead them in the struggles.'[3] If there are any lessons to be learned from the story of industrial transformation it is that unions need to have the public on side. They have to make their struggle, the people's struggle.

Community and Nation since 1984

Since 1984, the rallying cries of community and nation have continued to be heard in both the United States and Canada. Yet these years also saw the wholesale retreat of North American governments from the economic sphere. Deregulation, privatization, and continental free trade were the orders of the day. The 1990s also saw the revival of some of the hardest-hit industrial cities in the United States: warehouses were converted into loft apartments, old red brick mills became swanky restaurants. Yet for every Pittsburgh, Kenosha, and Cleveland, there was an Akron, a Youngstown, and a Flint. The prosperity of the late 1990s never seemed to reach these deindustrialized places as nothing arrived to fill the void created by lost industries. As a result, young people moved elsewhere in search of employment. The emptying out of once-bustling industrial centres could be seen in Youngstown, whose population dropped from 170,000 in the 1950s to 92,671 in 1995.[4] Sam Donnorummo, a former Youngstown steelworker, lamented in 1991 that, 'all you have left in the Valley is senior citizens.'[5]

Despite the spatial unevenness of the economic boom in the United States, the Canadian economy has under-performed its southern neighbour since 1984. The recession of the early 1990s was worse in Canada than it was in the United States and unemployment has been consistently higher. Fully 338,000 manufacturing jobs were lost from 1989 to 1992.[6] This period also saw the closing of a large number of mills and factories, including the General Motors van plant in Scarborough, Ontario. The integrated steel mill at Sault Ste Marie would have closed as well, if the provincial government and the United Steelworkers had not interceded to save it. Nationally, the election of Brian Mulroney's Conservatives in 1984 saw the repudiation of the economic prescriptions of the past. This new political era was symbolized in the early going when Mulroney dismantled the Foreign Investment Review Agency, renamed it Investment Canada, and gave it the mission of attracting foreign investment.[7]

The accelerated shift from manufacturing to service industry has resulted in continued organizational challenges for trade unions in the

United States and Canada. Declining membership numbers in the United States, where less than 20 per cent of the non-agricultural labour force is now unionized, led to the merger of once-formidable industrial unions such as the United Steelworkers and the United Rubber Workers.[8] In fact, many unions diversified out of traditional industries to become general unions, representing a wide range of white- and blue-collar workers.[9] In Canada, thousands of unionized jobs disappeared in the 1990s when a tidal wave of plant closings and mass lay-offs struck the country. Trade union membership in Canada slumped, but it did not collapse, with the rate of unionization in Canada still nearly double that of the United States. Even so, Canadian-based unions also embarked on a strategy of consolidation and diversification.

The lack of consensus over political strategy that fatally sundered plant closing opponents in the United States during the 1970s and 1980s continues to divide American trade unionists and social activists today. Trade unionists are split between left-wing insurgents such as the New Directions caucus that arose within the UAW during the late 1980s, and the dominant traditionalist wings in the major private sector unions.[10] This trend may be changing, as the election of a reform slate to the leadership of the AFL-CIO in 1995 has allowed for new initiatives such as the Union Summer program – where college students work with trade unions – and new alliances, but differences remain. One of the biggest challenges, perhaps, is the uncertain place of American nationalism in the post-Vietnam era.[11] At present, localism continues to define most of the American political left.

Although labour historians have stressed communal solidarities since Herbert Gutman's pioneering work in the 1960s, there has been relatively little reflection on what community means.[12] Lucy Taksa suggests that the relationship between class and community has been cast in one of three ways: in opposition, in alliance, or in equation.[13] In the first instance, labour historians have claimed that the cross-class identification and cooperation implied in community has come at the expense of class solidarity. Others, however, have seen labour and community as potential allies. This tendency is particularly common in studies of local resistance to plant closings in the United States. Community-based struggles need not be community-defined ones, noted Bruce Nissen.[14] He cites the example of the Calumet Project for Industrial Jobs in northwestern Indiana which gave workers and community 'a small degree of bargaining power with corporations.'[15] The third approach assumes that class and community are one and the same.

Historian Elizabeth Faue has written that many labour historians in the United States have understood community in this sense, working-class 'communities of interest' in various local settings.[16]

This equation underpins the scholarship of Faue and the other contributors to *'We Are All Leaders': Alternative Unionism in the Early 1930s*, edited by Staughton Lynd. The stated objective of the book's contributors was to show that community-based unionism was, and is, a viable alternative to the hierarchical 'business unionism' of the AFL-CIO.[17] For Lynd, mainstream unionism does not 'meet the needs of working people at the end of the twentieth century.' The same false dichotomy between virtuous community-based working-class organizations on the one hand and bureaucratic unions on the other has animated the New Left since the 1960s.[18] *'We Are All Leaders'* reveals that the old divisions between the New Left and the mainstream AFL-CIO have yet to disappear.

Can local community solidarity be a viable alternative to national or internationally based trade unions? Much has changed since the early successes of alternative unionism in the 1930s. The motive power of communal solidarity still has much to offer, but if the experience with plant closings during the 1970s and 1980s have taught anything it is that local communities are no match for multinational corporations. More heroic defeats are not the answer.

But the answer does not rest with the buy Americanism of the AFL-CIO either. As historian Dana Frank has persuasively argued, nationalist shopping did not save jobs, rebuild the economy, or sustain healthy communities.[19] Blaming Japanese imports provided an excuse for American companies shutting plants or moving production out of the country. It also created the impression that American companies and American workers were playing for the same team and that the solution was more teamwork. Some scholars in the United States have rejected economic nationalism for this reason, as it runs counter to a 'more class-based challenge to transnational corporations.'[20] American patriotism has long been associated with the political right, most recently with the virulent protectionism of Pat Buchanan and Ross Perot.

This blanket condemnation of economic nationalism has spilled over into Canada. In the millennial issue of *Labour/Le Travail*, sociologist Murray E.G. Smith condemned economic nationalism on two counts, for 'class collaboration' and for the erosion of international labour solidarity.[21] Smith argues that economic nationalism – 'whether espoused by "America-first" demagogues or "socialist" political economists [in Canada]' – is a tool used by elites to manipulate an unsuspecting public. While this is sometimes the case, it is simply wrong to suggest, as Smith does, that nothing distinguishes the economic nationalisms of Canada and the United States.

Economic nationalism in Canada has ebbed and flowed in the nearly two decades since 1984. North American free trade, an idea that has been in circulation for more than a century, was resurrected in the fall of 1985 when a Royal Commission headed by former Liberal finance minister Donald S. Macdonald endorsed free trade in its final report. The chief objective of a free trade agreement with the United States, from the Canadian vantage point, was to guarantee access to the huge U.S. market. The commission's report was followed by intense trade negotiations that culminated in the Canada–United States Free Trade Agreement that went into effect on 1 January 1989.[22] In exchange for a bilateral trade dispute settlement mechanism, Canada lowered its tariffs, liberalized its controls on foreign investment, and extended national treatment to U.S. firms operating in Canada. The United States also secured access to Canada's natural resources.[23]

The signing of the agreement did not come about without debate. The November 1988 federal election quickly became a referendum over the free-trade deal. The nationalist Pro-Canada Network, formed in April 1987 at the alternative Maple Leaf summit, brought together thirty-five feminist, trade union, church, environmental, and other organizations in opposition to the agreement.[24] This non-partisan coalition urged Canadians to vote for either the Liberals or the New Democrats, as both parties opposed the agreement. But free-trade opponents faced an unusually united business community that poured money into third-party advertising and into the ruling Progressive Conservative party. In the end, the election saw the government returned with 43 per cent of the vote and a strong parliamentary majority.[25]

This defeat represented a political Waterloo of sorts for economic nationalists in Canada. Since then, a nationalist story of battles lost has taken hold. According to political scientist Jeffrey Ayres, economic nationalists in Canada 'remained caught up in the discourse of job losses, spending cuts and so on; they had difficulty developing a positive narrative for their side.'[26] In the 1990s, with the federal Liberals embracing free trade, economic nationalism became associated with the New Democratic Party and the trade-union movement. The marginalization of the political left following the 1993 federal election further blunted the political impact of old economic nationalist arguments.[27] A decade of constitutional turmoil, resurgent regional and ideological cleavages in English-speaking Canada, and Quebec separatism have all no doubt contributed to this result. Accordingly, economic nationalism has faded into the background.

It would be a mistake, however, to conclude that economic nationalism is dead in Canada. Although defeated at the polls, free trade opponents mobilized large numbers of Canadians for their cause. The membership base of the nationalist Council of Canadians grew from 16,000 in 1988 to 100,000 in 1999.[28] The lingering influence of economic nationalism is also apparent on the shop floor where it not only continues to shape how workers interpret plant closings and job loss, but remains a powerful weapon in the trade union arsenal.

The closing of Toronto's Inglis appliance factory in 1989 is a case in point. In *Working at Inglis: The Life and Death of a Canadian Factory*, David Sobel and Susan Meurer reveal the continuing salience of the Canadian workers versus American bosses opposition. This nationalist line surfaces repeatedly in the visual sketches drawn by Inglis workers and in the authors' text. Not surprisingly, Sobel and Meurer note that most of the workers at Inglis blamed the recently enacted free trade agreement for the closing. The authors argue instead that 'the foreign management felt no loyalty to the Inglis name in Canada.'[29]

The contrast between these two explanations goes to the heart of what once distinguished the economic nationalisms of Canada and the United States. In a highly influential 1981 article, Denis Stairs suggested that economic nationalism in Canada had two main variants, 'investment nationalism' and 'trade nationalism.'[30] During the 1970s and early 1980s, public concern over foreign investment and later, disinvestment, predominated. After free trade, this was no longer the case. In giving a political face to a host of problems ranging from globalization to deindustrialization, the fight against free trade (and the more recent fights against the World Trade Organization) served to shift attention away from investment and towards trade. Arguably, the focus of economic nationalists today is more on buy Canadian protectionism than it is on foreign ownership. This shift from a political discourse centred on ownership and production to one on trade and consumption has meant that economic nationalisms in Canada and the United States are more alike today than they had been during the 1970s or early 1980s.

Canadian economic nationalism nonetheless played a key role in the negotiation of a plant-closing agreement at Inglis between the United

Steelworkers of America (USWA) and U.S.-based Whirlpool, the parent company.[31] Like at Columbus McKinnon in the late 1970s, the union intended to play the nationalist card for all it was worth. The USWA set a deadline of 1 September 1989 for the conclusion of negotiations. If no improvement in the severance packages was granted, it threatened to launch a Canada-wide consumer boycott of Whirlpool products on Labour Day. Steelworker's District 6 director Leo Gerard and the president of the company – Gerard did not remember his name, 'but he's an American' – met at the Delta Hotel in Toronto where the company reluctantly agreed to a 'very good' plant-closing agreement in exchange for a written promise not to launch a boycott. Economic nationalism also contributed to the union's decision to investigate reopening the plant under worker ownership. 'Stick the Steelworkers' flag on the backs and the Canadian flag on the front, and we'll sell more fucking washing machines than Sears,' Leo Gerard suggested. The effort failed. Yet Gerard's colourful language reflected the lingering usefulness of economic nationalism to Canadian workers and their unions in the post–free trade era.

Appendix

INTERVIEW GUIDE*

Name: **Date of Birth:**

Family:
Where were your parents born? What did they do for a living? What kind of neighbourhood did your family live in? Was it a close-knit area? Did everybody's parents work at the same place? Did you want to work there when you grew up?

Work History:
What jobs have you worked in over the years? What did you do? Could you describe the plant (exterior and interior)? Did you like your job? Was it a safe place to work? Did you ever see any accidents? Did you see any discrimination against women or people of colour? How did you get along with management? Were there many layoffs at your workplace before the final closure?

Union:
Was your workplace unionized? What was the name of the union? Were you active in the union? What were meetings like? Did the union do a good job? How did it affect work? Did you ever go out on strike? What do you think of the union?

Recreation:
Did people socialize after their shift? Were there any recreational activities planned by the company or the union?

---

*My style of interviewing tends to be informal. This guide represents only a general reference to the range of possible questions and themes in an interview.

Closure:
Did you anticipate the plant shutdown? Please describe the day that the announcement to close the plant was made. Why did it happen? Who was to blame? Could it have been avoided? Did you get severance pay? A pension? Health benefits? How did your family react to the news? How did the union respond? Was there any attempt to save the plant? Did the community or union help your family through the crisis or were you pretty much on your own? How was the town's economy at the time? Did you have any friends leave town to find work? Where did they go? Why? Did you ever think of leaving too? Why did you stay?

Aftermath:
How has life changed since the plant closed? How has the town changed since those days? Do you feel a strong attachment to your city? Did your wife/ husband work before the closure? Did that change afterwards? Did your children follow you into the plants? Do you still see your old friends from the plant?

Conclusion:
Has your opinion of the closure changed since your last shift in the plant? Is there anything else you would like to add before we end the interview?

Notes

Introduction

1 Richard Ellers, 'Ohio Works Furnaces, Era Are Dynamited into Dust,' *Youngstown Vindicator*, 24 April 1982.
2 George Reiss, 'Says Industrial Diversification to Follow Demise of Furnaces,' *Youngstown Vindicator*, 29 April 1982.
3 Ibid.
4 Jon C. Teaford, *Cities of the Heartland: The Rise and Fall of the Industrial Midwest* (Bloomington: Indiana University Press, 1994), vii.
5 William Serrin, *Homestead: The Glory and Tragedy of an American Steel Town* (New York: Vintage Books, 1994), 9.
6 Dana Frank, *Buy American: The Untold Story of Economic Nationalism* (Boston: Beacon Press, 1999), 131, and Peter Dicken, *Global Shift: Industrial Change in a Turbulent World* (London: Harper and Row, 1986), 314.
7 George Richardson, interview by Donna DeBlasio in 1991. The videotape recording is held at the Youngstown Historical Center of Industry and Labor.
8 Gary McDonogh, 'The Geography of Emptiness,' in Robert Rotenberg and Gary McDonogh, eds., *The Cultural Meaning of Urban Spaces* (Westport, CT: Bergin and Garvey, 1993), 7.
9 Historian Joy Parr reminds us that we 'come from a long tradition in the west which finds meaning by specifying differences, and clarity by concentrating and amplifying presence and absence. We subordinate continuity and diversity so as to feature our world as a series of fixed opposition.' Joy Parr, *The Gender of Breadwinners: Women, Men, and Change in Two Industrial Towns, 1880–1950* (Toronto: University of Toronto Press, 1990), 8–9.
10 Daniel Bell, *The Coming of Post-Industrial Society: A Venture in Social Forecasting* (New York: Basic Books, 1973).

11 Joseph A. Schumpeter. *Capitalism, Socialism and Democracy* 1942; reprint, (Toronto: Harper and Row, 1976), 83.

12 Robert M. Laxer, ed. *(Canada) Ltd. The Political Economy of Dependency* (Toronto: McClelland and Stewart, 1973), 9, 146.

13 Wayne Roberts, 'Shutdowns: Canadian Workers Are Virtually Unprotected from Take-the-Money-and-Run Multinationals,' *The Facts* 7, 4 (1985), 22.

14 Barry Bluestone and Bennett Harrison, *The Deindustrialization of America: Plant Closings, Community Abandonment, and the Dismantling of Basic Industry* (New York: Basic Books, 1982), 6. See also John C. Raines, Lenora E. Berson, and David McI. Grace, eds., *Community and Capital in Conflict: Plant Closings and Job Losses* (Philadelphia: Temple University Press, 1982).

15 John T. Cumbler, *A Social History of Economic Decline: Business, Politics and Work in Trenton* (New Brunswick, NJ: Rutgers University Press, 1989), 182.

16 Bluestone and Harrison, *The Deindustrialization of America*, 6.

17 Robert Z. Lawrence, 'Is Deindustrialization a Myth?' in Paul D. Staudohart and Holly E. Brown, eds., *Deindustrialization and Plant Closure* (Lexington, MA: Lexington Books, 1987), 28.

18 Barry Bluestone, 'In Support of the Deindustrialization Thesis,' in ibid., 41.

19 Ian Robertson MacLachlan finds that foreign owned plants closed more frequently in Ontario, but not in the numbers once suggested. 'Industrial Plant Closure and Competitive Strategy in Ontario, 1981–1986' (PhD diss., University of Toronto, 1990), 26.

20 Cumbler, *A Social History of Economic Decline*, 182–3.

21 Kathryn Marie Dudley, *The End of the Line: Lost Jobs, New Lives in Postindustrial America* (Chicago: University of Chicago Press, 1994), 177.

22 This point is raised in Geoff Eley and Keith Nield, 'Farewell to the Working Class?' *International Labor and Working-Class History* 57 (spring 2000), 1.

23 Thomas Dunk, *It's a Working Man's Town: Male Working-Class Culture* (Montreal: McGill-Queen's University Press, 1991), 45.

24 Anthony D. Smith, 'The Origins of Nation,' in Geoff Eley and Ronald Grigor Suny, eds., *Becoming National: A Reader* (New York: Oxford University Press, 1996), 105.

25 Historian Christine Stansell called the idea of 'womanhood' in the nineteenth century a 'magnificent fiction' because it enabled women to overcome differences. See 'Woman in Nineteenth Century America,' *Gender and History* 11, 3 (1999), 420.

26 Jonathan F. Vance, *Death So Noble: Memory, Meaning, and the First World War* (Vancouver: UBC, Press, 1997), 8.

27 E.P. Thompson, 'The Moral Economy of the English Crowd in the Eighteenth Century,' *Past and Present* 50 (1971), 76–136. For a discussion of

community in the work of Thompson and Natalie Zemon Davis see Suzanne Desan, 'Crowds, Community, and Ritual in the Work of E.P. Thompson and Natalie Davis,' in Lynn Hunt, ed., *The New Cultural History* (Berkeley: University of California Press, 1989).

28 Thompson, 'The Moral Economy of the English Crowd,' 78. Historian Suzanne Desan suggests that Thompson's study may at times 'suggest a more cohesive and united community than in fact existed.' See 'Crowds, Community and Ritual.'

29 The concept of community is examined fully in John C. Walsh and Steven High, 'Rethinking the Concept of Community,' *Histoire sociale/Social History* 17, 64 (1999), 255–74.

30 These are the key elements of community proposed by Walsh and High, ibid., 255. See the discussion of social network theory in Craig Calhoun, 'History, Anthropology, and the Study of Communities: Some Problems in Macfarlane's Proposal,' *Social History* 3 (1978), 363–73. Community as a social and spatial process is explored in Pierre Bourdieu, 'Social Space and Symbolic Power,' *Sociological Theory* 7 (1989), 14–25, and Henri Lefebvre, *The Production of Space* (Oxford: Blackwell, 1991 [1974]).

31 Joy Parr makes the important point that social identities and 'conceptions of common predicament and purpose' are 'forged in particular spatial and temporal settings.' *The Gender of Breadwinners*, 9.

32 This cultural approach has dominated our thinking of nationalism in recent decades. See Alon Confino's superb discussion of nationalism as cultural artifact in *The Nation as Local Metaphor: Wurttemberg, Imperial Germany, and National Memory, 1871–1918* (Chapel Hill: University of North Carolina Press, 1997), 4. For a good review of how the meaning of nationalism has undergone revision see Geoff Eley and Ronald Grigor Suny, 'Introduction: From the Moment of Social History to the Work of Cultural Representation,' in Eley and Suny, eds., *Becoming National*, 4–6. For a cross-border comparative example between Canada and the United States see Barbara Lorenzkowski, 'Border Crossings: The Making of German Identities in the New World, 1850–1914' (PhD diss., University of Ottawa, 2002).

33 Benedict Anderson, *Imagined Communities: Reflections on the Origins and Spread of Nationalism* (1983; reprint, New York: Verso, 1991), 5–6.

34 Ibid., 7. But as Cecelia Elizabeth O'Leary reminds us, nationalism is never neutral. *To Die For: The Paradox of American Patriotism* (Princeton: Princeton University Press, 1999), 4.

35 Eric Hobsbawm, *Nations and Nationalism since 1780: Programme, Myth, Reality* (Cambridge: Cambridge University Press, 1990), 163.

36 If national and local communities confer solidarity and group cohesion, they do so by constructing difference with others. Prasenjit Duara, 'Historicizing National Identity, or Who Imagines What and When,' in Eley and Suny, eds., *Becoming National*, 151–77.

37 Francis Fukuyama, 'The Great Disruption: Human Nature and the Reconstitution of Social Order,' *Atlantic Monthly*, May 1999, 72.

38 Christopher Lasch, 'The Communitarian Critique of Liberalism,' in Charles H. Reynolds and Ralph V. Norman, eds., *Community in America* (Berkeley: University of California Press, 1988), 177. See also Peter Clecak, *America's Quest for the Ideal Self: Dissent and Fulfilment in the 60s and 70s* (New York: Oxford University Press, 1983).

39 Lasch, 'The Communitarian Critique of Liberalism,' 177.

40 The following works all feature the loss of local community after mill or factory closures: Bill Bamberger and Cathy N. Davidson, *Closing: The Life and Death of an American Factory* (New York: W.W. Norton, 1998); Judith Modell and Charlee Brodsky, *A Town without Steel: Envisioning Homestead* (Pittsburgh: University of Pittsburgh Press, 1998); Steven P. Dandaneau, *A Town Abandoned: Flint, Michigan Confronts Deindustrialization* (Albany: State University of New York Press, 1996); Allison Zippay, *From Middle Income to Poor: Downward Mobility among Displaced Steelworkers* (New York: Praeger, 1991); Gregory Pappas, *The Magic City: Unemployment in a Working-Class Community* (Ithaca: Cornell University Press, 1989); and David Bensman and Roberta Lynch, *Rusted Dreams: Hard Times in a Steel Community* (Berkeley: University of California Press, 1988).

41 Milton Rogovin and Michael Frisch, *Portraits in Steel* (Ithaca: Cornell University Press, 1993), 11–12.

42 In his fascinating study of the personal testimonies of Central American refugees, William Westerman finds that their first person narratives contributed to the rapid growth of the Sanctuary movement of the mid-1980s: 'by performing their life stories, the refugees presented themselves as fully human; and as they described their pain and their experience they encouraged identification, sympathy, and empathy.' See William Westerman, 'Central American Refugee Testimonies and Performed Life Histories in the Sanctuary Movement,' in Robert Perks and Alistair Thomson, eds., *The Oral History Reader* (New York: Routledge, 1998), especially 224–9.

43 Resistance in Youngstown is recorded in Thomas G. Fuechtmann, *Steeples and Stacks: Religion and Steel, Crisis in Youngstown* (Cambridge: Cambridge University Press, 1989) and Staughton Lynd, *The Fight against Shutdowns: Youngstown's Steel Mill Closings* (San Pedro, CA: Singlejack Books, 1982). Resource mobilization theory is applied to Youngstown and Johnstown, Pennsylvania, in Scott D. Camp, *Worker Response to Plant Closings: Steel-*

workers in Johnstown and Youngstown (New York: Garland Publishers, 1995). The local campaign against plant closings in the Pittsburgh area is detailed in Dale A. Hathaway, *Can Workers Have a Voice? The Politics of Deindustrialization in Pittsburgh* (University Park: Pennsylvania State University Press, 1993). Finally, the community coalition in the Calumet region of northwestern Indiana is examined in Bruce Nissen, ed., *Fighting for Jobs: Case Studies of Labor, Community Coalitions Confronting Plant Closings* (Albany: State University of New York Press, 1995).

44 Mark McCulloch quoted in Paul Clark et al., 'Deindustrialization: A Panel Discussion,' *Pennsylvania History* 58, 3 (1991), 197.

45 Elizabeth Faue, 'Community, Class, and Comparison in Labour History and Local History,' *Labour History* (Australia) 78 (May 2000), 160. This article is part of a special issue on labour history and local history. See also Lucy Taksa, 'Like a Bicycle, Forever Teetering between Individualism and Collectivism: Considering Community in Relation to Labour History,' ibid., 7–32.

46 Rianne Mahon, *The Politics of Industrial Restructuring: Canadian Textiles* (Toronto: University of Toronto Press, 1984).

47 See, for example, J. Paul Grayson, *Plant Closures and De-Skilling: Three Case Studies* (Ottawa: Science Council of Canada, 1986), Daniel Drache, *The Deindustrialization of Canada and Its Implications for Labour* (Ottawa: Canadian Centre for Policy Alternatives, 1989), and Jane Jenson and Rianne Mahon, eds., *The Challenge of Restructuring: North American Labor Movements Respond* (Philadelphia: Temple University Press, 1993).

48 David Sobel and Susan Meurer, *Working at Inglis: The Life and Death of a Canadian Factory* (Toronto: James Lorimer and Company, 1994).

49 Sam Donnorummo, interview by Donna DeBlasio, 1991. The videotape recording is held by the Youngstown Historical Center of Industry and Labor.

50 For an assertion of a 'working-class moral economy' in the twentieth century see Bradon Ellem and John Shields, 'Making a "Union Town": Class, Gender and Consumption in Inter-War Broken Hill,' *Labour History* (Australia) 78 (May 2000), 116–40.

51 Sue Doro lost her much-loved job as a machinist at the Milwaukee Railroad in the mid–1980s. See her poem 'Kittens,' in Sue Doro, *Blue Collar Goodbyes* (Watsonville, CA: Papier-Mache Press, 1992), 49–52.

1: Gold Doesn't Rust: Regions of the North American Mind

1 Michael Moore (producer), *Roger and Me* (Warner Brothers, 1989).

2 Wilbur Zelinsky, 'North America's Vernacular Regions,' *Annals of the Association of American Geographers* 70, 1 (1980), 1.

3 Frederick C. Luebke, 'Regionalism and the Great Plains: Problems of Concept and Method,' *Western Historical Quarterly* 15, 1 (1984), 19.

4 William Westfall, 'On the Concept of Region in Canadian History and Literature,' *Journal of Canadian Studies* 15, 2 (1980), 11.

5 Despite the multiplicity of images projected onto a spatial area at any one time, R. Douglas Francis has argued that historians can ascertain the prevailing image of a region. See *Images of the West: Responses to the Canadian Prairies* (Saskatoon: Western Producer Prairie Books, 1989), xvii.

6 James Shortridge, *The Middle West: Its Meaning in American Culture* (Kansas: University of Kansas Press, 1989), 10.

7 Wallace E. Akin, *The North Central United States* (Princeton, NJ: D. Van Nostrand Co., 1968), 151.

8 Dale Maharidge, *Journey to Nowhere*, with photos by Michael Williamson (Garden City, NY: Dial Press, 1985).

9 David D. Anderson, 'The Dimensions of the Midwest,' *MidAmerica* 1 (October 1973), 9–10.

10 Lucien Stryck, *Heartland II: Poets of the Midwest* (DeKalb: Northern Illinois University Press, 1975).

11 Paul Bonnifield, *The Dust Bowl: Men, Dirt and Depression* (Albuquerque: University of New Mexico Press, 1979), vii.

12 Clarence L. Barnhart, *The New Century Cyclopedia of Names* (New York: Appleton-Century-Crofts, 1954).

13 *The Columbia Encyclopedia*, 5th ed. 2383.

14 The recurring need of the mass media to refer to new manifestations of Dust Bowl was demonstrated frequently: 'New Dust Bowl in the West,' *U.S. News and World Report*, 21 January 1955, 71–2; 'Fifty Million Acres – Dust Bowl Danger Zone,' *Newsweek*, 8 March 1954, 68–9; 'Oklahoma 1970: The Dust Bowl of the 1930s Revisited,' *Time*, 26 January 1970, 16–17; and Shona Mckay, 'Return of the Dust Bowl,' *Maclean's*, 6 August 1984, 17.

15 Donald Worster, *Dust Bowl: The Southern Plains in the 1930s* (New York: Oxford University Press, 1979), 4.

16 See, for example, Barry Broadfoot, *Ten Lost Years, 1929–1939: Memories of Canadians Who Survived the Depression* (Markham, ON: Paperjacks, 1975); and Studs Terkel, *Hard Times: An Oral History of the Great Depression* (New York: Pantheon, 1970).

17 Clarence L. Barnhart, *The Second Barnhart Dictionary of New English* (New York: Harper & Row, 1980).

18 James Cobb, 'From Muskogee to Luckenbach: Country Music and the Southernization of America,' *Journal of Popular Culture* 16 (1982), 81.

19 Bernard Schwartz (producer), *Coal Miner's Daughter* (Universal Studios, 1980).

20 *The Nation*, 1.
21 Bob Seger and the Silver Bullet Band, 'Boomtown Blues,' on *The Distance* (1982) and, Bobby Bare, n.d. 'Detroit City,' on *Detroit City and Other Hits*.
22 Bernard Weinstein, 'The Divided States of America,' *Current*, July–August 1980, 52–3.
23 Shortridge, *The Middle West*, 85.
24 Joel Garreau, *The Nine Nations of America* (Boston: Houghton Mifflin, 1981), xv.
25 John R. Borchert, *Northern Heartland* (Minneapolis: University of Minnesota Press, 1987), 4–5.
26 Allan C. Ornstein, 'Decline of the Frostbelt,' *Dissent* 30, 3 (1983), 373.
27 *Time*, 10 December 1979, 79.
28 Jon C. Teaford, *Cities of the Heartland. The Rise and Fall of the Industrial Midwest* (Bloomington: Indiana University Press, 1994), vii.
29 Earl Shorris, 'The Empty House,' in Earl Shorris, ed., *While Someone Else Is Eating* (Garden City, NY: Anchor Press, 1984), 70.
30 Tom Wayman, 'Detroit Poem,' in *Counting the Hours: City Poem* (Toronto: McClelland and Stewart, 1983). Permission to use courtesy of Tom Wayman.
31 Barry Bluestone and Bennett Harrison, *The Deindustrialization of America: Plant Closings, Community Abandonment, and the Dismantling of Basic Industry* (New York: Basic Books, 1982), 33.
32 Janice Castor, 'Book Audits,' *Time*, 23 May 1983, 44.
33 Garreau, *Nine Nations*, xv.
34 Ibid., 57.
35 *Time*, 13 December 1982, 54–5.
36 'A More Severe Slump,' *Time*, 26 May 1980, 40–1.
37 Christopher Byron, 'The Idle Army of Unemployed,' *Time*, 27 December 1980, 44–9.
38 Charles Alexander, 'Gathering Gloom for Workers,' *Time*, 14 December 1981, 64–5.
39 Christopher Byron, 'Booms, Busts and Birth of a Rust Bowl,' *Time*, 27 December 1982, 44–9.
40 Christopher Byron, 'Big Steel's Winter of Woes,' *Time*, 24 January 1983, 58–9.
41 *Historical Atlas of the United States* (Washington, DC: National Geographic Society, 1988), 164–5.
42 James Guimond, *American Photography and the American Dream* (Chapel Hill: University of North Carolina Press, 1991), 281.
43 Maharidge, *Journey to Nowhere*.
44 *The Business of America* (California Newsreel. Resolutions Inc., 1984).

45 Barry Spikings and Michael Deeley (producers), *The Deer Hunter* (Universal Pictures, 1978); Robert J. Wunsch and Stephen Friedman (producers) *Slapshot* (Universal Pictures, 1977).
46 *All the Right Moves* (20th Century Fox, 1983).
47 S. Lichter, Linda Robert, and Stanley Rothman, *Watching America* (New York: Prentice-Hall, 1989), 113.
48 Bob Seger and the Silver Bullet Band, 'Makin' Thunderbirds,' on *The Distance* (1982).
49 Billy Joel, 'Allentown,' on *The Nylon Curtain* (1982).
50 Bruce Springsteen, *Born to Run* (1975).
51 Bart Testa, 'Born to Run, Fight and Win,' *Maclean's*, 22 December 1980, 50–1.
52 Bruce Springsteen, *The River* (1980).
53 Bruce Springsteen, 'Johnny 99,' on *Nebraska* (1982).
54 Bruce Springsteen, 'My Hometown,' on *Born in the USA* (1984).
55 'Attacking Mr. Reagan's economic policies, Mr. Mondale said: "His ... policies are turning our great industrial base of this ... country ... into a rust bowl." This was picked up in the media and repeated as Rust Belt.' *Oxford Dictionary of New Words*, 1981.
56 *The Columbia Encyclopedia*. A generic definition of historical and geographic associations was given by *The American Heritage Dictionary of the English Language* (Boston: Houghton Mifflin, 1992). This trend can be seen in recent academic scholarship that has explored rust belts as far away as Russia and Japan. Recent examples of publications focused on so-called rust belts outside of the United States include: Rose Brady, 'The Great Russian Depression of 1992?' *Business Week*, 20 April 1992, 47; and Roger Schreffler, 'The New Rust Belt,' *Automotive Industries* 174 (1994), 22.
57 *Oxford Dictionary of New Words* (1981).
58 R. Douglas Hurt, 'Ohio: Gateway to the Midwest,' in James H. Madison, ed., *Heartland: Comparative Histories of the Midwestern States* (Bloomington: Indiana University Press, 1988), 222–3.
59 R. Douglas Francis, 'Regionalism and the Region,' in Mel Watkins, ed., *Canada* (New York: Facts on File, 1993), 236.
60 Ontario, *Ontario: Canada's Heartland of Industry, Finance, Culture* (Toronto: Department of Travel and Publicity, 1961), 1.
61 *Seaway to the Heartland* (National Film Board, Fred Gorman Films, 1975).
62 A thorough discussion of the many variations of the 'metropolitan thesis' can be found in Donald F. Davis, 'The "Metropolitan Thesis" and the Writing of Canadian Urban History,' *Urban History Review* 14, 3 (1985), 95–113.

63 L.D. McCann, *Heartland and Hinterland: A Geography of Canada* (Scarborough, ON: Prentice-Hall, 1982), 9.

64 Ibid., 102.

65 Sometimes Canadians spoke of a rural heartland in the Prairie breadbasket. See for example Ottmar Bierwagon and Mark Abley, *Heartland: Prairie Portraits and Landscapes* (Vancouver: Douglas and McIntyre, 1989).

66 Ralph R. Krurger, 'The Disappearing Niagara Fruit Belt,' *Canadian Geographic* 5, 4 (1959). See also *Dictionary of Canadian English: A Dictionary of Canadianisms on Historical Principles* (Toronto: Gage Education Publishing, 1991), 297.

67 Francis, 'Regionalism and Region,' 237.

68 John C. Van Nostrand, 'The Queen Elizabeth Way: Public Utility versus Public Space,' *Urban History Review* 7, 2 (1983), 13.

69 *Maclean's*, April 1970, 56.

70 Maurice Yeates, 'The Industrial Heartland in Transition,' in *Heartland and Hinterland*, ed. L.D. McCann (Scarborough, ON: Prentice-Hall, 1982), 105.

71 John Bacher and Wayne Roberts, 'The Unlucky Horseshoe,' *Canadian Dimension* 15, 7 (1981), 13.

72 Patrick Allen and Joan Howard, *Canada's Golden Horseshoe: An ESL/Geography Module* (Toronto: OISE Press, 1982).

73 W.P. Anderson, 'The Changing Competitive Position of the Hamilton Steel Industry,' in *Steel City: Hamilton and Region*, ed. M.J. Dear (Toronto: University of Toronto Press, 1987), 216.

74 If there was a Canadian equivalent to the Rust Belt in the early 1980s, it would have been the Montreal area. Despite the fears that Montreal was experiencing deindustrialization and industrial decline, the Rust Belt label was explicitly rejected by Pierre Lamonde and Mario Polèse, 'L'évolution de la structure économique de Montréal, 1971–1981: déindustrialisation ou réconversion?' *L'Actualité économique* 60, 4 (1984), 490; Benjamin Higgins, *The Rise and Fall? of Montreal* (Moncton: Canadian Institute for Research on Regional Development, 1986), 170; Paul-André Linteau, *Histoire de Montréal: dépuis la Confédération* (Montréal: Boréal, 1992), 433; and William J. Coffey and Mario Polèse, 'Le déclin de l'empire Montréalais: regard sur l'économie d'une métropole en mutation,' *Recherches sociographiques* 34, 3 (1993), 435.

75 David Bercuson and J.L. Granatstein, *The Collins Dictionary of Canadian History, 1867 to Present* (Toronto: Collins, 1988), 67.

76 David C. Jones, *Empire of Dust: Settling and Abandoning the Prairie Dry Belt* (Edmonton: University of Alberta Press, 1987), 16.

77 Desmond Morton, 'Responsibility or Trusteeship,' *Canadian Forum* (May 1972), 24.

78 N. H. Lithwick, 'Housing: In a Search of a Crisis,' *Canadian Forum* (February 1969), 250.
79 *Webster's Ninth New Collegiate Dictionary* 251, 1093.
80 John Richards and Larry Pratt, *Prairie Capitalism: Power and Influence in the New West* (Toronto: University of Toronto Press, 1979), 174.
81 Francis, 'Regionalism and the Region,' 237.
82 Glen Norcliffe, 'In a Hard Land: The Geographical Context of Canadian Industrial Landscape Painting,' in Paul Simpson-Housley and Greg Norcliffe, eds., *A Few Acres of Snow: Literary and Artistic Images of Canada* (Toronto: Dundurn Press, 1992), 79–80.
83 W.J. Keith, *Literary Images of Ontario* (Toronto: University of Toronto Press, 1992).
84 David McFadden, *A Trip around Lake Erie* (Toronto: Coach House, 1980), 71.
85 Don Hopkins and David Springbett (producers), *Shutdown* (National Film Board, 1980).
86 On the cover of *Our Times*, October 1984.

2: Transplanted Identities

1 Bricklayer #4, interview by author, during the 'community interview' arranged by the Steelworkers' Organization of Active Retirees (SOAR), Lackawanna, New York, April 1998.
2 Diane Garner, interview by author, Detroit, 24 February 1998. I have arranged to have the videotaped interviews donated to archives in each of the towns where interviews occurred. These institutions are the Walter Reuther Library at Wayne State University in Detroit, the Windsor municipal archives, and the archives of McMaster University in Hamilton. The interview guide and consent form were approved by the University of Ottawa's Committee on Ethical Research on Human Subjects.
3 Jim McHale, interview by author, Detroit, 24 February 1998.
4 The geographic breakdown of oral history interviews is as follows: ten in Ottawa; eight in Hamilton; eight in Windsor; ten in Detroit; seventeen in Buffalo (this was the number of participants in the community interview who shared their stories with me after the plenary was over); and eighty-four in Youngstown.
5 The approach that I have taken to oral history has been profoundly influenced by Alessandro Portelli, *The Death of Luigi Trastulli and Other Stories: Form and Meaning in Oral History* (Albany: State University of New York Press, 1991), Michael Frisch, *A Shared Authority: Essays on the Craft and Meaning of Oral and Public History* (Albany: State University of New York

Press, 1990), and Studs Terkel, *Working* (New York: Pantheon Books, 1972).

6 Ruth Milkman, *Farewell to the Factory: Auto Workers in the Late Twentieth Century* (Berkeley: University of California Press, 1997), 134.

7 Gabriel Solano, interview by author, Detroit, 24 February 1998.

8 Reverend Charles Gordon, Pastor, East Market Street United Church of Christ, Akron, United Rubber Workers Collection, Research Box 2, University of Akron Archives.

9 This feeling was a 'pervasive experience' during the 1980s observed Sharon Zukin in *Landscapes of Power: From Detroit to Disney World* (Berkeley: University of California Press, 1991), 28–9. Just how pervasive remains an open question.

10 Victor W. Turner, *The Ritual Process: Structure and Anti-Structure* (New York: Aldine de Gruyter, 1995 [1969]), 94.

11 Twenty years ago a debate raged over whether immigrant ties to their homelands were sundered or carried over with them. Although John Bodnar's 'transplanted' immigrants have largely displaced Oscar Handlin's 'uprooted' ones, some of what Handlin had to say is worth revisiting. See Oscar Handlin, *The Uprooted* (New York: Grosset and Dunlap, 1951), 6, and John Bodnar, *The Transplanted: A History of Immigrants in Urban America* (Bloomington: Indiana University Press, 1985).

12 Victor Turner, 'Variations on a Theme of Liminality,' in Sally F. Moore and Barbara G. Myerhoff, eds., *Secular Ritual* (Assen: Van Gorcum, 1977), 37.

13 Ruby Kendrick, interview by author, Southpark, Michigan, 25 February 1998. The videocassette will be donated to the Walter Reuther Library. For similar findings see Jacquelyn Dowd Hall, James Leloudis, Robert Korstad, et al., *Like a Family: The Making of a Southern Cotton Mill World* (Chapel Hill: University of North Carolina Press, 1987), xvii, and Tamara Hareven and Randolph Langenbach, *Amoskeag: Life and Work in an American Factory-City* (New York: Pantheon Books, 1978), 12.

14 The frequent references to home and family present us with two metaphors laden with ideological meanings that shape, and are shaped by, the perspectives of those who invoked them. According to Ruth Smith and Eric Eisenberg, root metaphors provide 'rich insight' into the origins of conflict as they present 'symbolic frames that provide an inferential base for understanding more discrete attitude and behaviour.' Root metaphors, in other words capture a fundamental, underlying world view. Ruth C. Smith and Eric M. Eisenberg, 'Conflict at Disneyland: A Root-Metaphor Analysis,' *Communications Monographs* 54, 4 (1987), 369. For a social psychological discussion of the importance of metaphor see George Lakoff, 'What Is a Conceptual System?' in Willis F. Overton and David S. Palermo,

eds., *The Nature and Ontogenesis of Meaning* (Hillsdale, NJ: Lawrence Erlbaum Associates, 1994), 84.

15 James C. Davis, interview by Donna DeBlasio, Youngstown, 26 September 1991.

16 Reverend Fred Williams, interview by Donna DeBlasio, Youngstown, 27 September 1991.

17 What it meant to be a steelworker in the Mahoning Valley before the mills closed is explored in Robert Bruno, *Steelworker Alley: How Class Works in Youngstown* (Ithaca: Cornell University Press, 1999).

18 Marilyn McCormack, interview by author, Troy, Michigan, 23 February 1998.

19 Jim McHale and Dolores McHale, interview by author, Detroit, 24 February 1998.

20 David Christopherson, interview by author, Hamilton, 6 February 1998. A resident of Akron similarly recalls growing up in that city: 'You'd go downtown and you could smell the odor of rubber mingled with the sweet scent of Quaker Oats ... Dad cured tires at Goodyear's Plant One. When he came home, you could smell him coming up the sidewalk.' Quoted in Norman Mlachak, 'Can Akron Survive more Plant Closings?' *Cleveland Press*, 26 March 1980.

21 John Livingstone, interview by author, Hamilton, 7 February 1998.

22 Steelworker 'A,' interview by author, Buffalo, April 1998. The videotape recording of the community interview is in the possession of the author. Growing up in Flint, where General Motors employed most adult men, Ben Hamper recalls in his autobiography that no matter how much he loathed the thought, he knew by grade ten that he would follow his father and eight other family members into the plant. See *Rivethead: Tales from the Assembly Line* (New York: Time Warner, 1991 [1986]), 1–3.

23 Dorothy Routenberg, interview by author, Hamilton, 6 February 1998.

24 Marilyn McCormack, interview by author, Troy, Michigan, 23 February 1998.

25 Diane Garner, interview by author, Detroit, 24 February 1998.

26 Ibid. Virtually all of the women interviewed turned out to be the breadwinners for their families.

27 Steelworker 'J,' interview by author, Buffalo, April 1998.

28 David Christopherson, interview by author, Hamilton, 6 February 1998.

29 Although rarely mentioned by the interviewees, this working-class world was also racialized. The work of David Roediger in the United States and Thomas Dunk in Canada has demonstrated that whiteness was often a prerequisite for being included under the 'working-class' label. Thomas W.

Dunk, *It's a Working Man's Town: Male Working-Class Culture* (Montreal: McGill-Queen's University Press, 1991); and David Roediger, *Wages of Whiteness: Race and the Making of the American Working Class* (New York: verso, 1991).

30 Basil Adili, interview by author, Hamilton, 8 February 1998.

31 Floyd Harris, interview by author, Windsor, 22 February 1998.

32 Hamper, *Rivethead*, 33.

33 Peter Bailey, 'Breaking the Sound Barrier: A Historian Listens to Noise,' *Body and Society* 2, 2 (1996), 49–50.

34 Marilyn McCormack, interview by author, Detroit, 23 February 1998.

35 David Christopherson, interview by author, Hamilton, 6 February 1998.

36 Willy Eady, interview by author, Troy, 23 February 1998.

37 Dorothy Routenberg, interview by author, Hamilton, 6 February 1998. For a more general look at house ownership in Hamilton see Michael Doucet and John Weaver, *Housing the North American City* (Montreal: McGill-Queen's University Press, 1991), 12.

38 Lisa M. Fine, '"Our Big Factory Family": Masculinity and Paternalism at the Reo Motor Car Company of Lansing, Michigan,' *Labor History* 34, 2–3 (1993), 274–91. The paternalism of an employer of non-union women is superbly shown in Joan Sangster, *Earning Respect: The Lives of Working Women in Small-Town Ontario, 1920–1960* (Toronto: University of Toronto Press, 1995).

39 Paul Hansen, interview by author, Windsor, 22 February 1998.

40 And yet, racism divided working people. Ed Mann recalled that discrimination was common in the open hearth department of his Youngstown steel mill: 'We would work in a gang, in a circle – each shovel[ed] then you'd walk over and get a shovel full of material, walk around in a circle, shovel again: almost a rhythm. The first helper had control of that furnace. He'd pull that door up a little higher when the black guy would come by. He would set the damper in the hole and the flame would shoot out the door instead of out the stack.' Ed Mann, interview with Donna DeBlasio, 16 April 1991. For more on race see Thomas J. Sugrue, *The Origins of the Urban Crisis: Race and Inequality in Post-war Detroit* (Princeton: Princeton University Press, 1997), and the symposium on Sugrue's work in *Labor History* 39, 1 (1998).

41 Anonymous worker #2, interview by author, Lackawanna, April 1998.

42 Ed Lawrenson, interview by author, St. Clair Shores, 26 February 1998.

43 Floyd Harris, interview by author, Windsor, 22 February 1998.

44 John R. Gillis, *A World of Their Own Making: Myth, Ritual and the Quest for Family Values* (New York: Basic Books, 1996), xv.

45 This was particularly true for former workers of Beach Foundry, a stove and furnace manufacturer in the close-knit 'Mechanicsville' neighbour-hood of Ottawa. The factory occupied a special place in the workers' memories. See interviews with Marc Desrochers, Raymond Fauvelle, and Omer Pletilic, City of Ottawa Archives.

46 Yi-Fu Tuan, *Space and Place: The Perspectives of Experience* (Minneapolis: University of Minnesota Press, 1978), 54.

47 Peter Wirth, interview by author, Windsor, 22 February 1998.

48 Sociologist Herbert Gans found in his study of slum clearances in West Boston in 1958–9 that the mainly Italian-American residents did not be-lieve that the city would demolish their neighbourhood to make way for luxury apartment complexes. Instead, they read the landscape around them for signs that the city would back down from its declared intention. Hence, the paving of city streets and the installation of new gas meters were seen as 'evidence' that supported what West Enders desperately wanted to believe. Herbert J. Gans, *The Urban Villagers: Group and Class in the Life of Italian-Americans* (New York: Free Press, 1982 [1962]), 330–42.

49 Ed Lawrenson, interview by author, St. Clair Shores, 26 February 1998.

50 Scott D. Camp, *Worker Response to Plant Closings: Steelworkers in Johnstown and Youngstown* (New York: Garland Publications, 1995), 14.

51 Frank Farizo, interview by Donna DeBlasio, Youngstown, 19 September 1991.

52 George Richardson, interview by Donna DeBlasio, Youngstown, 1991.

53 Basil Adili, interview by author, Hamilton, 8 February 1998.

54 Steelworker 'F,' interview by author, Buffalo.

55 Bill Fuller, interview by author, Hamilton, 7 February 1998.

56 Johnny Holmes, interview, 25 February 1993 cited in Jane Sferra's excellent thesis entitled 'A Way of Life Gone Forever: The Youngstown Steel Indus-try,' Master's thesis, Miami University, Oxford, OH, 1993, 10.

57 Francis McHugh, interview by Mary Kay Schulz, Youngstown, 29 January 1981. The transcript of the interview is held by the library of Youngstown State University.

58 David Christopherson, interview with author, Hamilton, 6 February 1998.

59 Ruby Kendrick, interview with author, Southpark, Michigan, 25 February 1998. In addition, the UAW research branch discovered that the company was a marginally profitable one. See Musick, letter to Harry Kujawski, International Rep, Region 1B, UAW Local 417, box 4, Folder 22, WRL.

60 Bernice Adams, interview by author, Troy, Michigan, 23 February 1998.

61 John Palermo, interview by Philip Bracy, Youngstown, 7 April 1981. The transcript of the interview is held at the library of Youngstown State University.

62 Michael J. Katula, interview by Philip Bracy, Youngstown, 28 December 1981. The transcript of the interview is held at the library of Youngstown State University.

63 Marvin Weinstock, interview by Donna DeBlasio, Youngstown, 7 May 1991.

64 'Shutdowns: This Is Our Story. The Steelworkers and Their Families of Youngstown.' Ohio AFL-CIO Papers, Box 95, File 3: Plant Closings, Save Jobs Committee, Ohio Historical Society (OHS). Youngstown steelworkers could be forgiven for being surprised when U.S. Steel announced the closing of its Youngstown and McDonald Works. *Fortune* magazine had only the week before run a feature article entitled 'Youngstown Bounces Back.'

65 Lawrence Quinn, 'Stunned Workers Critical of "No Warning" at S&T,' *Youngstown Vindicator*, 24 September 1977.

66 Larry Smith, testimony at plant closing hearing to Rep. Perry Bullard, 11 May 1981, UAW Region 1B collection, Box 307-7, WRL. Two of those displaced were Ed Brosofski, age sixty-five, with forty-two years' seniority, and his wife, Rose, age sixty, who worked in the plant for twenty-five years. They were left with no pension, no medical coverage, no severance pay, 'simply nothing.'

67 Ed Lawrenson, interview by author, St. Clair Shores, 26 February 1998.

68 Bernice Adams, interview by author, Troy, 23 February 1998.

69 Bill Scandlon, interview by author, Hamilton, 7 February 1998.

70 Transcript of story, CHCH-TV, Hamilton, 6 January 1984. Ontario Ministry of Labour, RG 7, Interim Box 26, File: Stelco Inc. Canada Works, Hamilton, Archives of Ontario (AO).

71 Paul Hansen, interview by author, Windsor, 22 February 1998.

72 When the unemployment office misfiled his records, the person behind the desk did not believe him when he said he had worked at Bendix. In frustration, Ed exploded: 'Like, Christ, I've been there ten years.' Not persuaded, the unemployment officer replied: 'You've never worked there before.' Ed Lawrenson, interview by author, St. Clair Shores, 26 February 1998.

73 Harlan R. Cagle, president of Sahlin, to Leonard Montford, Local 417, 7 August 1972, Box 8, File 25, UAW Local 417, WRL.

74 Ralph Brubaker, interview by author, Clawson, Michigan, 25 February 1998.

75 Diane Garner, interview by author, Detroit, 24 February 1998.

76 Jim McHale, interview by author, of Detroit, 24 February 1998.

77 These letters emanated from across Ohio and Michigan. Most told the stories of displacement in small towns like Logan, Ohio. There, the 1977 relocation to Virginia of Coffman Stain Co. resulted in the permanent

layoff of 239 area residents. While the numbers being displaced paled next to the huge steel layoffs in the Mahoning Valley, they had a devastating impact nonetheless.

78 Louis A. Hancotte of Garden City, MI, letter to Governor Milliken, 21 May 1975, RG 88-269, Box 256, File 3 Labour, State Archives of Michigan (SAM).

79 Raymond J. Boza of Harper Woods, MI, letter to Senator R. Griffin, 28 February 1972, RG-88-269, Box 124, File Labor-D, SAM.

80 Ramie E. Phillips of Detroit, letter to Governor Milliken, 25 March 1976, RG 88-269, Box 292, File: Economic Expansion, M-P., SAM. The writer, fifty-four years of age, worked at Whitman & Barnes in Plymouth, MI.

81 Mrs. Bernice Kordynski, letter to Governor Milliken, April 1973. Her husband worked for Briggs Manufacturing in Detroit. RG 88-269, Box 160, File: Labor K-L, SAM.

82 Laura L. Towne, letter to Governor Milliken, 28 April 1975, RG 88-269, Box 246, file: OEC 1975, SAM.

83 Pat McCarthy, 'Dear Citizen: The Governor's Mailbag,' *Detroit News*, 2 April 1975.

84 Employees of Bower Division, letter to Sam McArthur and Tom Russell received by Governor Milliken's office, 1 March 1973, RG 88-269, Box 159, File Labor A-B, SAM.

85 Letter from a male worker to Mr. Galvin of Wheel Trueing Tool Co., Windsor, 17 October 1983, Ontario Ministry of Labour. RG 7-11-0-54, Interim Box 26, AO.

86 Dan McCarthy, interview by author, Detroit, 23 February 1998.

87 Harry Kujawski to Ken Morris, 27 May 1971, UAW Local 417, Box 4, File 22, WRL.

88 Jim McHale, interview by author, Detroit, 24 February 1998.

89 The closing of the town's auto assembly plant in 1987 sparked a redefinition of place. Anthropologist Kathryn Marie Dudley concludes that industrial workers had become 'Primitive Americans' in a post-industrial era. In so doing, they act as a constant reminder of what was lost. See Dudley's *The End of the Line: Lost Jobs, New Lives in Postindustrial America* (Chicago: University of Chicago Press, 1994), 161, 177.

90 Gregory Pappas, *Magic City: Unemployment in a Working-Class Community* (Ithaca: Cornell University Press, 1989), 161.

91 Michel Foucault, *The Order of Things: An Archaeology of the Human Sciences* (1970; reprint, New York: Vintage Books, 1973), 195–8.

92 'Shutdowns: This Is Our Story,' OHS.

93 John Barbero, 'Hundreds of Thousands of Steelworker Jobs Are on the

Line,' *Brier Hill Unionist*, October–November 1977. Others, like Dave Snyder who worked at Sieberling Tire in Barberton, Ohio, until it closed in 1981, saw themselves reduced to being 'migrant worker[s].' Steve Hoffman and Bill O'Connor, 'Labor of Love Lost and a New Start,' *Akron Beacon Journal*, 25 January 1981.

94 Michael Robinson, 'Tough Times Are Afloat Downriver,' *Detroit News*, 25 October 1981.

95 Robert Beauregard, *Voices of Decline: The Postwar Fate of U.S. Cities* (Cambridge: Blackwell, 1993), xi.

96 Willy Eady, interview by author, Detroit, 23 February 1998.

97 Steelworker 'F,' interview by author, Buffalo, April 1998.

98 Sam Donnorumo, interview by Donna DeBlasio, Youngstown, 1991.

99 Diane Garner, interview by author, Detroit, 24 February 1998.

100 Marilyn McCormack, interview by author, Detroit, 23 February 1998.

101 Bricklayer #4, interview by author, Buffalo, April 1998.

102 Claire Sferra quoted in Jane Sferra's excellent MA thesis, 'A Way of Life Gone Forever: The Youngstown Steel Industry' (Master's thesis, Miami University, Oxford, OH, 1993).

103 Sheldon Friedman to Marc Stepp, 17 December 1979, UAW. Research. Box 34-20, File: Plant Closings, 1975–80, WRL.

104 Gabriel Solano, interview by author, Detroit, 24 February 1998.

105 Ibid.

106 Ibid.

107 Ibid.

108 Diane Garner, interview by author, Detroit, 24 February 1998.

109 Ibid.

110 Ibid.

111 John Livingstone, interview by author, Hamilton, February 1998.

112 The textile-mill town of Paris, Ontario, was one of these exceptions. For a perceptive study of this community see Joy Parr, *The Gender of Breadwinners: Women, Men, and Change in Two Industrial Towns, 1880–1950* (Toronto: University of Toronto Press, 1990), and Rianne Mahon, *The Politics of Industrial Restructuring: Canadian Textiles* (Toronto: University of Toronto Press, 1984).

113 Ed Lawrenson, interview by author, St. Clair Shores, 26 February 1998.

114 Andy Morocko, interview by author, Windsor, 27 February 1998.

115 Ed Lawrenson, interview by author, St. Clair Shores, 26 February 1998.

116 Brian Hill, interview by Ken Clavette, Ottawa, 1996. The videotape is held at the City of Ottawa Archives.

117 David Christopherson, interview by author, Hamilton, February 1998.

3: Back to the Garden

1 Manuel Castells and Peter Hall, *Technopoles of the World: The Making of 21st Century Industrial Complexes* (London: Routledge, 1994), 1.
2 Changes in production in earlier eras have sometimes produced 'a new aesthetic of industry.' See David E. Nye, *American Technological Sublime* (Cambridge, MA: MIT Press, 1994), 107. A post-industrial aesthetic thus infuses Castells and Hall's judgment of 'quiet good taste.'
3 Samuel P. Hayes, *Beauty, Health, and Permanence: Environmental Politics in the United States, 1955–1985* (Cambridge: Cambridge University Press, 1987), 2–3.
4 Progress has often been understood as the conquest of nature. See for example Richard White, 'The Nature of Progress: Progress and the Environment,' in Leo Marx and Bruce Mazlish, eds., *Progress: Fact or Illusion* (Ann Arbor: University of Michigan Press, 1996), 121.
5 The collapsing of the division between the new and old economies has its antecedent in the various attempts at a urban-rural synthesis. James L. Machor, *Pastoral Cities: Urban Ideals and the Symbolic Landscape of America* (Madison: University of Wisconsin Press, 1987).
6 The American Society for the Encouragement of Domestic Manufacturers (1817) quoted in Thomas Bender, *Toward an Urban Vision: Ideas and Institutions in Nineteenth-Century America* (Lexington: University Press of Kentucky, 1975), 19.
7 Thomas Jefferson quoted in Bender, *Toward an Urban Vision*, 19.
8 Americans in the early republic apparently saw no contradiction between their 'professed love of nature' and their 'passionate embrace of the machine.' See John F. Kasson, *Civilizing the Machine: Technology and Republican Values in America, 1776–1900* (1976; reprint, New York: Hill & Wang, 1999), 8, 174.
9 Donald Worster, *Nature's Economy: A History of Ecological Ideas* (Cambridge: Cambridge University Press, 1994), especially chapter 2.
10 A connection between the 'garden setting' and the ascendant English middle-class is drawn in Leonore Davidoff and Catherine Hall, *Family Fortunes: Men and Women of the English Middle Class, 1780–1850* (Chicago: University of Chicago Press, 1987), 370.
11 Ramsay Cook, '1492 and All That: Making a Garden out of a Wilderness,' in Chad Gaffield and Pam Gaffield, eds., *Consuming Canada: Readings in Environmental History* (Toronto: Copp Clark, 1995), 62, 69–73.
12 Daniel Nelson, *Managers and Workers: Origins of the Twentieth-Century Factory System in the United States, 1880–1920* (Madison: University of

Wisconsin Press, 1995). An outstanding study of the environmental effects of this early phase of industrialization can be found in Theodore Steinberg, *Nature Incorporated: Industrialization and the Waters of New England* (Amherst: University of Massachusetts Press, 1991).

13 Traveller Alexander MacKay quoted in Marvin Fisher, *Workshops in the Wilderness: The European Response to American Industrialization, 1830–1860* (Oxford: Oxford University Press, 1967), 93.

14 Ibid., 92.

15 Marianne Doezema, *American Realism and the Industrial Age* (Cleveland: Cleveland Museum of Art, 1980), 36.

16 For a discussion of rationalization see Lindy Biggs, *The Rational Factory: Architecture, Technology, and Work in America's Age of Mass Production* (Baltimore: Johns Hopkins University Press, 1996), 6. Biggs writes that: 'rationalization in industry has a more specific meaning: it refers to the introduction of predictability and order – machinelike order – that eliminates all questions of how work is to be done, who will do it, and when it will be done. The rational factory, then, is a factory that runs like a machine.'

17 The massive River Rouge complex on the outskirts of Detroit was comprised of 23 main buildings, 93 miles of track, 53,000 machines and 75,000 employees. David L. Lewis, *The Public Image of Henry Ford: An American Folk Hero and His Company* (Detroit: Wayne State University Press, 1976), 160. The two other major studies of factory design are Grant Hildebrand, *Designing for Industry: The Architecture of Albert Kahn* (Cambridge, MA: MIT Press, 1974), and David A. Hounshell, *From the American System to Mass Production: The Development of Manufacturing Technology in the United States, 1800–1932* (Baltimore: Johns Hopkins University Press, 1984). Unfortunately, there is still no equivalent study of factory architecture in Canada.

18 For more on Charles Sheeler see Miles Orvell, *After the Machine: Visual Arts and the Erasing of Cultural Boundaries* (Jackson: University Press of Mississippi, 1995) and Karen Lucic, *Charles Sheeler and the Cult of the Machine* (Cambridge: Harvard University Press, 1991).

19 Daniel Bell, *The Coming of Post-Industrial Society: A Venture in Social Forecasting* (1973; reprint, New York: Basic Books, 1976), 37. The post-industrial label was further popularized by Alvin Toffler's best-selling *The Third Wave* (New York: William Morrow, 1980). However, the post-industrial idea is not without its critics. Fred Block has concluded that the post-industrial label is mainly used as a 'relatively empty synonym for modernity.' See *Postindustrial Possibilities: A Critique of Economic Discourse* (Berkeley: University of California Press, 1990).

20 The origins and implications of technological progress are explored in Merritt Roe Smith and Leo Marx, eds., *Does Technology Drive History? The Dilemma of Technological Determinism* (Cambridge, MA: MIT Press, 1994).

21 Michael L. Smith, 'Recourse of Empire: Landscapes of Progress in Technological America,' in Smith and Marx, eds., *Does Technology Drive History?* For a cross-disciplinary discussion of the iconography of landscape see Denis Cosgrove and Stephen Daniels, eds., *The Iconography of Landscape: Essays on the Symbolic Representation, Design and Uses of Past Environments* (New York: Cambridge University Press, 1988). Sharon Zukin has noted that an industrial landscape was a 'moral order' in *Landscapes of Power: From Detroit to Disney World* (Berkeley: University of California Press, 1991), 254–6.

22 Joel A. Tarr, *The Search for the Ultimate Sink: Urban Pollution in Historical Perspective* (Akron: University of Akron Press, 1996), xxx.

23 Editorial, *Industrial Development* (November–December 1972), 2–6.

24 Daniel Patrick Moynihan, 'The Federal Government and the Economy of New York State' (15 July 1977), 6.

25 David Proulx, *Pardon My Lunch Bucket: A Look at the New Hamilton ... With a Bit of the Old Thrown In* (Hamilton: City of Hamilton, 1971), i.

26 Ibid.

27 Windsor was hurt by its reputation as a 'Blue Collar' town according to 30 per cent of respondents, by 'No Jobs' in 29 per cent, by being 'Too American' in 16 per cent, by 'Bad Press' in 2 per cent, and by people 'Leaving City' in 5 per cent. The city's opinion leaders were even more likely to point to the city's 'lunch bucket' image than ordinary residents. Donald J. MacTavish, ed., *Windsor and Essex County Blueprint for a Brighter Tomorrow* (Windsor: Windsor Star, 1982).

28 Allison Zippay, *From Middle Income to Poor: Downward Mobility among Displaced Steelworkers* (New York: Praeger, 1991), 2–3.

29 Stuart Hall, 'The Question of Cultural Identity,' in Stuart Hall, David Held, and Kenneth Thompson, eds., *Modernity: An Introduction to Modern Societies* (Oxford: Blackwell Publishers, 1997), 596.

30 In a commissioned history of Eaton Corporation, the old alienating urban factories of the 1960s were compared to the 'new environment' created at the company's plant in rural Nebraska. As the company president notes in his preface to the book, Eaton was 'constantly creating, and recreating, the workplaces.' Donald N. Scobel, *Creative Worklife* (London: Gulf Publishing Company, 1981), ix, 1–3.

31 Gordon B. Carson, ed., *Production Handbook* (New York: Ronald Press, 1958), 32. See also Nye, *American Technological Sublime,* 107–12.

32 'An Enlightened Look at a Factory,' (c. 1948) reprinted in Architectural
    Record, *Building for Industry: An Architectural Record Book* (Westport, CT:
    Greenwood Press, 1972), 15.
33 See, for example, Frank L. Whitney, 'Newer Trends in Industrial Build-
    ings,' in ibid., 3.
34 Ibid., 2.
35 Michael F. Roberts, 'Building For Industry,' *Industrial Canada* (December
    1970), 31.
36 James M. Moore, *Plant Layout and Design* (New York: Macmillan Company,
    1962), 71.
37 K.G. Lockyer, *Factory and Production Management* (1962; reprint, London:
    Pitman, 1974), 92–3.
38 'Factors Affecting Industrial Building Design' (c. 1954), reprinted in Archi-
    tectural Record, *Building for Industry*, 8–9.
39 'The Canadian Plant of the 70s: No.1 – Plant Engineering,' *Industrial
    Canada* (February 1970), 15.
40 The post-industrial facade was very much on display in the pages of
    Canadian Architect. See for example 'Levi Strauss Manufacturing Plant,
    Stoney Creek, Ontario,' *Canadian Architect* 26, 10 (1981).
41 Minesinger to H.H. Leckler and Leckler to Minesinger, 6 September 1978,
    Acme Cleveland Corp. (1969–1982), Container 5, Folder 76, Western
    Reserve Historical Society Archives (WRHS).
42 Ian Duke, interview by author, Windsor, 27 February 1998.
43 Robert Lewis, 'Running Rings around the City: North American Industrial
    Suburbs, 1850–1950,' in Richard Harris and Peter J. Larkham, eds., *Chang-
    ing Suburbs: Foundation, Form and Function* (London: E & FN Spon, 1999),
    148.
44 David C. McNary, 'Industrial Parks: If They're Well-planned, They're
    Profitable,' *Industrial Development* (March/April 1970), 7–11.
45 Ibid., 10.
46 A survey of industrial park owners found that nine in ten regulated the
    aesthetics of industrial buildings and property. Linda Liston, 'Proliferating
    Industrial Parks Spark Plant Location Revolution,' *Industrial Development*
    (March/April 1970), 7–11.
47 Advertisement, 'A "Custom-Made" Industrial Site?,' *Industrial Canada*
    (April 1969), 69.
48 'See How They Grow: A Survey of Industrial Park Development Trends,'
    Industrial Development (July/August 1978),13.
49 A 1975 survey found that manufacturers in the following sectors were
    most likely to relocate to industrial parks: food, electrical, appliances, tires,

and distribution warehouses. Van G. Whaler, 'What Are Today's Industrial Parks Like?' *Industrial Development* (July/August 1975), 21–3.

50 Moore, *Plant Layout and Design*, 37.

51 Pete J. Barber, 'The Site Selection Process at Honeywell,' *Industrial Development* (November/December 1982), 9.

52 Del Morgano, 'Organizing for Facility Planning and Real Estate Management, part 1, The One Man Operation,' *Industrial Development* (March/April 1979), 18–19.

53 Editorial, *Site Selection Handbook* (1972), 2.

54 Early twentieth-century factory owners used the common artistic formula of exaggerated edifices to convey 'heroic size' in their publicity. See Dominic T. Alessio, 'Capitalist Realist Art: Industrial Images of Hamilton, Ontario, 1884–1910,' *Journal of Urban History* 18, 4 (1992), 442.

55 In 1972, the editors of the *Handbook* began a separate and unique volume covering environmental factors and design. *Site Selection Handbook: Industry's Guide to Geo-Economic Planning* (1972), 2.

56 Advertisement, *Site Selection Handbook* (1972), 43.

57 Advertisement for Raritan Center Industrial Park in Newark, New Jersey, Ibid., 124.

58 St Louis–San Francisco Railway Company Advertisement, ibid. (1977).

59 Other selling points included the availability of reliable non-union workers, a central location (often used by representatives of older industrial areas), and great historical events and icons. Thus, Boston pilgrims vied with Daniel Boone and coonskin-capped pioneers for the attention of corporate executives.

60 An image analysis of factories showcased in this column between 1969 and 1984 was conducted. Virtually identical visual images can be found in *Industrial Canada*, the newsletter of the Metropolitan Toronto Industrial Commission and the photographic archives of Windsor's Industrial Commission. Windsor-Essex County Development Commission Records, MS 42, Windsor Municipal Archives (WMA).

61 See the architectural drawing of the Applied Devices Corporation plant in Orlando, Florida. *Industrial Development* (March/April 1976), 27.

62 See the drawing of the Westinghouse Electric Corporation plant in Coral Springs, Florida. Ibid. (May/June 1978), 25.

63 Ibid. (March/April 1970), 29.

64 Historian Bryan Palmer wryly observed that the proposed Goodyear Tire plant in Napanee, Ontario, was depicted as a kind of resort. Landscaped lawns and trees made the atmosphere 'deceptively congenial.' Bryan D.

Palmer, *Capitalism Comes to the Backcountry: The Goodyear Invasion of Napanee* (Toronto: Between the Lines, 1994), 147.

65 *Industrial Development* (March/April 1971), 30.

66 Ibid. (January/February 1975), 30.

67 Ibid. (January/February 1974), 26.

68 David E. Nye, *Image Worlds: Corporate Identities at General Electric, 1890–1930* (Cambridge, MA: MIT Press, 1985).

69 Donald F. Davis, *Conspicuous Production: Automobiles and Elites in Detroit, 1899–1933* (Philadelphia: Temple University Press, 1988), x; John N. Ingham, *The Iron Barons: A Social Analysis of an American Urban Elite, 1874–1965* (Westport, CT: Greenwood Press, 1977), xviii; Philip Scranton, 'Large Firms and Industrial Restructuring: The Philadelphia Region, 1900–1980,' *Pennsylvania Magazine of History and Biography* 116, 4 (1992), 419, 461–2.

70 Philip Scranton, *Proprietary Capitalism: The Textile Manufacturer at Philadelphia* (Cambridge: Cambridge University Press, 1983), 418.

71 John T. Cumbler, *A Social History of Economic Decline: Business, Politics and Work in Trenton* (New Brunswick, NJ: Rutgers University Press, 1989), 7.

72 W. Lawrence Weeks, interview by Donna DeBlasio, Youngstown, 1991. See also interview with Tom Cleary, vice president of operations by Youngstown Sheet & Tube, 20 September 1991. The videotapes are held at the Youngstown Historical Center for Industry and Labor.

73 Ralph Nader and William Taylor, *The Big Boys: Power and Position in American Business* (New York: Pantheon Books, 1986), 13.

74 Ibid., 60–1.

75 Alfred Chandler, *Scale and Scope: The Dynamics of Industrial Capitalism* (Cambridge: Belknap Press of Harvard University Press, 1990), 622–3.

76 Zukin, *Landscapes of Power*, 74.

77 Ibid., 256.

78 Anthony Giddens, *The Consequences of Modernity* (Stanford, CA: Stanford University Press, 1990), 16–19.

79 Stephen Kern, *The Culture of Time and Space, 1880–1918* (Cambridge: Harvard University Press, 1983), 2–3. David Harvey, 'On the History and Present Condition of Geography: An Historical Geography Manifesto,' *Professional Geographer* 36 (1984), 1–11.

80 Doreen Massey, 'A Global Sense of Place,' *Marxism Today* (June 1991), 25–6.

81 Chandler, *Scale and Scope*, 607.

82 Stephen V. Ward, *Selling Places: The Marketing and Promotion of Towns and Cities, 1850–2000* (London: Routledge, 1998), 182.

4: The Deindustrializing Heartland

1 Barry Bluestone and Bennett Harrison, *The Deindustrialization of America*: *Plant Closings, Community Abandonment, and the Dismantling of Basic Industry* (New York: Basic Books, 1982), 141.
2 Jane Jenson and Rianne Mahon, 'North American Labour: Divergent Trajectories,' in Jenson and Mahon, eds., *The Challenge of Restructuring: North American Labor Movements Respond* (Philadelphia: Temple University Press, 1993), 2–3. These challenges were also facing other countries such as France. See W. Rand Smith, *The Left's Dirty Job: The Politics of Industrial Restructuring in France and Spain* (Pittsburgh: University of Pittsburgh Press; Toronto: University of Toronto Press, 1998).
3 Anne R. Markusen and Virginia Carlsen, 'Deindustrialization and the American Midwest: Causes and Responses,' in Lloyd Rodwin and Hidehiko Sazanami, eds., *Deindustrialization and Regional Economic Transformation* (Boston: Unwin Hyman, 1989), 29. Also see Ann Markusen, Peter Hall, Sabina Deitrick, and Scott Campbell, *The Rise of the Gunbelt* (New York: Oxford University Press, 1991).
4 Manuel Castells and Peter Hall, *Technopoles of the World: The Making of 21st Century Industrial Complexes* (London: Routledge, 1994).
5 Needless to say, Canada's military-industrial complex, such as it was, did not have a similarly profound influence on industrial location.
6 U.S. Secretary of Labor, *Economic Adjustment and Worker Dislocation*, 19–20. The census districts included New England, Middle Atlantic, East North Central, West North Central, South Atlantic, East North Central, West South Central, Mountain, and Pacific.
7 Bluestone and Harrison, *The Deindustrialization of America*, 4.
8 Markusen and Carlson, 'Deindustrialization in the American Midwest,' 31.
9 Sheldon Friedman, Director of Research Department to Congressman William D. Ford, 13 March 1984, United Auto Worker (UAW) Collection, Research Branch, Box 33-14. Walter Reuther Libary (WRL). The displaced-worker surveys of the 1980s conducted by the Bureau of Labor Statistics have improved the situation, but in the absence of routinely generated government information many researchers have turned to the Dun and Bradstreet database that tracked closings. Most researchers agree, however, that this source of information is only partial.
10 Stephen McBride, *Not Working: State, Unemployment, and Neo-Conservatism in Canada* (Toronto: University of Toronto Press, 1992), 5.
11 Garnett Picot and Ted Wannell, *Job Loss and Labour Market Adjustment in the Canadian Economy* (Ottawa: Statistics Canada, 1987), 3. A helpful discussion

of restructuring can be found in Doreen Massey and Richard Meegan, *The Anatomy of Job Loss* (London: Methuen, 1982), 9.

12 F. Siddiqui, 'Review of Mass Lay-Offs Covered by Termination of Employment Legislation During 1972,' December 1973, 1, RG 7-67, Box 3, File 2: Termination/Severance Pay Legislation Review, 1972–74, Ontario Ministry of Labour, Archives of Ontario (AO).

13 Ibid.

14 John E. Ullman, *The Anatomy of Industrial Decline: Productivity, Investment, and Location in U.S. Manufacturing* (New York: Quorum Books, 1988), 129.

15 Advertisement in the *New York Times*, nd, United Electrical Workers Archives, Research Box 1805, File: New Plant, the South, 1960–62, University of Pittsburgh Archives (UPA).

16 The right-to-work states included: Alabama, 1953; Arizona, 1947; Nevada, 1951; North Carolina, 1947; Texas, 1947; Wyoming, 1963; Florida, 1944; Georgia, 1944; Iowa, 1947; North Dakota, 1947; South Carolina, 1954; Utah, 1955; Kansas, 1958; Mississippi, 1954; Nebraska, 1947; South Dakota, 1947; Tennessee, 1947; and Virginia, 1947. Other states adopted right-to-work laws and then repealed them: Delaware (1947–9), Indiana (1957–65), Louisiana (1956), Maine (1947–8), and New Hampshire (1947–9). United Steelworkers of America Archives, Legislative Department, Box 61, File 15, Office Files – Runaway Plants under 14 (b) [Right to Work] – District Inquiries. D31 American Can Co. Rockdale Illinois and USWA. Penn State U. Leg Box 79, File 54, General Right to Work (1980) – June 1980 list, Penn State University Archives (PSUA).

17 Bluestone and Harrison, *The Deindustrialization of America*,136.

18 Borg Warner Corporate document, 30 May 1974, UAW Collection, Research Branch, Box 87-18 Borg Warner, 1965–76, WRL. See also Leon Potok to Richard Prosten, research director, 26 May 1977, UAW Collection, Research Branch, Box 93-16, Caterpillar, 1970–1977.

19 North American Rockwell, *Annual Reports*, 1970–84. Displacement was prolonged for years for many employees as the company's national agreement with the UAW allowed employees preferred hiring rights at other unionized shops. When workers lost their jobs at Detroit Transmission, Axle and Forge plants in June 1973, they were given the option of going to Oshkosh, Wisconsin, Newark, Ohio, Marysville, Ohio, Ashtabula, Ohio, or Winchester, Kentucky. W.E. St. Clair, Plant Manager, Rockwell Standard Division to all hourly employees. November 7, 1972, MG 28, I119, Canadian Auto Workers, Volume 36, File 14, Rockwell International, National Archives of Canada (NAC).

20 Montieth M. Illingworth, 'Eaton's Drive to Cut Costs Begins to Pay Off,'

Barron's, 15 August 1983; Jeffrey J. Zygmont, 'A Slimmer Eaton Poised for Future Growth,' *Ward's*, 3 October 1983. The closing of Eaton's Battle Creek transmission plant resulted in the layoff of 1800 employees. See James V. Higgins, 'Eaton to Close Michigan Plant in Cutback,' *Detroit News*, 27 January 1983.

21 James Rubenstein, *The Changing U.S. Auto Industry: A Geographical Analysis* (New York: Routledge, 1992), 132. 'Parts Makers Resist UAW,' *New York Times*, 4 August 1981. The auto parts sector was dominated by a dozen big multinational companies including Federal Mogul, Duplate, Gulf & Western, Kelsey-Hayes, Bendix, Budd, Champion Spark Plugs, Dana, Eaton, Eltra, Ex-Cell-O, Essex, Bundy, Eltra, and Borg Warner.

22 Jack Norman, 'Why do Companies Leave?' *Milwaukee Journal*, 4 May 1982. According to leaked documents, the corporation favoured Topeka, Kansas, for seven reasons, six of which related to labour: 'competitive labor advantage,' 'better labor climate,' 'right-to-work state,' 'skilled workers,' 'lower labor cost community,' and 'break inflexible UAW position.'

23 Clipping from *Wall Street Journal*, 10 June 1983, 27, UAW Collection, Research Branch, Box 93-21, Caterpillar Clippings, 1982, WRL.

24 Sheldon Friedman, director of research, to Howard Young, 'Regarding the Impact of US–Canadian Exchange Rate Fluctuation on Supplier Plant,' 19 January 1979, UAW, Research, Box 107, File 21: Eaton Corporation, 1975–1983, WRL.

25 *Windsor Daily Star*, 7 April 1954.

26 W.J. Patrick to D.P.W. Wood, assistant director, Mechanical Transport Branch, April 17, 1972, Department of Industry, Trade and Commerce, RG 20 Accession 1983–84/228 Volume 162, File 8001-260/A4-1 pt 2, and NAC. D.N. Mott, Iron and Steel Division to W.B. Horovitz, Materials Branch, 14 December 1966, RG 20 Accession 1983–4/228 Volume 166, File 8001-260/ J1 pt 1, Industrial Development – Iron Foundry Industry, 1965–66. NAC.

27 *Windsor Daily Star*, 27 April 1949. Essex Wire complained to Windsor's mayor that the wage rate of $1.62 per hour for female employees far surpassed that of its competition, which was said to range from $0.93 to $1.25. As a result, the company shifted production to Dunnville, Ontario, less than an hour's drive from Buffalo. Thirty years later, when faced with union demands for better wages and benefits, Essex Wire picked up and moved again.

28 John McArthur, 'The Chrysler Truck Plant,' *Guardian* 19, 3 (1978).

29 'A Confidential Report,' October 1961, MS 42 II/3, Windsor-Essex County Development Commission, Confidential Files, Windsor Municipal Archives (WMA).

30 Report of the Joint Manpower Planning Committee, 28 July 1972, R.D. Fraser, Chairman, RG 7-91, Interim Box 28, File: Aerovox-Hamilton; National Archives of Canada, RG 118, Volume 2, File 3837-1/A18 Technological and Economic Change Adjustment Assistance-Aerovox Canada Ltd, AO.

31 Issues of workplace inequality between men and women have usually been considered in terms of wage differentials and discriminatory hiring practices by employers, yet rarely in terms of differential job security. Canadian sociologist Pat Armstrong, for example, responded to the question 'who suffers during an economic crisis?' by arguing that men bore the brunt of the recession in the early 1980s as they were concentrated in declining sectors of the economy. Pat Armstrong, *Labour Pains: Women's Work in Crisis* (Toronto: Women's Press, 1984), 97. While the sex labelling of employment began to break down during the 1970s, Bonnie J. Fox and John Fox have indicated that sexual segregation continued to be the norm in Canada. See Bonnie J. Fox and John Fox, *Occupational Gender Segregation of the Canadian Labour Force, 1931–1981* (Toronto: York University Institute for Social Research, 1987), 1.

32 William F. Scanlon, letter to M. Fenwick, 22 January 1970, United Steelworkers of America, District 6 Records, Box 101a, File: Hamilton folder 3, McMaster University Archives (MUA).

33 Ibid., Scanlon to Gordon Milling, 10 March 1970.

34 Dorothy Routenberg, interview by author, Hamilton, 6 February 1998. Bill Scandlon, interview by author, Hamilton, 7 February 1998.

35 In St Catharines, the inflexibility of the sexual division of labour resulted in the indefinite layoff of high-seniority women at McKinnon Industries at the same time as men were being hired off the street. The Royal Commission on the Status of Women heard a brief from twelve women at McKinnon who claimed that the sex labelling of job classifications, determined by union men in consultation with the company, led to women bearing the brunt of industrial restructuring. It appears that production lines with women wage earners were being transferred elsewhere, while those areas designated for men were expanding. Sharon Jarvis, 'Woman Predicts End of Women on McKinnon Production Lines,' *St Catharines Standard*, 6 June 1968. For the union response to this article see James Connell, president of Local 199 to Douglas Hamilton, secretary-treasurer of the Ontario Federation of Labour, 10 June 1968, MG 28 I 119, Canadian Auto Workers, Volume 165, File 16: Local 199, St Catharines, Ontario, Correspondence, 1968–70, NAC.

36 Floyd Fell, international representative to Robert Andras, president of the

Quinte District Labour Council, United Steelworkers of America District 6, Box 101 (a), File: Kingston Area, MUA.

37 United Steelworkers of America District 6, Box 147 (b), File 7313: Amplifone Canada Ltd, Belleville, MUA.

38 Organization for Economic Cooperation and Development, *Regional Policies in Canada* (Paris: OECD, 1980), 15.

39 Martin Kenney and Richard Florida, *Beyond Mass Production: The Japanese System and Its Transfer to the U.S.* (New York: Oxford University Press, 1993), 200.

40 Richard E. Zeller, research associate, 'The Steel, Glass, and Rubber and Plastics Industries in Ohio,' MSS 1857, Box 30, File 3, Statistics – Plants Leaving, 1976, Ohio Historical Society (OHS).

41 Wilford L'Esperance and Arthur E. King, 'Bulletin,' 1, MSS 1857, Box 30, File 3, OHS.

42 Douglas F. Campbell and John J. Nicholson, 'The Sydney Steelworkers' Adjustments to Economic Insecurity,' paper presented to meeting of Atlantic Provinces Sociologists and Anthropologists, 1969. See also Robert W. Sexty, *Public Enterprise and Employment in Canada* (Ottawa: Labour Market Development Task Force, 1981), 5, 11.

43 Confidential report memo to Cabinet on Industrial Growth Opportunities by Minister of Industry, Trade and Commerce, 11 March 1970, 5, Department of Industry, Trade and Commerce, RG 20, Volume 103, File 25/500-2, NAC.

44 Lawrence J. White, 'Regulation and Policy Issues Involving the Motor Vehicle Industry in the 1980s' (draft), for the U.S. Regulatory Council, February 1980, 3, Bernick, Box 3, File Auto Studies, Jimmy Carter Presidential Library (Carter).

45 *Time*, 8 January 1979, 39 and 7 January 1980, 88–9. The global shift in auto making could be seen in changing American and Japanese production figures. In 1960, the United States produced more than half of the world's automobiles. By 1982, however, that figure had plunged to 18 per cent. Japan, by contrast, accounted for 1.3 per cent of world automotive manufacturing in 1960 and 18 per cent in 1975. By 1980, Japan had surpassed the United States as the world's largest auto maker. Peter Dicken, *Global Shift: Industrial Change in a Turbulent World* (London: Harper and Row, 1986), 281.

46 Memo to president Carter from G. William Miller, 1 July 1980, White House, Office of the Counsel to the President, Box 53, Automobile Industry – 7–11/80, Carter.

47 Charlotte Yates, 'Curtains or Encore: Possibilities for Restructuring in the Canadian Auto Industry,' in Jenson and Mahon, eds., *The Challenge of Restructuring*, 345.

48 'History of Ford of Canada,' n.d., Ford Public Relations document, Historical Pamphlet #89, Windsor Public Library.

49 *Windsor Daily Star*, 31 October 1951. See also UAW Collection. Region 7,
Box 32, File 3, WRL.

50 Brief on industrial location presented to Windsor city council by UAW
Area Plant Movement Committee, 16 May 1962, UAW Collection. Region
7. Box 32, File 7, WRL.

51 Even though the Big Three tentatively began to terminate US–based
operations in the 1950s, the consolidation process lagged behind their
efforts in the smaller Canadian market. Ford terminated its operations in
Buffalo, Long Beach, California, Memphis, Tennessee, Somerville, Massachusetts, and Chester, Pennsylvania, while Chrysler shuttered plants in
San Leandro, California, and Evansville, Indiana. However, the 1960s and
1970s saw few additional closures. Between 1962 and 1978, General Motors
closed an assembly plant in Oakland, California, Chrysler closed its Los
Angeles plant, Ford its Dallas operation and Studebaker, on its way out of
the auto making business, closed its South Bend, Indiana, and Hamilton
plants.

52 Greg Donaghy, 'A Continental Philosophy: Canada, the United States, and
the Negotiation of the Autopact, 1963–1965,' *International Journal* (summer
1998), 441–64.

53 Ibid., 464.

54 Ibid.

55 John Holmes, 'Restructuring in a Continental Production System,' in John
Britton, ed., *Canada and the Global Economy: The Geography of Structural and
Technological Change* (Montreal: McGill-Queen's University Press, 1996), 232.

56 K.C. Kau, executive director to executive committee, 18 April 1980, George
C. Eads, Box 2, File Autos – Background, Cabinet Economic Policy Group,
Carter.

57 Closed Chrysler plants included an assembly plant in St Louis, two forging plants in Illinois, another in Ohio, eight parts plants, one engine and
two assembly operations in Michigan, and one engine plant in Windsor.

58 Rubenstein, *The Changing U.S. Auto Industry*, 98. Also see Nancy Abner,
'After Day of Rumors Bad News Comes,' *Detroit News*, 4 January 1972.

59 Ben Bedell, 'Black Jobless at All-time High Level,' *Guardian*, 15 September
1982.

60 Plant closings had a similarly disproportionate effect on minorities working in steel. Letter to Anthony Barbieri, international representative, from
attorney Michael Gottesman, 29 June 1971, USWA Records, Secretary-
Treasurers Records, Box 34, File 11: Bethlehem-Lackawanna, PSUA.

61 Gregory D. Squires, *Capital and Communities in Black and White: The Intersections of Race, Class and Uneven Development* (Albany: State University of New York Press, 1994), 3.

62 Remarks of Marc Stepp at a public hearing on plant closings in Philadelphia, 16 February 1980, UAW Archival Collection, Box 114-1, WRL.

63 Rubenstein, *The Changing U.S. Auto Industry*. Among the Big Three, General Motors replaced obsolete plants four times and Chrysler once.

64 The Poletown experiment proved to be a highly contentious one as mainly white neighbourhood activists and consumer advocates like Ralph Nader were pitted against mainly black trade unionists and powerful local politicians such as Detroit mayor Coleman Young.

65 Sam Ginden to all service representatives, Canadian Region, 26 November 1974, MG 28 I 119, Canadian Auto Workers, Box 316, File 3, Layoffs in Auto Industry, Correspondence, memoranda, reports (1), 1974–8, NAC.

66 Sam Ginden, district research director to Robert White, UAW-Canada director, 13 June 1980, Canadian Auto Workers, Volume 316, File 5, Layoff in Automotive Industry, M.R., Clippings, 1979–81, NAC.

67 Rubenstein, *The Changing U.S. Auto Industry*, 135.

68 In the Detroit area Chrysler's Jefferson Street plant had been built in 1907 and the Dodge brothers opened Dodge Maine in 1914. Auto bodies in the Kenosha AMC-Chrysler facility were welded and painted in a five-storey former mattress factory built in the 1890s and moved by truck to the main plant constructed in 1902.

69 The invention of the radial tire revolutionized tire making. Most notably, radial tires wore out after 40,000 miles, whereas bias-belted tires needed to be replaced after 23,000 miles. Goodyear Tire Collection, Property Box 2, Textile in Tires (n.d.), University of Akron Archives (UAA).

70 'South Appeals Financially to Business, Study Shows,' *Rubber and Plastics News* (13 April 1981).

71 Cabinet Economic Policy Group Memorandum from Randall K.C. Kau, executive director, to executive committee et al., 18 April 1980, George C. Eads, Box 2, File Autos–Background, Carter.

72 Michael J. French, *The U.S. Tire Industry: A History* (Boston: Twayne Publishers, 1990), 104.

73 Just a few minutes' drive south of Akron is Barberton, Ohio. Once popularly known as the 'Magic City' (as it grew like magic), and home to the Seiberling Tire Company (a division of Firestone), Barberton had lost its magic by the beginning of the 1980s. Anthropologist Greg Pappas has documented the effect of its closing in March 1980, leaving nearly a thousand people out of work. Gregory Pappas, *The Magic City: Unemployment*

in a Working-Class Community (Ithaca: Cornell University Press, 1989), 7. Also see Richard Ellers, 'Barberton Lost Its Magic When It Lost Its Factories,' *Cleveland Plain Dealer*, 17 May 1986.

74 Letter from J.W. Reynolds, director of Industrial Relations for BF Goodrich, to George Cunningham, president of URW Local 5, URW, Research Box 2. File: Plant Closings or Permanent Curtailments, 1971–8, UAA.

75 Allan Gerlat, 'General Tire Plans to Close Akron Plant, Ending City's Tire Era,' *Rubber and Plastic News*, 8 March 1982. The closure represented a broken promise by the company after it wrung concessions amounting to $0.36 per hour in 1979 in exchange for the promise of a new facility in Akron.

76 Richard Manning and John McCormack, 'The Blue Collar Blues,' *Newsweek*, 4 June 1984.

77 Ibid. The effect of plant shutdowns on local schooling has been examined in two dissertations completed at the University of Akron, Donald Richard Castle, 'The Response of the Mansfield City Schools to Local Deindustrialization, 1968–84' (PhD diss., University of Akron, 1990) and Donald Paul Spayd, 'The Economic Impact of Deindustrialization on Financial Decisions of the Warren City Schools, 1975–89' (PhD diss., University of Akron, 1991).

78 Kenney and Florida, *Beyond Mass Production*, 194.

79 'Many Benefits will Continue after Closing,' *Firestone Non-Skid* 65, 6, 1980, 1.

80 'Firestone Canada Plant Closes July 18 in Whitby,' *Firestone Non-Skid* 65, 7, 1980, 1.

81 Paul G. Engel, 'Going Flat: U.S. Tire Plant Closings Continue,' *Industry Week*, 28 April 1986.

82 Plant Closing or Permanent Curtailment Report, n.d., URW, Research Box 2, UAA.

83 See also Kenney and Florida, *Beyond Mass Production*, 200.

84 'Trouble in Rubber City: Akron About to Lose Its Image?' *Modern Tire Dealer*, February 1978.

85 Editorial, 'Not a Very Good Year,' *Akron Beacon Journal*, 14 November 1978.

86 John Leo Kosher, 'Mohawk Closing in Akron Will Idle 318,' *Cleveland Plain Dealer*, 14 November 1978.

87 'More Losses Force Mansfield to Shut Oh Plant,' *Rubber and Plastic News*, 21 August 1978.

88 Dicken, *Global Shift*, 256.

89 Ibid., 262–3.

90 W.P. Anderson, 'The Changing Competitive Position of the Hamilton Steel

Industry,' in M.J. Dear, J.J. Drake, and L.G. Reeds, eds., *Steel City: Hamilton and Region* (Toronto: University of Toronto Press, 1987), 204.

91 Dicken, *Global Shift*, 271.

92 Irwin M. Marcus, 'The Deindustrialization of America: Homestead, A Case Study, 1959–1984,' *Pennsylvania History* 52, 3 (1985), 162. In addition, the steel industry has received attention from David Brody, 'On the Decline of American Steel,' *Pennsylvania Magazine of History and Biography* 113, 4 (1989), 627–33, Peter Michael Dodson, 'Import Challenge, Sectoral Response and the Decline of American Integrated Steelmaking, 1959–82,' (PhD diss., University of Virginia, 1985), Douglas Arnold Schuler, 'Corporate Political Involvement for Managing Industrial Decline: The Case of the U.S. Steel Industry and Steel Policy' (PhD diss., University of Minnesota, 1992).

93 Judith Stein, *Running Steel, Running America: Race, Economic Policy and the Decline of Liberalism* (Chapel Hill: University of North Carolina Press, 1998), 236.

94 See, for example, Paul A. Tiffany, *The Decline of American Steel: How Management, Labor and Government Went Wrong* (New York: Oxford University Press, 1988), viii, and John P. Hoerr, *And the Wolf Finally Came: The Decline of the American Steel Industry* (Pittsburgh: University of Pittsburgh Press, 1988).

95 Stu Eizenstadt and Bob Ginsburg to the President, 12 october 1977, Box 284, File Steel, [O/A 6343], Carter.

96 Anthony M. Solomon, Report to the President, 'A Comprehensive Program for the Steel industry,' White House Office of Counsel to the President, Box 46, F. Steel Policy (1977), 11/77–1/78, Carter.

97 Stein, *Running Steel, Running America*, 240.

98 Alfred E. Kahn, 'Government Policies Toward the Steel Industry' paper, 5 December 1979, Eizenstadt, Box 283, File Steel (CF O/A 731), 2, Carter.

99 Charles Bradford quoted in Daniel Rosenheim and James Warren, 'Why South Works Declined,' *Chicago Sun Times*, 30 October 1983.

100 U.S. Steel, *Annual Report* (1979).

101 K.J. Rea, *The Prosperous Years: The Economic History of Ontario, 1939–1975* (Toronto: University of Toronto Press, 1985), 210.

102 Anderson in Dear, Drake and Reeds, eds., *Steel City*, 209. See also note to file by W.J.H. Purcell, International Commodities and Special Projects Division, RG 20, Volume 89, File 8730-TB-120 pt 3, 29 May 1969, NAC.

103 Stelco's decision in the 1970s to build a new integrated steel plant one hour's drive south of Hamilton on the north shore of Lake Erie at Nanticoke naturally generated considerable concern back in Hamilton.

104 M.J. Webber, 'Regional Production and the Production of Regions: The Case of Steeltown,' in Allen J. Scott and Michael Storper, eds., *Production, Work, Territory: The Geographical Anatomy of Industrial Capitalism* (Boston: Allen and Unwin, 1986), 197.

105 Michael Webber and Ruth Fincher, 'Urban Policy in Hamilton in the 1980s,' in Dear, Drake, and Reeds, eds., *Steel City*, 238. In 1971, 38 per cent of the city's industrial employees worked in the steel industry, followed by 14 per cent in metal products industries, 6 per cent in textile mills and 9 per cent in the electrical industry. Robert E. Drass and Norman Shulman, Final Report, August 1975, RG 127 Volume 106. File 2101-D1 pt 2, External Research, NAC.

106 Roy Lubove, *Twentieth Century Pittsburg*, vol. 2, *The Post Steel Era* (Pittsburgh: University of Pittsburgh Press, 1996), 7.

107 Domestic Steel Industry: Spot Statistics, n.d., Box 63, File American Iron and Steel Institute, Carter.

108 Lykes-Youngstown Corporation, *Annual Report* (1975).

109 Stein, *Running Steel, Running America*, 243.

110 John Logue, 'When They Close the Factory Gates: How Big Steel Scrapped a Community,' *The Progressive* (August 1980).

111 Seeing the company's annual reports today, it appears that it was never serious about modernizing its Youngstown facilities. Instead, the reports showcased the modern steelmaking operations at Indiana Harbor. A year before closing the Campbell Works, the company dropped 'Youngstown' from its name and 'deferred' its BOF plan indefinitely, thus disassociating itself from the Mahoning Valley. Lykes-Youngstown Corporation, *Annual Reports* (1969–80).

112 J.J. Koss, interview by Philip Bracy, November 1981, Youngstown State University Shutdown Project. The transcript of the interview is held at the library of Youngstown State University.

113 Besides being burdened with aging equipment, older mills and factories usually had aging (high seniority) workforces and unions. While academic studies have established that the effects of job loss were hardest on older workers and that the age of those displaced in a plant closing tended to be older, the evidence suggests that aging workforces may very well have contributed to the closing of well-established mills and factories. Undoubtedly, these additional costs put many plants into the red in intracorporate assessments. According to Robert Dennis Hiscott, 'Plant Closures and Employee Displacement: A Case Study of the Beach Appliance Plant Closure' (MA thesis, Queen's University, 1982), displaced older workers were also more likely to earn less at their new jobs. See also

Myron Kramar, *The Impact of Plant Closures on Older Workers, Consolidated Bathurst: A Case Study* (Hamilton: Social Planning and Research Council, 1984), 24–5.

114 John N.H. Britton, 'Introduction,' in Britton, ed., *Canada and the Global Economy*, 21–2.

115 Michael Bliss, 'Canadianizing American Business: The Roots of the Branch Plant,' in Ian Lumsden, ed., *Close the 49th Parallel etc: The Americanization of Canada* (Toronto: University of Toronto Press, 1970), 32.

116 Kari Levitt, *Silent Surrender: The Multinational Corporation in Canada* (Toronto: Macmillan, 1970), 6.

117 A.E. Safarian, 'Foreign Investment in Canada: Some Myths,' *Journal of Canadian Studies* (1971), 6.

118 The expansion of foreign direct investment in Canada in the immediate post-war period is explored in Lawrence Aronsen, 'An Open Door to the North: The Liberal Government and the Expansion of American Foreign Investment, 1945–1953,' *American Review of Canadian Studies* 22, 2 (1992), 167–97.

119 Fred Caloren, *Layoffs, Shutdowns and Closures in Ontario Manufacturing, Mining and Trade Establishments, January 1971–June 1972* (Ottawa: University of Ottawa, 1974), 1–2.

120 J. Paul Grayson, *Corporate Strategy and Plant Closures: The SKF Experience* (Toronto: Our Times, 1985), especially chapter 2.

121 Ian Robertson MacLachlan, 'Industrial Plant Closure and Competitive Strategy in Ontario, 1981–1986' (PhD diss., University of Toronto, 1990), 26.

122 Ibid., 111.

123 Ian MacLachlan, 'Organizational Restructuring of U.S.-based Manufacturing Subsidiaries and Plant Closure,' in Britton, ed., *Canada and the Global Economy*, 196.

124 Rianne Mahon, *The Politics of Industrial Restructuring: Canadian Textiles* (Toronto: University of Toronto Press, 1984), 17.

125 Pierre Bougault, *Innovation and the Structure of Canadian Industry* (Background Study No. 23, Science Council of Canada, 1972).

126 R.G. Head, assistant deputy minister to J.F. Grandy, deputy minister of Industry, Trade and Commerce, RG 20 Acc. 1983–4/228, Box 181, File 8001-270/711 part 2, Development Operation: Massey Ferguson Ltd, NAC.

127 Department of Industry, Trade and Commerce, 'Problems of the Modern Society – Industry,' Prepared for the OECD council ministers meeting, 12–14 February 1969.

128 Memorandum to Cabinet by the minister of Industry, Trade and Commerce, 11 March 1970, RG 20, Volume 103, File 25/500-2 part 1, NAC.

129 Editorial, 'Instead of Paying Welfare,' *Ottawa Evening Journal*, 29 June 1973 and Richard Gwyn, '$4 Billion for New Industries Is All Carrot and No Stick,' *Toronto Daily Star*, 30 June 1978.

130 C.B. Landstreet, report, RG 118 Acc 19875–6/076 Box 5 F, 3837-1/G41 Tech and Econ Ch Adj Assist-Glendale Spinning Mills, NAC.

131 Harry N. Shardlow to Rex G. Porter, director of the Plant Closure Review and Employment Adjustment Branch of the Ministry of Labour, 12 August 1981, RG 7.91, File Glendale Spinning Mills, Hamilton, AO. Those displaced in the plant's closing received no pension, severance pay, life insurance, or adjustment assistance of any kind.

132 Garnett Picot and Wendy Pyper, *Permanent Layoffs and Displaced Workers: Cyclical Sensitivity, Concentration, and Experience Following the Layoff* (Ottawa: Statistics Canada, 1993), 16.

133 Philip Scranton, 'Large Firms and Industrial Restructuring: The Philadelphia Region, 1900–1980,' *Pennsylvania Magazine of History and Biography* 116, 4 (1992), 454.

134 J. Paul Grayson, *Plant Closures and De-Skilling: Three Case Studies* (Ottawa: Science Council of Canada, 1986), 7.

5: In Defence of Local Community

1 See, for example, Kim Moody, *An Injury to All: The Decline of American Unionism* (New York: Verso, 1988).

2 Dale A. Hathaway, *Can Workers Have a Voice? The Politics of Deindustralization in Pittsburgh* (University Park, PA: Pennsylvania State University Press, 1993), ix.

3 David Bensman and Roberta Lynch, *Rusted Dreams: Hard Times in a Steel Community* (Berkeley: University of California Press, 1988), 202.

4 *Outlook for the Auto Industry and Its Impact on Employment, Industries and Communities Dependent Upon It*, written remarks from senator John Kelly, hearings before the Subcommittee on Economic Development of the Committee on Public Works and Transportation, House of Representatives. 97th Congress, 1st Session, 21 December 1981, Lansing, Michigan, Library of Congress (LOC).

5 One can see the dampening effect that the Cold War had on organized labour in Ronald L. Filipelli and Mark D. McColloch, *Cold War in the Working Class: The Rise and Decline of the United Electrical Workers* (Albany: State University of New York Press, 1995).

6 Christopher Lasch, 'The Communitarian Critique of Liberalism,' in Charles H. Reynolds and Ralph V. Norman, eds., *Community in America* (Berkeley: University of California Press, 1988), 177. The communitarian

critique of liberalism coincided with the adoption of the community strategy by plant closing opponents in the United States. Philosopher Alasdair MacIntyre claimed that the loss of community – once 'constituted by a set of shared stories about virtue and vice' – made it impossible to agree on a shared concept of justice. See *After Virtue: A Study of Moral Theory* (Notre Dame: University of Notre Dame Press, 1981).

7 Susan S. Fainstein, 'Local Mobilization and Economic Discontent,' in Michael Peter Smith and Joe R. Feagin, eds., *The Capitalist City: Global Restructuring and Community Politics* (Oxford: Blackwell, 1987), 328. For the neighbourhood movement see Harry C. Boyte, *The Backyard Revolution* (Philadelphia: Temple University Press, 1980), and Manuel Castells, *The City and the Grassroots* (Berkeley: University of California Press, 1983).

8 The United Auto Workers proved to be a partial exception as the union helped forge the 'Progressive Alliance' that brought together a wide variety of organizations in support of the proposed Full Employment Act. It was the Progressive Alliance that commissioned Bluestone and Harrison to write *The Deindustrialization of America*.

9 Christopher L. Tomlins, *The State of the Unions: Labor Relations, Law and the Organized Labor Movement in America, 1880–1960* (Cambridge: Cambridge University Press, 1985), William E. Forbath, *Law and the Shaping of the American Labor Movement* (Cambridge: Harvard University Press, 1991), and Victoria C. Hattam, *Labor Visions and State Power: The Origins of Business Unionism in the United States* (Princeton: Princeton University Press, 1993).

10 Forbath, *Law and the American Labor Movement*, 6–7.

11 Michael C. Harper, 'The Scope of the Duty to Bargain Concerning Business Transformations,' in Samuel Estreicher and Daniel G. Collins, eds., *Labor Law and Business Change: Theoretical and Transactional Perspectives* (New York: Quorum Books, 1988), 25.

12 Peter G. Nash and Scott W. Schattenfield, 'Plant Closings, Relocations, and Transfers of Unit Work: A Management View,' in Estreicher and Collins, eds., *Labor Law and Business Change*, 208.

13 This decision overturned the 1965 *Textile Workers Union of America* v. *Darlington Manufacturing Co.* that held that an employer's anti-union animus only counted if it chilled labour relations in another location. In other words, an employer's actions could only be deemed an unfair labour practice if the shutdown was partial.

14 In the case of *Local 1330 USWA* v. *U.S. Steel Corp*, for example, the judge ruled in 1980 that 'this Court has spent many hours searching for a way to cut to the heart of the economic reality – that obsolescence market forces

demand the close of the Mahoning Valley plants, and yet the lives of 3,500 workers and their families and the supporting Youngstown community cannot be dismissed as inconsequential. United States Steel should not be permitted to leave the Youngstown area devastated after drawing from the lifeblood of the community for so many years. Unfortunately, the mechanism to reach this ideal settlement ... is not now in existence in the code of laws of our nation.' The union local had asked the court to prevent U.S. Steel from removing machinery from the Brier Hill mill until the community could buy the mill. Peter Pitegoff, *Plant Closings: Legal Remedies When Jobs Disappear* (Sommerville, MA: Industrial Cooperative Association, 1981), n.p.

15 Bernice Adams, interview by author, Troy, Michigan, 23 February 1998.

16 Marilyn McCormack, interview by author, Troy, Michigan, 23 February 1998.

17 Due process is a concept laden with legal and cultural meaning. On the one hand due process originated with the English idea of 'natural justice' as articulated in the Magna Carta, namely, the right to be heard and tried fairly. The American concept of 'procedural due process,' on the other hand, refers to the judicial power to review the fairness of state action. Frederick F. Schauer, 'English Natural Justice and American Due Process: An Analytical Comparison,' in Sidney R. Peck, ed., *Due Process: Introductory Material for a Seminar on Due Process* (Toronto: Osgoode Hall Law School, 1994), B4. See also William D. Preston Jr. and Gerson B. Mehlman, 'The Due Process Clause as a Limitation on the Reach of State Legislation: An Historical and Analytical Examination of Substantive Due Process,' *Baltimore Law Review* 8, 1 (1978).

18 Meyer Bernstein to Clinton Pialt of New Boston, 14 August 1970, USWA, Legislative Department, Box 46, File 10 TAA – Detroit Steel, Portsmouth Division Case (1969–71), Penn State University Archives (PSUA).

19 Lawrence E. Rothstein, *Plant Closings: Power, Politics and Workers* (London: Auburn House Publishing Co., 1986), 17–18.

20 Dana Frank, *Buy American: The Untold Story of Economic Nationalism* (Boston: Beacon Press, 1999), 136.

21 Ibid., 148.

22 William D. Ford, 'Coping with Plant Closings,' *Labor Law Journal* 36, 6 (1985), 323–6.

23 John T. Addison and Pedro Portugal, 'Advance Notice,' in John T. Addison, ed., *Job Displacement: Consequences and Implications for Policy* (Detroit: Wayne State University Press, 1991), 203.

24 Linda D. McGill, 'State Laws Extend Warn Provisions,' *Employment Rela-*

tions Today 18, 2 (1991), 253. The WARN Act of 1988 made prenotification of mass terminations of over 500 workers mandatory in the United States and created labour-management committees modelled on the Canadian experiment of 1963.

25 'Some Historical Notes Regarding Pensions,' n.d., USWA Records, Legislative Department, Box 52, Pensions, File 12 PR, AFL-CIO Meeting (1975), PSUA. For an excellent overview of this tragedy see Steven A. Sass, *The Promise of Private Pensions: The First Hundred Years* (Cambridge: Harvard University Press, 1997), especially chapter 8.

26 I.W. Abel to all USWA district directors, staff representatives and local union secretaries, August 17, 1971, USWA Records, Legislative Department, Box 49, File 3, PSUA. Throughout the campaign, the AFL-CIO was immobilized by the opposition of the teamsters as well as the clothing and building trades, all of whom relied on multi-employer plans and did not want to pay higher pension contributions. USWA Records, Legislative Department, Box 50, File 5, Pension Reform–General, 12 February 1974, PSUA.

27 *Pension Asset Raids*, Hearing before the Select Committee on Aging, House of Representatives, 98th Cong., 1st sess., 28 September 1983, LOC 1984. The 114 plan terminations occurred between 1 January 1980 and 1 August 1983.

28 *Corporate Raiding of Worker Pension Plans.* Hearing before a Subcommittee of the Committee on Government Operation, House of Representatives, 100th Cong., 2nd sess., 28 September 1988, Chairman Tom Lantos.

29 William Alonso, 'Deindustrialization and Regional Policy,' in Lloyd Rodwin and Hidehiko Sazanami, eds., *Deindustrialization and Regional Economic Transformation: The Experience of the United States* (Boston: Unwin Hyman, 1989), 222–3. The Nixon administration was keenly aware of these policy failures. Toward a National Urban Policy, 3, Nixon Papers, FG 6-12, Council for Urban Affairs, Box 1, 2/23/69, Urban Affairs Council, 3 February 1969, National Archives and Records Administration (NARA).

30 Yet trade union leaders looked at employee ownership with a jaundiced eye. For the leadership of the USWA and the UAW, Employee Stock Ownership Plans (ESOPs) and other forms of community ownership threatened the high salaries and dues prevalent in their respective industries. As institutions representing members in hundreds of towns and cities across North America, the unions regarded calls for communal solidarity as naive and counterproductive and were deeply sceptical about the wide assortment of fringe groups lined up behind some of these local campaigns.

31 Although at least thirteen state AFL-CIO union centrals were involved in

plant-closing legislation by 1981 (Alabama, Iowa, Maine, Michigan, Mississippi, Montana, New York, Ohio, Oregon, Pennsylvania, Vermont, Wisconsin, and Washington), twenty others were not.

32 United in their opposition were the Ohio Manufacturers' Association, the Ohio Council of Retail Merchants, the Chamber of Commerce, the Ohio Department of Economic and Community Development, and the Cleveland Growth Association.

33 Carl Dimengo, 20 March 1981, URW, Research, File: Plant Closures or Permanent Curtailments, 1981–2, University of Akron Archives (UAA).

34 Many of these bills featured 'community' in their titles to situate the issue in a context other than labour law. The Ohio Public Interest Campaign, for example, lobbied unsuccessfully in 1977 for the passing of the 'Community Readjustment Bill.' Ronald G. Ehrenberg and George H. Jacubson, 'Advance Notification of Plant Closings: Does It Matter?' *Industrial Relations: A Journal of Economy and Society* 28, 1 (1989), 60. See also Kenneth A. Kovach and Peter E. Millspaugh, 'The Plant Closing Issue Arrives at the Bargaining Table,' *Journal of Labor Research* 4, 4 (1983), 370, and Edward Kelly, 'Plant Closings Legislation: The Ohio Experience,' in William Schweke, ed., *Plant Closings: Issues, Politics and Legislation* (Boston: Conference on Alternative State and Local Policies, 1980).

35 The state of Connecticut required in 1983 that non-bankrupt firms maintain employee health insurance benefits for a 120 day period, whereas Rhode Island required that laid-off employees be paid wages owing within 24 hours. Roger Kerson and Greg LeRoy, *State and Local Initiatives on Development Subsidies and Plant Closings* (Chicago: Federation for Industrial Retention and Renewal, 1989), 25.

36 Michael Shippani, 'Creative Alternatives to Plant Closings: The Massachusetts Experience,' *Labor Law Journal* 38, 8 (1987), 462.

37 Nancy R. Folbre, Julia L. Leighton, and Melissa R. Roderick, 'Plant Closings and Their Regulation in Maine, 1971–1982,' *Industrial and Labor Relations Review* 37, 2 (1984), 190.

38 Kerson and LeRoy, *State and Local Initiatives*, 25.

39 Norton L. Berman, director of the Department of Commerce to governor William G. Milliken, 22 December 1981, RG 86–51, Box 9, File 3: SF-Economic Development, 1981–2, State Archives of Michigan (SAM).

40 William J. Giles to Tom Turner, president of Detroit AFL-CIO, 7 May 1981, Metro Detroit AFL-CIO Council Collection (Part 4) Accession 53, Box 108, File 108-55, 1981, Walter Reuther Library (WRL).

41 Roy Lubove, *Twentieth Century Pittsburgh*, vol. 2, *The Post-Steel Era* (Pittsburgh: University of Pittsburgh Press, 1996), 20–1.

42 Lloyd Rodwin, 'Deindustrialization and Regional Economic Transforma-
    tion,' in Rodwin and Sazanami, eds., *Deindustrialization and Regional
    Economic Transformation*, 21.
43 George F. Lord and Albert C. Price, 'Growth Ideology in a Period of De-
    cline: Deindustrialization and Restructuring, Flint Style,' *Social Problems* 39,
    2 (1992), 155.
44 John Portz, *The Politics of Plant Closings* (Lawrence: University Press of
    Kansas, 1990), 165–6.
45 James F. Fitzpatrick, ed., *WARN Act and State Plant-Closing Handbook*
    (Washington: Bureau of National Affairs, 1993), n.p.
46 The plant-closing manual directed locals to negotiate the decision to close
    with the company before moving to the effects of the decision. If the
    company refused to furnish responses to union questions, international
    representatives were told to file an unfair labour practice charge with the
    National Labour Relations Board: 'The charge can strengthen the union's
    bargaining position in negotiating shutdown benefits.' Douglas Fraser,
    president, to department heads and international representatives, 1 May
    1981, UAW, Community Services Department, Box 9, File 5: Plant Clos-
    ings, General Information, January 1980–January 1991, WRL. UAW Plant
    Closing Manual (For Confidential Use of UAW International Representa-
    tives), February 1981, UAW, Community Services Department, Box 9, File
    6: Plant Closings, General Information, January 1980–January 1991, WRL.
47 Leonard Page and Judith Scott, *The Law of Plant Shutdowns* (Detroit: United
    Auto Workers, 1981).
48 John T. Addison, 'Job Security in the United States: Law, Collective Bar-
    gaining, Policy and Practice,' *British Journal of Industrial Relations* 24, 3
    (1986), 399. According to Addison, 'Historically ... unions have sought to
    establish job rights through a seniority system underwritten by severance
    payments. In recent years, this passive approach to job security has
    changed. Plant closing issues have gained in importance and unions have
    often been granted decision bargaining rights.'
49 William D. Torrence, 'Plant Closing and Advance Notice: Another Look at
    the Numbers,' *Labor Law Journal* 37, 8 (1986), 462–3.
50 If previous administrations were unsympathetic to the plight of displaced
    workers and their unions, the Reagan administration was outright hostile.
    Even more than the Chrysler bailout concessions, the crushing of the
    PATCO air controllers' strike put U.S. trade unions on the defensive. Jeff
    Stansbury, 'Putting the Brakes on a Runaway Shop,' *Solidarity* (February
    1983).
51 *Time*, 24 January 1983, 58–9.

52 Several scholars have pointed to the deradicalization of the union movement during the anti-communist purges of the Cold War. See Scott D. Camp, *Worker Response to Plant Closings: Steelworkers in Johnstown and Youngstown* (New York: Garland Publishers, 1995), and Filipelli and McColloch, *Cold War in the Working Class*, 1.

53 Typically, the last membership meetings dealt exclusively with the mechanics of job loss: severance pay, pension eligibility, health and life insurance extension, and the liquidation of union assets. There was no hint of defiance. Minute-book, 1950–72, USWA Archives, Cancelled Local Unions, District 13, Box 6, Local 4384, Monessen, PA, PSUA.

54 Robert Saute, 'The Fight-back against "Give-backs,"' *Guardian* (16 March 1983).

55 Leona Sibelman, industrial relations specialist and Elaine Davis, Southeastern regional representative to Steve Clem, director of research, URW, 17 September 1986, URW, Box 2, File: Plant Closing or Permanent Curtailment, 1979–80, UAA.

56 John Fillion to Owen Bieber, 30 June 1983, UAW, Region 1, Box 221, File 1: Plant Closings, WRL.

57 Bernice Adams, interview by author, Troy, Michigan, 23 February 1998.

58 Opposition was swift: critics circulated flyers entitled 'First They Closed the Plant – We Lost Our Jobs! Now They Are Abolishing Our District – We Are Losing Our Union!' Leaflet from the 'Committee to Preserve D. 26,' Gerald Dickey Collection, Box 1, File: USWA Flyers, Youngstown Historical Center of Industry and Labor (YHCIL).

59 UAW, Region 1, Box 221, File 1: Plant Closings, 27 June 1983, WRL.

60 Proceedings, USWA 21st Constitutional Convention, 20–4 September 1982, Atlantic City, NJ, 75, Delegate Rich (LU 6787, District 31).

61 Moody, *An Injury to All*, 4.

62 William T. Dickens and Jonathan S. Leonard, 'Accounting for the Decline in Union Membership, 1950–1980,' *Industrial and Labor Relations Review* 38, 3 (1985), 326.

63 Barry Bluestone and Bennett Harrison, *The Deindustrialization of America: Plant Closings, Community Abandonment, and the Dismantling of Basic Industry* (New York: Basic Books, 1982), 19.

64 Ibid., 50.

65 The local community's solidarity was on display during the Fourth of July parade that year, rededicated to the campaign to keep the mill operating. Parade floats devoted to employee ownership followed more traditional fare beneath the green ribbons and huge green flags lining Main Street that were said to represent community rebirth. William Serrin, 'Town Rallies

for Workers Trying to Buy Plan,' *New York Times*, 6 June 1982. A similar parade was held in Taunton, Massachusetts, after the announcement that Paragon Gears would close. There, the parade opened with local veterans holding aloft U.S. flags, and included beauty queens, floats, fire engines, and five school bands. Joan S. Lublin, 'Unions Try New Kinds of Resistance as Anger over Plant Closings Grows,' *Wall Street Journal*, 27 January 1982.

66 Staughton Lynd, 'The Genesis of the Idea of a Community Right to Industrial Property in Youngstown and Pittsburgh, 1977–1987,' *Journal of American History* 74, 3 (1987), 926.

67 The Dayton plant had been the base of operations for the company since 1921. By 1970, Frigidaire employed 17,000 people in the Dayton area and paid $5,554,000 in local taxes that year. Rex Smith to V.E. Lewis, industrial relations manager, Frigidaire Collection, Box 68, File 79-10.8-23, General Motors Institute (GMI) Archives.

68 Typed 'Plan of Action' not on company letterhead, no author identified. However, written notations appear to be in Rex Smith's handwriting, Frigidaire Collection, Box 68, File 79-10.8-21, GMI.

69 Statement by Harold W. Campbell, General Motors vice president and general manager of Frigidaire, 12 June 1971, Frigidaire Collection, Box 67, File 79-10.8-2, GMI.

70 Larry Froelich, 'Dayton Citizens Saved Worker Jobs,' *Akron Beacon Journal*, 7 December 1971.

71 Frank G. Anger to All Interested Citizens, 28 June 1971, Frigidaire Collection, Box 68, File 79-10.8-10 Labor Relations: Save Frigidaire Committee, GMI.

72 George T. Lytle to Frank G. Anger, Frigidaire Collection, Box 68, File 79-10.8-10, Labor Relations: Save Frigidaire Committee, GMI.

73 Martha Murphy to Frank G. Anger, Frigidaire Collection, Box 68, File 79-10.8-10, Labor Relations: Save Frigidaire Committee, GMI.

74 C. Thomas to Frank G. Anger, Frigidaire Collection, Box 68, File 79-10.8-10, Labor Relations: Save Frigidaire Committee, GMI.

75 A good example of this point can be seen in a letter written by Josephine McDermid: 'It never occurred to me to buy other than Frigidaire; but if the appliance lines leave Dayton believe me I will.' Josephine McDermid to Frank G. Anger, Frigidaire Collection, Box 68, File 79-10.8-10, Labor Relations: Save Frigidaire Committee, GMI.

76 See the letter written by Mrs. Paul J. Maple who advised Frigidaire to 'get a woman designer. We want simple operations, and less clutter.' Mrs. Paul

J. Maple to Frank G. Anger, Frigidaire Collection, Box 68, File 79-10.8-18, Labor Relations: Save Frigidaire Committee, GMI.

77 General Motors press statement. 16 July 1971, Frigidaire Collection, Box 68, File 79-10.8-10, GMI.

78 WAVI Radio. Memo, 18 June 1971, Frigidaire Collection, Box 68, File 79-10.8-15, GMI.

79 Smith to Groehn, 13 July 1971 [first of two reports that day], Frigidaire Collection, Box 68, File 79-10.5-15, GMI.

80 Rex Smith to Thomas Groehn, Director, news relations staff at General Motors, 22 July 1971, Frigidaire Collection, Box 68, File 79-10.8-15, GMI.

81 Smith to Groehn, 13 July 1971 [second of two reports that day], Frigidaire Collection, Box 68, File 79-10.8-15, GMI.

82 Smith to Groehn, 15 July 1971, Frigidaire Collection, Box 68, File 79-10.8-15, GMI.

83 Smith to Groehn, 10 September 1971, Frigidaire Collection, Box 68, File 7-10.8-16, GMI.

84 Smith to Groehn, 13 September 1971, Frigidaire Collection, Box 68, File 79-10.8-16, GMI.

85 Statement to the media, Frigidaire Division, 13 September 1971, and Smith to Groehn, 10 September 1971, Frigidaire Collection, Box 68, File 79-10.8-16, GMI. The entire statement read as follows: 'Obviously the Union is not willing to meet the problem halfway now and consider having a long-range plan to achieve labor cost parity later. As a result we find it necessary now to pursue possible alternatives.' However, had the membership gone along with concessions Frigidaire would have released the following press statement: 'We have already explained the situation relating to the appliance business and the alternatives available under the existing labor agreement to Union officials. Also, in response to a question from the Union, we have ex-pressed a willingness to consider a Union proposal that would meet the problems halfway now and a long-range plan to achieve labor cost parity later. We stand ready to continue the talks with the Union officials on this basis.'

86 'Frigidaire Showdown,' *Dayton Journal Herald*, 14 September 1971.

87 Editorial, 'Frigidaire Settlement ... a Boon to the Community,' *Dayton Journal Herald*, 23 November 1971.

88 Rex Smith, Memorandum, 'The Frigidaire Situation: A Review of the Public Relations Aspects Before and After the Unique Labor Settlement,' 16 March 1972, Frigidaire Collection, Box 68, File 79-10.8-4, GMI.

89 Rex Smith, PR director, Frigidaire, An Estimate of the Public Relations

Shock Effects of a Business Failure, n.d., Frigidaire Collection, Box 67, File 79-10.8-3, Labor Relations–Special Project, 1971, GMI.

90 Notes taken by Bill Pierce at meeting on Frigidaire, 28 July 1971, Frigidaire Collection, Box 67, File 79-10-8-1, GMI.

91 'Frigidaire Renaissance: A Marketing Plan for Rebuilding Frigidaire Leadership in the Appliance Industry,' 22 October 1971, Frigidaire Collection, Box 67, 79-10.8-2 Labor Relations Miscellaneous, 1971, GMI.

92 Jim Good, 'Akron Tries to Copy Dayton Bounce,' *Dayton News*, 17 January 1972.

93 Jim Good, 'It's Whole New Tennis Match, with Management Serving,' *Dayton Daily News*, 23 January 1972.

94 Ralph Orr, 'A Growing Trend: Asking Union Aid to Save Companies,' *Akron Beacon Journal*, 30 January 1972.

95 For an assessment of the social impact of the mill closure see Terry F. Buss and F. Stevens Redburn, *Shutdown at Youngstown: Public Policy for Mass Unemployment* (Albany: State University New York Press, 1983).

96 Sergio Lalli, 'Campbell Works More than Jobs: Steel Way of Life Is Disappearing,' *Youngstown Vindicator*, 26 September 1977.

97 The religious response in Youngstown is very well explained in Thomas G. Fuectmann, *Steeples and Stacks: Religion and Steel, Crisis in Youngstown* (Cambridge: Cambridge University Press, 1989). The fight against the mill's closing is considered in the context of social movement theory in Camp, *Worker Response to Plant Closings*.

98 Jack C. Hunter, interview by Philip Bracy, Youngstown, 24 April 1981. The transcript of the interview is held at the library of Youngstown State University. Historian Judith Stein has sketched out the various factions within the valley's political leadership as well as within the local district of the USWA in *Running Steel, Running America: Race, Economic Policy and the Decline of Liberalism* (Chapel Hill: University of North Carolina Press, 1998), 244–7.

99 Anthony C. Centofanti, interview by Philip Bracy, Youngstown, 1981. The transcript is held in the library of Youngstown State University.

100 Mr. Sullivan, Philip Bracy, interview by Youngstown, 1981. The transcript of the interview is held by the library of Youngstown State University.

101 Bluestone and Harrison, *The Deindustrialization of America*, 252.

102 *Problems in U.S. Steel Market*, Field Hearings before Subcommittee on Trade of the Committee on Ways and Means, House of Representatives, 96th Cong., 1st Sess., in Youngstown 27 December 1979 (Washington, 1980), 140, LoC.

103 Bishop W. Malone to members of Youngstown Religious Coalition with

an attached copy of the pastoral message prepared by the committee, 22 November 1977, William J. Carney Papers, Box 5, Folder 5, YHCIL. The original draft was written by John Carr of the U.S. Catholic Conference. See also the transcript of an oral history interview with Bishop Malone by Philip Bracy, 8 April 1981. Held at the library of Youngstown State University.

104 Irwin M. Marcus, 'An Experiment in Reindustrialization: The Tri-State Conference on Steel and the Creation of the Steel Valley Authority,' *Pennsylvania History* 54, 3 (1987), 181.

105 Reverend Robert Campbell, interview by Philip Bracy, Youngstown, 28 April 1981. The transcript is held at the library of Youngstown State University.

106 Father Edward Stanton, interview by Philip Bracy, Youngstown, 5 April 1981. The transcript is held in the library of Youngstown State University.

107 Bishop James W. Malone, interview by Philip Bracy, 8 April 1981. The transcript is held by the library of Youngstown State University.

108 'The Fight against Black Monday' (ABC TV, 1978). For a brief summary of the program see Terry F. Buss, F. Stevens Redburn, and George E. Cheney, 'Studying the Politics of Economic Decline,' *Teaching Political Science* 8, 4 (1981), 511–16. *Bill Moyer's Journal* also featured worker efforts to purchase Youngstown mills on 26 June 1980, 'It's Not Working' (PBS, WNET/Thirteen, New York).

109 Dale Peskin, 'Many Have Looked at Youngstown, but Few Have Seen,' *Youngstown Vindicator*, 17 September 1978, B3. Peskin argues that the outside media overstated the hardships faced by area residents after Black Monday with the result that the 'Youngstown story' then being told was only 'half a story.'

110 *Preserving Jobs and Communities in Michigan*, Conference on Alternative State and Local Policies, 25 June 1981, Vertical File: 'Employment '82,' Michigan State Library, Lansing.

111 Ibid.

112 James W. Smith to Lloyd McBride regarding a feasibility study for re-opening Campbell Works, Youngstown Sheet and Tube, 19 December, 1977, USWA, Lloyd McBride, Box 20, File 4, PSUA.

113 Sam Donnorummo, interview by Donna DeBlasio, Youngstown, 1991.

114 United Steelworkers of America. *Convention Proceedings*, 18–22 September 1978, Atlantic City, Resolution 16, The Shutdown of Steel Plants.

115 United Steelworkers of America. *Convention Proceedings*, 1980.

116 For example, he was advised of the 'political ramifications' of various responses to the Youngstown Sheet and Tube closing by Stu Eizenstat and

Bob Ginsburg. Memo for president from Stu Eizenstat and Bob Ginsburg, 12 October 1977, Box 284, File: Steel, [O/A 6343]. See also Carter. Memo to president, Subject: Organizing ourselves on the steel problem, 29 September 1977, Box 284, File: Steel [O/A 6343], Carter.

117 Jerry Jasinowski to Stu Eizenstat, 5 August 1980, Box BE-5, File BE 3 6/1/ 80–1/20/81, Carter. Handwritten notes by Jimmy Carter on a memo from Stu Eizenstat to president, 14 December 1977. Box 292, File: Trade Adjustment Assistance [O/A6237-2], Carter. Faced with a delegation from Mahwah, New Jersey, in May 1980 wanting to discuss Ford's closing of an auto assembly plant there, Carter's domestic policy adviser Stu Eizenstat urged him to appear 'personally concerned' as the closing had become 'a major political issue in the primary on June 3rd, particularly since Senator Kennedy visited the plant last Monday. Gov. Byrne feels strongly that you should show your deep concern for this problem so that he can carry that message to the voters in the next few weeks.' Ralph Schlosstein to Stu Eizenstat re: Mahwah Ford closing, 8 May 1980, Box 163, File: Auto Industry, Carter.

118 The Commission for a National Agenda for the Eighties, named by Carter, called the decline of the cities of the heartland 'inevitable' and urged the federal government to facilitate the relocation of the urban poor to the Sunbelt. Large industrial cities had been rendered 'obsolete.' *Time*, 12 January 1981, 19.

119 Memo for the president from Douglas M. Costle, director, U.S. Environmental Protection Agency, 30 September 1977, Box 284, File: Steel, [O/A 6343], Carter.

120 Barbara Blum, deputy administrator to Stuart Eizenstat, asst. to president for Domestic Affairs and Policy, Box 284, Steel/Chrome, [CF O/A 24-3], US EPA, Carter. The EPA had allowed a one-time exemption for the Mahoning Valley mills from its effluent guidelines. The decision sparked considerable public controversy and court challenges. George Humphreys, Associate Director for Environment, to Jim Cannon, 27 May 1976, Box 22, File Mahoning Valley, Ohio, Gerald Ford Presidential Library (Ford).

121 Most Reverend James W. Malone to President Carter, 21 May 1979, M19 Ecumenical Coalition of the Mahoning Valley, Inc., Records, Box 3, File 5: General Record–Memos, YHCIL.

122 For an excellent analysis of these events see Lynd, 'The Genesis of the Idea,' 926–58.

123 Ibid., 945.

124 Ibid., 926–58. The Pittsburgh area experimented with the use of eminent

domain to achieve worker or community ownership of closing mills in the early 1980s. See Marcus, 'An Experiment in Reindustrialization,' 180.

125 Tri-State Conference on Manufacturing (or Steel) Records, 1982–93, Box 53 (green dot 9053) unprocessed. Folder: 'Campaign for Human Development, 1981–2' proposal and resumes, University of Pittsburgh Archives (UPA).

126 The competing memories of these mill closings are examined in two recent works: Steven High, 'Deindustrializing Youngstown: Memories of Resistance and Loss in the Decades following "Black Monday," 1977–97,' *History Workshop Journal* 54 (2002), and Sherry Lee Linkon and John Russo, *Steeltown, USA: Work and Memory in Youngstown.* Lawrence: University of Kansas Press, 2002.

127 J. Philip Richley, interview by Donna DeBlasio, Youngstown, 12 June 1991 and 11 December 1991.

128 Ohio Public Interest Campaign, *Public Interest Report*, November/December 1979, 'No More Youngstowns,' VAA. URW Research, RG 15, Box 2, File: Plant Closings or Permanent Curtailments, 1979–80. See also Buss and Redburn, *Shutdown at Youngstown*, 25. The anti-shutdown movement failed to reopen the Campbell Works, according to Buss and Redburn, for five principle reasons: (1) the resistance of the steel companies, (2) the opposition of the USWA, (3) the lack of grassroots support demonstrated by poorly attended rallies, (4) its association with political radicalism, and (5) the political divisions in the Valley.

129 John C. Raines, Leonora Berson, and David McI.Grace, eds., *Plant Closings and Job Losses* (Philadelphia: Temple University Press, 1982), *Community and Capital in Conflict*, 28.

130 Frank, *Buy American*, 181.

131 Dana Frank suggests that the International Ladies Garment Workers Union played the 'race card' when it produced an advertising campaign that featured a U.S. flag juxtaposed with the bold letters 'Made in Japan.' Frank, *Buy American*, 137.

6: 'I'll Wrap the F*#@ Canadian Flag around Me'

1 Noah Meltz, 'Unionism in the Private-Service Sector: A Canada–US Comparison,' in Jane Jenson and Rianne Mahon, eds., *The Challenge of Restructuring: North American Labor Movements Respond* (Philadelphia: Temple University Press, 1993), 210.

2 John Holmes and A. Rusonik have shown that these economic differences resulted in dramatically different bargaining positions in 'The Break-up of

an International Labour Union: Uneven Development in the North American Auto Industry and the Schism in the UAW,' *Environment and Planning A* 23 (1991), 9.

3 Kim Moody, *An Injury to All: The Decline of American Unionism* (New York: Verso, 1988), and Ian Robinson, 'Economic Unionism in Crisis: The Origins, Consequences, and Prospects of Divergence in Labour Management Characteristics,' in Jenson and Mahon, eds., *The Challenge of Restructuring*, 19.

4 Stephen Azzi, *Walter Gordon and the Rise of Canadian Nationalism* (Montreal: McGill-Queen's University Press, 1999), 167.

5 This was evident in the popularity of George Grant's *Lament for a Nation: The Defeat of a Nation* (Ottawa: Carleton University Press, 1965).

6 Walter L. Gordon, *A Choice for Canada: Independence or Colonial Status* (Toronto: McClelland and Stewart, 1966).

7 It should be noted that Canadian economic nationalism was strongest in Ontario. In Quebec, of course, there was a competing nationalism at work. In the West and in the Atlantic provinces, the manufacturing sectors were weak and foreign ownership was less pronounced. The debate over deindustrialization was thus concentrated in Canada's most heavily industrialized and populous province.

8 Mel Watkins, 'Foreign Ownership and the Structure of Canadian Industry,' in Dave Godfrey and Mel Watkins, eds., *Gordon to Watkins to You, a Documentary: The Battle for Control of our Economy* (Toronto: new press, 1970), 65.

9 Canada, *Royal Commission on Canada's Economic Prospects* (Walter Gordon, Chairman) (Ottawa: Queen's Printer, 1958); Canada, *Foreign Ownership and the Structure of Canadian Industry.* Report of the Task Force on the Structure of Canadian Industry (M. Watkins, Chairman) (Ottawa: Queen's Printer, 1968); and Canada, Department of Industry, Trade and Commerce. *Foreign-Owned Subsidiaries in Canada, 1964–1969* (Ottawa: Information Canada, 1972).

10 Abraham Rotstein and Gary Lax, *Independence: The Canadian Challenge* (Toronto: Committee for an Independent Canada, 1972), 127.

11 Mahon, *The Politics of Industrial Restructuring*, 17–18.

12 Robert M. Laxer, ed., *(Canada) Ltd.: The Political Economy of Dependency* (Toronto: McClelland and Stewart, 1973), 7–8. Many left-nationalists in Canada had ties to the Old Left either within the Canadian Communist Party or other left-wing organizations. The resilience of the traditional left no doubt contributed to the resurgence of trade union militancy in Canada during the 1970s.

13 Jim Laxer and Doris Jantzi, 'The De-Industrialization of Ontario' in Laxer, ed., *(Canada) Ltd.*, 150.

14 The Waffle believed that only the federal government had the power, through the nationalization of major industries, to counteract American investment that threatened Canada's independence. See John Bullen, 'The Ontario Waffle and the Struggle for an Independent Socialist Canada: Conflict within the NDP,' *Canadian Historical Review* 64, 2 (1983), 188–215.

15 John Herd Thompson and Stephen J. Randall, *Canada and the United States: Ambivalent Allies* (Montreal: McGill-Queen's University Press, 1994), 253.

16 Jack Granatstein suggested that nationalism has been employed almost exclusively by Canada's elite in *Yankees Go Home? Canadians and Anti-Americanism* (Toronto: HarperCollins, 1996), x.

17 Jane Jenson and Rianne Mahon, 'Legacies for Labour of Two Decades of Crisis,' in Jenson and Mahon, eds., *The Challenge of Restructuring*, 73; Don Wells, 'The Impact of the Postwar Compromise on Canadian Unionism: The Formation of an Auto Workers Local in the 1950s,' *Labour/Le Travail* 36 (fall 1995), 147–73; Judy Fudge and Eric Tucker, *Labour before the Law: The Regulation of Workers' Collective Actions in Canada, 1900–1948* (Oxford: Oxford University Press, 2001).

18 Fudge and Tucker, *Labour before the Law*, 5.

19 Michael C. Harper, 'The Scope of the Duty to Bargain Concerning Business Transformations,' in Samuel Estreicher and Daniel G. Collins, eds., *Labor Law and Business Change: Theoretical and Transactional Perspectives* (New York: Quorum Books, 1988), 25.

20 The common law principle of advance notice in cases of individual termination was formalized by legislation in Saskatchewan (1929), Manitoba (1951), Nova Scotia (1964), and Newfoundland (1969). Memo, p. 4, Department of Labour, RG 27, Box 4465, File 47-2-4 pt 1, National Archives of Canada (NAC).

21 Jeffrey Sack and C. Michael Mitchell, *Ontario Labour Relations Board: Law and Practice* (Toronto: Butterworths, 1985).

22 Research Branch, Ontario Department of Labour, 'Background Information on Advance Notice and Severance Pay,' 20 January 1970, Ontario Ministry of Labour, RG 7-20-0, Box 2, File 69: Plant Closures and Layoffs, 1970–1, Archives of Ontario (AO).

23 Memo from deputy minister L.E. Couillard to the minister 8 June 1970; Department of Employment and Immigration, RG 118, Accession 1985–86/071, Box 90, File 3325-2-3 pt 1, NAC; and Arthur Krugar, *Human Adjustment to Industrial Conversion* (draft study prepared for the Task Force on Labour Relations), April 1968.

24 The Quebec Manpower Vocational Training and Qualification Act of 1969 provided advance notice of mass terminations of more than 10 employees

on a sliding scale of 4 months for terminations of more than 300 workers, 3 months for the lay-off of 100 to 299 employees, and 2 months for the dismissal of 10 to 99 employees. Jean Sexton, *Fermetures d'usines et reclassement de la main-d'oeuvre au Québec* (Quebec: Ministère du travail, 1975).

25 'Discussion on Technological Change,' 12 January 1970, Ontario Ministry of Labour, RG 7-20-0, Box 2, File 69, Plant Closures and Layoffs, 1970–71, AO.

26 D.C. McNeill, special projects officer to T.M. Eberlee, deputy minister, 5 October 1970. Dunlop's Toronto factory specialized in the manufacture of industrial rubber products such as conveyor belting and hosing. Ontario Ministry of Labour, RG 7-91 Interim Box 28, File: Dunlop of Canada, AO.

27 Editorial, 'Time of Grace,' *Toronto Star*, 10 April 1970.

28 Alexander Ross, 'Tale of a Plant Closure: No Pat Answers for 597,' *Financial Post*, 28 March 1970.

29 Ontario Labour Relations Board, *Annual Report* (Toronto, 1970), 356. The case was *Local 130 United Rubber, Cork, Linoleum and Plastic Workers of America* v. *Dunlop of Canada Limited and Scott-Atkinson International Ltd.*

30 'Students Protest Dunlop Closing,' *Oakville Journal Record*, 22 April 1970; and 'Negotiations Falter on Offer to Purchase, Operate Dunlop Plant,' *Globe and Mail*, 24 April 1970.

31 Harold Greer, 'Queen's Park Report,' *Brockville Recorder Times*, 21 March 1970.

32 Editorial, 'The Dunlop Caper,' *Peterborough Examiner*, 17 April 1970. See Jack Cahill, 'Foreign-controlled Companies Blamed for Most Layoffs,' *Toronto Daily Star*, Thursday 19 November 1979; and 'Foreign Control Called Unemployment Cause,' *Toronto Daily Star*, 12 December 1970.

33 Harold Greer, 'Queen's Park Report,' *Brockville Recorder Times*, 21 March 1970.

34 Editorial, 'The Government Has a Duty,' *Globe and Mail*, 1 April 1970.

35 Ross, 'Tale of a Plant Closure.'

36 Canada, *Hansard*, March 13, 1970, RG March 19, 1970, NAC. Federal NDP leader Tommy Douglas called on the government to 'take over and operate this plant, as was done with the Dosco steel plant in Sydney, at least until such time as the feasibility of the operation can be established and a course of action mapped out.' At the time, the steel plant was still widely seen as a public ownership success story.

37 Stephen Clarkson to Prime Minister Pierre Trudeau, 14 April 1970. Clarkson refers to a Liberal Party of Ontario resolution entitled 'Man and Social Change,' adopted in 1966, that stated, in part, that due to the effects of automation and technological change there should be 'obligations for

employers to provide advance notice in case of shutdown or re-location.'
Department of Industry, Trade and Commerce, RG 20, Volume 1609, File 6-
41, 1c, NAC.

38 Editorial, 'Mackasey Package on Labor Laws,' *London Free Press*, 10 March
1971.

39 But the agency was a 'toothless dragon' as it operated in a policy vacuum
during its ten year existence. Glen Norcliffe, 'Foreign Trade in Goods and
Services,' in John N.H. Britton, ed., *Canada and the Global Economy: The
Geography of Structural and Technological Change* (Montreal: McGill-Queen's
University Press, 1996), 26.

40 M.L. Skolnik, director of research to Len Haywood, chief economist,
Briefing Notes on Termination Legislation, page 2, 21 January 1976, On-
tario Ministry of Labour, RG 7-67, Box 3, File: Termination/Severance Pay
Legislation Review, 1972–4, AO.

41 J.K. Reynolds, secretary to the Cabinet to Dalton A. Bales, minister of
Labour, 28 April 1970, Cabinet Office, RG 75-6, Box 1, 1970, Cabinet Deci-
sions, Memos, AO. See also: Cabinet Office, RG 75-14, Cabinet Minutes,
Box 40, File 1970 Labour, AO.

42 'Ontario Bill Makes Employers Give Advance Layoff Notice,' *Toronto Daily
Star*, 28 May 1970.

43 Ontario's advance notice of mass termination did not cover workers with
less than three months service, workers on fixed-term contracts or on
suspension for disciplinary reasons, workers laid off due to labour dis-
putes or bankruptcies, or workers with temporary layoffs of less than
thirteen weeks. John W. Eleen and Ashley G. Bernardine, *Shutdown: The
Impact of Plant Shutdown, Extensive Employment Terminations and Layoffs on
the Workers and the Community* (Toronto: Ontario Federation of Labour,
1971), 90–1.

44 Ronald S. Saunders, *Permanent Layoffs: Some Issues in the Policy Debate*
(Toronto: Ontario Economic Council, 1981), 5.

45 Memo, 11 August 1970, RG 3-26, Box 177, File: Employment Standards Act,
AO.

46 John Schreiner, *Financial Post*, 13 June 1970.

47 Stanley J. Randall to Dalton Bales, 3 April 1970, RG. 3-26, Box 376, File:
Trade and Industry Branch-Plant Closings, Trade and Development,
January–December, 1970, AO.

48 Report by Ian Welton, Advance Notice of Termination – Steel Company of
Canada Ltd. (Page-Hersey Works and Welland Tube), 5–6, 8 August 1974,
Ontario Ministry of Labour, RG 7-67, Box 3, File: Review of Termination
Legislation (Interviews), 1974, AO.

49 Report by Ian Welton, Advance Notice of Termination: Chrysler, 25 April 1974, RG 7-67, Box 3, File: Review of Termination Legislation (Interview), 1974, AO.
50 Report by Ian Welton, 11 September 1974, page 4, RG 7-67, Box 3, File: Review of Termination Legislation (Interview), 1974, AO. A Supplemental Unemployment Benefits (SUB) plan required an employer to establish a trust fund to top up the income of temporarily laid-off workers. SUB was designed to keep temporarily laid-off workers available for work.
51 Intra-Memo from J.R. Kinley, director of Research Branch, 8 October 1974, RG 7–67, Box 3, File: Review of Termination Legislation (Interview), 1974, AO.
52 Fred Caloren, 'Layoffs, Shutdowns and Closures in Ontario Manufacturing, Mining and Trade Establishments, January 1971–June 1972' (unpublished paper, University of Ottawa 1974), 252.
53 John Kinley, director of the Research Branch to R.D. Johnston, deputy minister of Labour, Memo on 'Mass Lay-Offs in Ontario During 1971,' 3, June 1972, Ontario Ministry of Labour, RG 7-12, Box 80, File: 4228, AO.
54 Cabinet Submissions, James M. Mackay, policy development co-ordinator, 29 April 1975 and 12 May 1975, Ontario Ministry of Labour, RG 7-67. Box 2, File 2: Review of Termination Legislation, 1975, AO.
55 D.E. Hushion, executive director, Employment Services Division, to J.R. Kinley, Research Branch, Pension Plan Termination Insurance, 26 March 1975, RG 7-67, Box 2, File 2: Review of Termination Legislation, 1975, AO.
56 Cliff Pilkey to John Moynahan, plant chair, Dominion Forge, UAW Local 195, Papers of Hugh Peacock, Box 7, File 78, University of Windsor Archives (UWA).
57 Laxer, ed., (Canada) Ltd.
58 Stewart Cook quoted in 'No One Was Happy as Closing Debated,' Oshawa Times Gazette, 13 July 1978. For how the deindustrialization thesis contributed to the politicization of industrial restructuring see Mahon, The Politics of Industrial Restructuring, 134.
59 Robert L. Perry, GALT, USA: The 'American Presence' in a Canadian City (Toronto: Maclean-Hunter Limited, 1971), 52.
60 Canadian Forum, Special Issue, April 1972 reprinted in H.V. Nelles and Abraham Rotstein, eds., Nationalism or Local Control: Responses to George Woodcock (Toronto: New Press, 1973), vi.
61 Christian Bay, 'The Perils of Patriotism,' in Nelles and Rotstein, eds., Nationalism or Local Control, 23–4.
62 Bruce Hodgins, 'Nationalism, Decentralism and the Left,' in Nelles and Rotstein, eds., Nationalism or Local Control, 43. The deindustrialization

thesis later came under attack from Toronto Marxists who dismissed it as a myth 'symbolic of the theoretical poverty of left-nationalism.' See Steve Moore and Debi Wells, 'The Myth of Canadian De-industrialization,' in Craig Heron, ed., *Imperialism, Nationalism and Canada* (Toronto: New Hogtown Press, 1977), 46.

63 Steve Moore and Debi Wells, *Imperialism and the National Question in Canada* (Toronto, 1975), 44–52.

64 In his autobiography, Bob White recalls that the company had demanded a 25 cent an hour rollback in wages. *Hard Bargains: My Life on the Line* (Toronto: McClelland and Stewart, 1987), 184.

65 Telegram from John Washuta, local president, and Fred Hancock, plant chairman to Robert White, UAW Canada director, 18 August 1978, Canadian Auto Workers, MG 28 I 119, Box 354, File 23: Columbus McKinnon Ltd. Memoranda and Correspondence, 1977–9, NAC.

66 B. Rovers, international representative, to Robert White, 6 December 1978, Canadian Auto Workers, MG 28 I 119, Box 354, File 23: Columbus McKinnon Ltd. Memoranda and Correspondence, 1977–9, NAC.

67 Gord Parker, international representative, to Robert White, 23 November 1978, Canadian Auto Workers, MG 28 I 119, Box 354, File 23, NAC.

68 Ed Robinson, president UAW Local 1474 (DAAL Specialties in Collingwood, Ontario), to company management, 5 October 1978, MG 28 I 119, Box 354, File 23, NAC.

69 Pat Clancy, international representative, to Robert White, November 1978, MG 28 I 119, Box 354, File 23, NAC.

70 William J. Marshall international representative, to Robert White, 2 November 1978, MG 28 I 119, Box 354, File 23, NAC.

71 Sheila McGovern, 'Gray, Weeks Seek Last-ditch Talks to Keep Bendix Here,' *Windsor Daily Star*, 21 June 1980.

72 Wendy Cuthbertson, '"This Is Our Real Estate": How They Fight Shutdowns in Ontario,' *Solidarity* (March 1982).

73 Julian Hayashi, 'UAW Eyes Plant Takeover to Fight Closures,' *London Free Press*, 23 June 1980.

74 White, *Hard Bargains*, 224.

75 Sheila McGovern, 'Bendix Powderkeg! Peace Talks Continue,' *Windsor Daily Star*, 24 June 1980. It was also reported that workers gathered outside the plant's gate complained that 'Canadians are always suffering at the hands of Americans.'

76 Ibid.

77 Andy Morocko, interview by author, Windsor, 27 February 1998. Ed Lawrenson, interview by author, St. Clair Shores, 26 February 1998.

78 White, *Hard Bargains*, 228.
79 Dave Elsila, 'Standing Up by Sitting Down,' *Solidarity* (5 September 1980).
80 'Kicked Out, They Kicked Back,' *Solidarity* (August 1980).
81 Editorial, 'Tougher Plant Closing Laws not Answer,' *Financial Times of Canada*, 25 August 1980.
82 *Newsletter*, Public Relations Department, Canada, UAW, Research Department, Box 116, Folder 116–17, Walter Reuther Library (WRL).
83 Publicity UAW Proposal (Houdaille sit-down), 6 September 1980, Laura Sky to Wendy, Buzz, and Doug, Canadian Auto Workers, MG 28 I119, United Auto Workers, Box 309, File 11, Films, NAC.
84 Charlotte Yates, 'North American Autoworkers' Response to Restructuring,' in Miriam Golden and Jonas Pontusson, eds., *Bargaining for Change: Union Politics in North America and Europe* (Ithaca: Cornell University Press, 1992), 112. Yates is supported by Sam Gindin, a former director of research for the Canadian UAW in *The Canadian Auto Workers: The Birth and Transformation of a Union* (Toronto: James Lorimer and Company, 1995).
85 Miriam Smith, 'The Canadian Labour Congress: From Continentalism to Economic Nationalism,' *Studies in Political Economy* 38 (summer 1992), 35–60.
86 The records of the United Steelworkers of America, District 6, the International Association of Machinists, and the International Union of Electrical Workers (IUE) all reveal nationalist agitation against plant closings. Several union locals facing plant closings also resorted to illegal strikes to ensure adequate severance packages. For example, members of IUE Local 508 at the Prestolite (Sangamo) plant in Guelph walked out on 21 April 1971. The Prestolite Company of Canada Ltd. Sarnia, Ontario, General Correspondence, 1970–1975, IUE, MG 28 I264, File 49-7, Local 508, NAC.
87 'Demonstrate! It Could Be Your Job Next,' *UE News (Canadian Edition)* 43, 15 (1980), 1.
88 William J. Marshall, international representative, to Robert White, 18 October 1980, Canadian Auto Workers, MG 28 I119, Box 324, File 2: Ontario Select Committee on Plant Shutdowns, 1980–2, NAC.
89 'Tory Measures on Plant Closings Termed Political Window-Dressing,' *UE News (Canadian Edition)* 43, 17 (1980), 1.
90 Robert White speech to OFL demonstration at Queen's Park, 18 October 1980, Canadian Auto Workers, MG 28 I119 Volume 250, File 2, NAC.
91 Transcript of Committee Hearings, 9 December 1980, RG 49-173, Box C-294, AO.
92 Canadian Federation of Independent Business, Exhibit 75-80, page 3, RG 49-173, Box C-295, AO.

93 Transcripts of Select Committee on Plant Shutdowns and Employee Adjustment, 5 November 1980, 1, Select Committees, RG 49-173, Box C-294, AO.

94 Select Committee on Plant Shutdowns and Adjustment, *Interim Report*, December 1980, 33, Select Committees, RG 49-173, Bx C-294, AO.

95 Harry N. Shardlow to File, 11 February 1982, RG 7-11, Box 54, File: Dominion Auto Accessories Ltd., AO.

96 Memo, Harry N. Shardlow, 4 November 1983, RG 7-11, Box 54, File: Severance Pay Preparation, 1983, AO.

97 Esther Thompson, UAW Local 195 recording secretary, RG 7-11, Box 54, File: Dominion Auto Accessories Ltd, AO. Amalgamated Local 195 represented workers in Windsor's troubled auto parts plants. It was thus devastated by plant closures. In fact, of the 2,700 members it represented in January 1981, only 1,371 were left by December 1981.

98 United States. Office of Technology Assessment, *Plant Closings: Advance Notice and Rapid Response, Special Report* (Washington, 1986), 37–8. The Conference Board of Canada, in turn, reported a 'developing consensus' among Canadian corporate executives in favour of severance pay, advance notice, extended health care, and out-placement. See: *Retrenchment and Beyond: The Acid Test of Resource Management* (Ottawa: Conference Board of Canada, 1982).

99 Sam Ginden, research director to Shirley Carr, executive vice-president of the Canadian Labour Congress, 13 November 1980, Canadian Auto Workers, MG 28 I 119, UAW, Box 326, File 1: Plant Closures, Reference Material, Correspondence (1), 1979–80, NAC.

100 'Windsor Plant Shuts Down Early,' *Windsor Daily Star*, 10 December 1981.

101 David Christopherson, interview by author, Hamilton, 6 February 1998.

102 Ontario, Ministry of Labour, *Preferential Hiring Rights in Business Relocations and Closures* (Toronto, June 1983), 1.

103 Andy Morocko, interview by author, Windsor, 27 February 1998.

104 White, *Hard Bargains*, 228.

105 *Final Offer: Bob White and the CAW Fight for Independence* (National Film Board, 1985).

106 See Sam Gindin, 'Breaking Away: The Formation of the Canadian Auto Workers,' *Studies in Political Economy* 29 (summer 1989), 64. For an American insider's perspective see S. Friedman, 'Discussion: IR developments in U.S. and Canada,' in *Proceedings of the 41st Annual Meeting of the Industrial Relations Research Association* (Madison: University of Wisconsin Press), 288.

107 Christine Stansell, 'Woman in Nineteenth Century America,' *Gender and History* 11, 3 (1999), 423

Conclusion

1 Reinhold Niebuhr quoted in Christopher Lasch, *The True and Only Heaven: Progress and Its Critics* (New York: W.W. Norton, 1991), 371.
2 Steve Early, 'Drawing the Line on Give Backs,' *NTN* (5 February 1983).
3 Jean Claude Parrot, 'Stopping Concessions: Our Survival as a Movement is at Stake,' *Our Times* (1983), 33–4. The militancy of this conference contrasted sharply with another organized by the labour mainstream. Nine days beforehand, Tom Turner, president of the Metropolitan Detroit AFL-CIO, admitted to affiliates that there were more legislators registered than delegates: 'Please, please do everything possible to encourage a turnout among your members ... if there is not a greater turnout than our current registrations indicate, the AFL-CIO is going to look ridiculous and our legislative program seriously damaged.' Tom Turner (president of council) to Brothers and Sisters, 27 February 1981, Metro Detroit AFL-CIO Council Collection (Part 4) Acc 53, Box 97, File 100-53, 1981 Uniroyal (Plant Closing) Along with Weatherization Curriculum, Walter Reuther Library (WRL).
4 George Walker, 'Steel Missed, Hearth and Soul,' Youngstown *Vindicator*, 14 September 1997, A5.
5 Sam Donnorummo, interview by Donna DeBlasio, 1991.
6 Lars Osberg, Fred Wien, and Jan Grude, *Vanishing Jobs: Canada's Changing Workplaces* (Toronto: James Lorimer, 1995), 31.
7 John N.H. Britton, 'Introduction,' in John N.H. Britton, ed., *Canada and the Global Economy: The Geography of Structural and Technological Change* (Montreal: McGill-Queen's University Press, 1996), 25–6.
8 Jane Jenson and Rianne Mahon, 'North American Labour: Divergent Trajectories,' in Jane Jenson and Rianne Mahon, eds., *The Challenge of Restructuring: North American Labour Movements Respond* (Philadelphia: Temple University Press, 1993), 9.
9 Kim Moody, *An Injury to All: The Decline of American Unionism* (New York: verso, 1988), 196–7.
10 Stephen Herzenberg makes this point in relation to the UAW, but it is true of others. 'Whither Social Unionism? Labor and Restructuring in the United States Auto Industry,' in Jenson and Mahon, eds., *The Challenge of Restructuring*, 320.
11 The U.S. labour movement's campaign against the North American Free Trade Agreement (NAFTA) ignited rank-and-file patriotism. American trade unionists directed their campaign against the export of jobs to Mexico. This patriotic response comes under heavy criticism from anti-

nationalists on the political left. Jefferson Cowie, 'National Struggles in a Transnational Europe: A Critical Analysis of U.S. Labor's Campaign Against NAFTA,' *Labor Studies Journal* 55, 4 (1996), 473–88.

12 Elizabeth Faue, 'Community, Class, and Comparison in Labour History and Local History,' *Labour History* (Australia) 78 (May 2000), 155.

13 Lucy Taksa, 'Like a Bicycle, Forever Teetering between Individualism and Collectivism: Considering Community in Relation to Labour History,' *Labour History* (Australia) 78 (May 2000), 17.

14 Bruce Nissen, *Fighting for Jobs: Case Studies of Labor-Community Coalitions Confronting Plant Closings* (Albany: State University of New York Press, 1995), 169.

15 Ibid., 8.

16 Faue, 'Community, Class, and Comparison,' 155.

17 The attraction of the 'community mobilization' model is best expressed in Faue's study of Minneapolis in the 1930s. Women played a leading and active role in alternative trade unionism: 'The community-based unionism that emerged in the 1930s drew on the configurations of gender and class embedded in local solidarities, it embraced familial and fraternal sanctions of activism for both men and women and legitimated struggle that was expressive of and rooted in the claims of community.' However, the subsequent shift in the base of working-class mobilization from the community to the workplace, and from the locally to nationally organized unions, acted to exclude and marginalize women.

18 As part of a symposium on Lynd's book see Roger Horowitz, 'What Did Workers Want in the 1930s, Anyway?' *Labor History* 38, 2–3 (spring–summer 1997), 169. For the most noteworthy of these earlier efforts see Alice Lynd and Staughton Lynd, eds., *Rank and File: Personal Histories of Working-Class Organizers* (Boston: Beacon Press, 1973).

19 Dana Frank, *Buy American: The Untold Story of Economic Nationalism* (Boston: Breacon Press, 1999), 132.

20 Ibid., 249.

21 Murray E.G. Smith, 'Political Economy and the Canadian Working Class: Marxism or National Reformism?' *Labour/Le Travail* 46 (fall 2000), 349.

22 For a revealing look at the negotiations see Bruce Doern and Brian Tomlin, *Faith and Fear: The Free Trade Story* (Toronto: Stoddart, 1991).

23 John Herd Thompson and Stephen J. Randall, *Canada and the United States: Ambivalent Allies* (Montreal: McGill-Queen's University Press, 1994), 288.

24 The best study of economic nationalist opposition to free trade is Sylvia B. Bashevkin, *True Patriot Love: The Politics of Canadian Nationalism* (Toronto: Oxford University Press, 1991). See also Jeffrey M. Ayres, 'Political Process

and Popular Protest: The Mobilization against Free Trade in Canada,' *American Journal of Economics and Sociology* 55, 4 (1996), 473–88.

25 Gerald P. Glyde, 'Canadian Labour and the Free Trade Agreement,' *Labor Studies Journal* 17, 4 (1993), 4.

26 Jeffrey M. Ayres, 'From National to Popular Sovereignty? The Evolving Globalization of Protest Activity in Canada,' *International Journal of Canadian Studies* 16 (1997), 122.

27 Sylvia Bashevkin, 'In the Shadow of Free Trade: Nationalism, Feminism and Identity Politics in Contemporary English Canada,' *Journal of Canadian Studies* 35, 2 (2000), 111.

28 Ayres, 'From National to Popular Sovereignty?' Economic nationalism also continues to be the rallying cry of the Canadian Labour Congress. Miriam Smith, 'The Canadian Labour Congress: From Continentalism to Economic Nationalism,' *Studies in Political Economy* 38 (summer 1992), 56.

29 David Sobel and Susan Meurer, *Working at Inglis: The Life and Death of a Canadian Factory* (Toronto: James Lorimer and Company, 1994), 7. Pro-labour economists such as Andrew Jackson have also argued that the wave of plant closings that struck industrial Ontario had little to do with the free trade agreement. Andrew Jackson, 'The Free Trade Agreement: A Decade Later,' *Studies in Political Economy* 58 (spring 1999).

30 Denis Stairs, 'North American Continentalism – Perspectives and Policies in Canada,' in David M. Cameron, ed., *Regionalism and Supranationalism: Challenges and Alternatives to the Nation-State in Canada and Europe* (Montreal: Institute for Research on Public Policy, 1981), 83–110.

31 Leo Gerard quoted in Sobel and Meurer, *Working at Inglis*.

Bibliography

Archival Sources

Canada

Archives of Ontario (AO), Toronto
  Cabinet Office, RG 75.
  Ministry of Industry and Tourism, RG 9.
  Ministry of Labour, RG 7.
  Ontario Economic Council, RG 34.
  Ontario Press Clippings, MG 755.
  Select Committees, RG 49.
McMaster University Archives (MUA), Hamilton
  Canadian Auto Workers Collection.
  Canadian Liberation Movement.
  Hamilton and District Labour Council Papers.
  Peter C. Newman Papers.
  Radical Archives.
  Richard Allen Papers.
  United Electrical, Radio and Machine Workers (UE), Local 504.
  United Steelworkers of America, District 6.
  United Steelworkers of America, Locals 1005, 2868, 3692.
  Westinghouse Canada Inc.
National Archives of Canada (NAC), Ottawa
  Beach Foundry Papers, MG 28 I 264.
  Canadian Auto Workers, MG 28 I 119.
  Canadian Chamber of Commerce, MG 28 III 62.
  Canadian Labour Congress, MG 28 I 103.
  Canadian Manufacturers' Association, MG 28 I 230.

Department of Employment and Immigration, RG 118.
Department of External Affairs, RG 25.
Department of Industry, Trade and Commerce, RG 20.
Department of Labour, RG 27.
Department of Urban Affairs, RG 127.
Economic Council of Canada, RG 75.
International Union of Electrical Workers Papers, MG 28 I 264.
Michael Fenwick Papers, MG 31 B 17.
Privy Council Office, RG 2.
Royal Commissions, RG 33.
Textile Workers Union of America, MG 28 I 219.
United Steelworkers of America, MG 28 I 268.
Queen's University Archives (QUA), Kingston
Canadian Federation of Mayors and Municipalities Papers.
Committee for an Independent Canada Papers.
Liberal Party of Ontario.
University of Windsor Archives (UWA), Windsor
Papers of Hugh Peacock.
Papers of Mayor Bert Weeks, 1975–82.
Windsor and District Chamber of Commerce.
Windsor Municipal Library–Archives (WMA)
Records of the City Clerk.
Windsor-Essex County Development Commission.

United States

Bentley Historical Library (BHL), Ann Arbor, Michigan.
James G. O'Hara Papers.
Governor Peter Milliken Papers.
Senator Philip A. Hart Papers.
Kettering University Archives / General Motors Institute (GMI), Flint, Michigan.
Dave Langdon Papers.
Frigidaire Collection.
Gerald Ford Presidential Library (Ford), Ann Arbor, Michigan.
Arthur F. Burns Papers.
Council of Economic Advisors.
John C. Vickerman Papers.
L. William Seidman Papers.
White House Records.

Jimmy Carter Presidential Library (Carter), Atlanta, Georgia.
  White House Records.
Library of Congress (LoC), Washington, DC.
  Proceedings of Government Hearings.
Michigan State Library, Lansing.

Milwaukee Historical Society (MHS), Milwaukee, Wisconsin.
  Allis-Chalmers Records.
National Archives and Records Administration (NARA), College Park,
  Maryland.
  Richard Nixon Papers.
Ohio Historical Society (OHS), Columbus, Ohio.
  Brush-McCoy Pottery, MSS 624.
  Department of Development, 4111.
  Donaldson Baking Company, MSS 818.
  Donna Pope, 1974–81, MSS 863.
  Federal Glass Company, MSS 665.
  Ohio AFL-CIO, MSS 252.
  Ray C. Bliss Papers, MSS 768.
  United Steelworkers of America, District 27, MSS 511.
  Youngstown Sheet and Tube Company, MSS 776.
Penn State University Archives (PSUA), State College, Pennsylvania.
  Clarence Eaton Papers.
  Industrial Site Renderings.
  Paul Ilig Papers.
  United Steelworkers of America Archives.
State Archives of Michigan (SAM), Lansing, Michigan.
  Commerce Department, Economic Development, RG 85-133.
  Commerce Department, Director's Office, RG 86-51.
  Governor Peter Milliken Papers, RG 88-269.
University of Akron Archives (UAA), Akron, Ohio.
  B.F. Goodrich Collection.
  Goodyear Tire and Rubber Collection.
  United Rubber Workers.
University of Pittsburgh Archives (UPA), Pittsburgh, Pennsylvania.
  Allegheny Conference on Human Development.
  Allegheny County Labor Council Records, 1961–85.
  Armor Workers Collection, 1983–85.
  Charles McCollester Collection.
  Denominational Ministry Strategy Records, 1982–96.

Environmentalists for Full Employment, 1977–82.
Robert 'Joe' Jurich Collection.
Tri-State Conference on Steel Records, 1982–94.
United Electrical Workers Archives.
United Electrical Workers Union Local 610, Campaign to Save Union Switch.
Women in Urban Crisis Pittsburgh Records, 1969–85.
Walter Reuther Library, Wayne State University (WRL), Detroit, Michigan.
Douglas A. Fraser Collection.
Metro Detroit AFL-CIO Council Collection.
Michigan AFL-CIO (William Marshall).
United Auto Workers Collection.
Western Reserve Historical Society (WRHS), Cleveland, Ohio.
Acme Cleveland Corporation, 1874–1982.
Buckeye Brass and Manufacturing Company, 1912–82.
Cyrus Stephen Eaton Papers, 1920–83.
Fisher Body-Coid Road Plant, 1920–83.
TRW Inc., 1900–69.
Youngstown Historical Center for Industry and Labor (YHCIL), Youngstown, Ohio.
Ecumenical Coalition of the Mahoning Valley, Inc. Records.
Gerald Dickey Collection.
Industrial Drawings and Blueprint Collection.
Lykes-Youngstown Corporation Audiovisual Archives.
Robert Wolfe Photo Collection.
Staughton Lynd Papers.
William Brown Papers.
William J. Carney Papers.
U.S. Steel Company-Ohio Works Photograph Collection.
Youngstown Industries Slide Collection.

Oral History Projects Consulted

Ottawa District Labour Council's Workers' Heritage Project. The Beach Foundry 'Made In Ottawa' component of the project included interviews with ten former employees. Ken Clavette (coordinator), 1996.
Youngstown Historical Center of Industry and Labor. This oral history project completed interviews with thirty-eight displaced steel mill workers. Donna DeBlasio (interviewer), 1991.
Youngstown State University. The Sheet and Tube Shutdown Project completed interviews with forty-six area residents about the mill's closing, 1981.

Published and Scholarly Sources

Adamson, Arthur. 'Identity through Metaphor: An Approach to the Question of Regionalism in Canadian Literature.' *Studies in Canadian Literature* 5 (September 1980), 83–99.

Addison, John T. 'Job Security in the United States: Law, Collective Bargaining, Policy and Practice.' *British Journal of Industrial Relations* 24, 3 (1986), 381–418.

– ed. *Job Displacement: Consequences and Implications for Policy.* Detroit: Wayne State University Press, 1991.

Alessio, Dominic T. 'Capitalist Realist Art: Industrial Images of Hamilton, Ontario, 1884–1910.' *Journal of Urban History* 18, 4 (1992), 442–69.

Allen, Patrick, and Joan Howard. *Canada's Golden Horseshoe: An ESL/Geography Module.* Toronto: OISE Press, 1982.

Altman, Irwin, and Setha M. Low, eds. *Place Attachment.* New York: Plenum Press, 1992.

The American Heritage Dictionary of the English Language. Boston: Houghton Mifflin, 1992.

Anderson, Benedict. *Imagined Communities: Reflections on the Origins and Spread of Nationalism.* New York: Verso, 1991.

Anderson, David. 'The Dimensions of the Midwest.' *MidAmerica* 1 (October 1973), 7–15.

Anderson, J.S. Duncan, and R. Hudson, eds. *Redundant Spaces in Cities and Regions?* London: Academic Press, 1983.

Anderson, Kay J. *Vancouver's Chinatown: Racial Discourse in Canada, 1875–1980.* Montreal: McGill-Queen's University Press, 1991.

Architectural Record. *Building for Industry: An Architectural Record Book.* Westport, CT: Greenwood Press, 1972.

Armstrong, Pat. *Labour Pains: Women's Work in Crisis.* Toronto: The Women's Press, 1984.

Aronsen, Lawrence, 'An Open Door to the North: The Liberal Government and the Expansion of American Foreign Investment, 1945–1953.' *American Review of Canadian Studies* 22.2 (1992), 167–97.

Aullett, Judy Root. 'Blue Collar Families in the 1981–1983 Recession: An Examination of Family and Gender in a Period of Economic Decline.' PhD diss., Michigan State University, 1986.

Ayres, Jeffrey M. 'From National to Popular Sovereignty? The Evolving Globalization of Protest Activity in Canada,' *International Journal of Canadian Studies* 16 (1997), 107–23.

– 'Political Process and Popular Protest: The Mobilization against Free Trade in Canada.' *American Journal of Economics and Sociology* 55 (1996), 473–88.

Azzi, Stephen. *Walter Gordon and the Rise of Canadian Nationalism*. Montreal: McGill-Queen's University Press, 1999.

Babson, Steve. *Working Detroit: The Making of a Union Town*. Detroit: Wayne State University Press, 1984.

Bailey, Peter. 'Breaking the Sound Barrier: A Historian Listens to Noise.' *Body and Society* 2, 2 (1996), 49–66.

Bamberger, Bill, and Cathy N. Davidson. *Closing: The Life and Death of an American Factory*. New York: W.W. Norton and Company, 1998.

Barnhart, Clarence L. *The New Century Cyclopedia of Names*. New York: Appleton-Century-Crofts, 1954.

– *The Second Barnhart Dictionary of New English*. New York: Harper and Row, 1980.

Baron, Ava, ed. *Work Engendered: Toward a New History of American Labor*. Ithaca, NY: Cornell University Press, 1991.

Barthes, Roland. *Mythologies*. Trans. Annette Lavers. 1952. Reprint, New York: Hill and Wang, 1972 [1952].

Bashevkin, Sylvia. 'In the Shadow of Free Trade: Nationalism, Feminism and Identity Politics in Contemporary English Canada.' *Journal of Canadian Studies* 35, 2 (2000).

– *True Patriot Love: The Politics of Canadian Nationalism*. Toronto: Oxford University Press, 1991.

Beauregard, Robert. *Voices of Decline: The Postwar Fate of U.S. Cities*. Cambridge: Blackwell, 1993.

Bell, Daniel. *The Coming of Post-Industrial Society: A Venture in Social Forecasting*. 1973. Reprint, New York: Basic Books, 1976.

Bender, Thomas. *Toward an Urban Vision: Ideas and Institutions in Nineteenth-Century America*. Lexington: University Press of Kentucky, 1975.

Bensman, David, and Roberta Lynch. *Rusted Dreams: Hard Times in a Steel Community*. Berkeley: University of California Press, 1988.

Bercuson, David, and J.L. Granatstein. *The Collins Dictionary of Canadian History, 1867 to Present*. Toronto: Collins, 1988.

Berry, Kimberley. 'She's No Lady: The Experience and Expression of Gender among Women Taxi Drivers.' Master's thesis, St Mary's University, 1996.

Biggs, Lindy. *The Rational Factory: Architecture, Technology, and Work in America's Age of Mass Production*. Baltimore: Johns Hopkins University Press, 1996.

Bliss, Michael. 'Canadianizing American Business: the Roots of the Branch Plant.' In Ian Lumsden, ed. *Close the 49th Parallel etc: The Americanization of Canada*. Toronto: University of Toronto Press, 1970.

Block, Fred. *Postindustrial Possibilities: A Critique of Economic Discourse*. Berkeley: University of California Press, 1990.

Bluestone, Barry, and Bennett Harrison. *Capital and Communities: The Causes and Consequences of Private Disinvestment*. Washington: Progressive Alliance, 1980.

Bluestone, Barry, and Bennett Harrison. *The Deindustrialization of America: Plant Closings, Community Abandonment, and the Dismantling of Basic Industry*. New York: Basic Books, 1982.

Bodnar, John. 'Power and Memory in Oral History: Workers and Managers at Studebaker.' *Journal of American History* 75 (1989), 1201–21.

– *Remaking America: Public Memory, Commemoration, and Patriotism in the Twentieth Century*. Princeton, NJ: Princeton University Press, 1992.

– *The Transplanted: A History of Immigrants in Urban America*. Bloomington: Indiana University Press, 1985.

Boers, Frank, and Murielle Demecheleer. 'A Few Metaphorical Models in (Western) Economic Discourse.' In Wolf-Andreas Liebert, Gisela Redeker, and Linda Waugh, eds. *Discourses and Perspectives in Cognitive Linguistics*. Amsterdam: John Benjamins Publishing Co., 1997.

Bonnifield, Paul. *The Dust Bowl: Men, Dirt and Depression*. Albuquerque: University of New Mexico Press, 1979.

Borchert, John R. *Northern Heartland*. Minneapolis: University of Minnesota Press, 1987.

Bothwell, Robert. *Canada and the United States: The Politics of Partnership*. Toronto: University of Toronto Press, 1992.

Bourgault, Pierre. *Innovation and the Structure of Canadian Industry*. Background Study No. 23, Science Council of Canada, 1972.

Boyte, Harry C. *The Backyard Revolution*. Philadelphia: Temple University Press, 1980.

Braverman, Harry. *Labor and Monopoly Capital: The Degradation of Work in the Twentieth Century*. New York: Monthly Review Press, 1974.

Breuilly, John. *Nationalism and the State*. New York: St Martin's Press, 1982.

Britton, John N.H., ed. *Canada and the Global Economy: The Geography of Structural and Technological Change*. Montreal: McGill-Queen's University Press, 1996.

Broadfoot, Barry. *Ten Lost Years, 1929–1939: Memories of Canadians Who Survived the Depression*. 1973. Reprint, Markham, ON: Paperjacks, 1975.

Brody, David. 'On the Decline of American Steel.' *Pennsylvania Magazine of History and Biography* 113, 4 (1989), 627–33.

Bruno, Robert. *Steelworker Alley: How Class Works in Youngstown*. Ithaca, NY: Cornell University Press, 1999.

Building for Industry: An Architectural Record Book. Westport, CT: Greenwood Press, 1972.

Bullen, John. 'The Ontario Waffle and the Struggle for an Independent Socialist Canada: Conflict within the NDP.' *Canadian Historical Review* 64, 2 (1983),
188–215.

Burke, Ronald J. 'The Closing at Canadian Admiral: Correlates of Individual
Well-being Sixteen Months after Shutdown.' *Psychology Reports* 55, 1 (1984),
91–8.

Buss, Terry F., and F. Stevens Redburn. *Shutdown at Youngstown: Public Policy
for Mass Unemployment*. Albany: State University of New York Press, 1983.

Buttimer, Anne. 'Home, Reach, and the Sense of Place.' In Anne Buttimer
and David Seamon, eds. *The Human Experience of Space and Place*. London:
Croom Helm, 1980.

Calhoun, Craig. 'History, Anthropology, and the Study of Communities: Some
Problems in Macfarlane's Proposal.' *Social History* 3 (1978), 363–73.

Caloren, Fred. 'Layoffs, Shutdowns and Closures in Ontario Manufacturing,
Mining and Trade Establishments, January 1971–June 1972.' University of
Ottawa: unpublished paper, 1974.

Camp, Scott D. *Worker Response to Plant Closings: Steelworkers in Johnstown and
Youngstown*. New York: Garland Publishers, 1995.

Campbell, Douglas F., and John J. Nicholson. 'The Sydney Steelworkers'
Adjustments to Economic Insecurity.' Paper presented to meeting of Atlantic Provinces Sociologists and Anthropologists, 1069.

Campbell, Robert. *The Full-Employment Objective in Canada, 1945–1985: Historical, Conceptual, and Comparative Perspectives*. Ottawa: Economic Council of
Canada, 1991.

Canadian Labour Market Productivity Centre. *Labour Adjustments in Canada*.
Ottawa: Government of Canada, 1986.

Carson, Gordon B., ed. *Production Handbook*. New York: Ronald Press, 1958.

Castells, Manuel. *The City and the Grassroots*. Berkeley: University of California
Press, 1983.

Castells, Manuel, and Peter Hall. *Technopoles of the World: The Making of 21st
Century Industrial Complexes*. London: Routledge, 1994.

Castle, Donald Richard. 'The Response of the Mansfield City Schools to Local
Deindustrialization, 1968–84.' PhD diss., University of Akron, 1990.

Chandler, Alfred. *Scale and Scope: The Dynamics of Industrial Capitalism*. Cambridge, MA: Belknap Press of Harvard University Press, 1990.

Chase, Susan E., and Collen Bell. 'Interpreting the Complexity of Women's
Subjectivity.' In Eva M. McMahan and Kim Lacy Rogers, eds. *Interactive Oral
History Interviewing*. Hillsdale, NJ: Lawrence Erlbaum, 1994.

Clark, Paul, et al. 'Deindustrialization: A Panel Discussion.' *Pennsylvannia
History* 58, 3 (1991), 181–211.

Clecak, Peter. *America's Quest for the Ideal Self: Dissent and Fulfillment in the 60s and 70s*. New York: Oxford University Press, 1983.

Clement, Wallace. *Continental Corporate Power: Economic Linkages Between Canada and the United States*. Toronto: McClelland and Stewart, 1977.

Cobb, James. 'From Muskogee to Luckenbach: Country Music and the Southernization of America.' *Journal of Popular Culture* 16 (1982), 81–91.

Coffey, William J., and Mario Polèse. 'Le déclin de l'empire Montréalais: regard sur l'économie d'une métropole en mutation.' *Recherches sociographiques* 34, 3 (1993), 417–37.

Cohen, Lizabeth. 'What Kind of World Have We Lost? Workers' Lives and Deindustrialization in the Museum.' *American Quarterly* 41, 4 (1989), 670–81.

Cohen, Stephen S., and John Zysman. *Manufacturing Matters: The Myth of the Post-Industrial Economy*. New York: Basic Books, 1986.

The Columbia Encyclopedia. 5th ed. New York: Houghton Mifflin, 1993.

Conference Board of Canada. *Retrenchment and Beyond: The Acid Test of Resource Management*. Ottawa: Conference Board of Canada, 1982.

Confino, Alon. *The Nation as Local Metaphor: Wurttemberg, Imperial Germany, and National Memory, 1871–1918*. Chapel Hill: University of North Carolina Press, 1997.

Connerly, Charles E. 'The Community Question: An Extension of Wellman and Leighton.' *Urban Affairs Quarterly* 20, 4 (1985).

Cooper and Lybrand. *Closing Plants: Planning and Implementing Strategies*. Financial Executives Research Foundation, 1987.

Cosgrove, Denis, and Stephen Daniels, eds. *The Iconography of Landscape: Essays on the Symbolic Representation, Design and Uses of Past Environments*. New York: Cambridge University Press, 1988.

Cowie, Jefferson. 'National Struggles in a Transnational Europe: A Critical Analysis of U.S. Labor's Campaign against NAFTA.' *Labor Studies Journal* 55, 4 (1996), 473–88.

Critchlow, Donald T. *Studebaker: The Life and Death of an American Corporation*. Bloomington: Indiana University Press, 1996.

Csikszentmihalyi, Mihaly, and Eugene Rochberg-Halton, eds. *The Meaning of Things: Domestic Symbols and the Self*. Cambridge: Cambridge University Press, 1981.

Cumbler, John T. *A Social History of Economic Decline: Business, Politics and Work in Trenton*. New Brunswick, NJ: Rutgers University Press, 1989.

Cunningham, Mary. *Power Play: What Really Happened at Bendix*. New York: Linden Press, 1984.

Davidoff, Leonore, and Catherine Hall. *Family Fortunes: Men and Women of the English Middle Class, 1780–1850*. Chicago: University of Chicago Press, 1987.

Davis, Donald F. *Conspicuous Production: Automobiles and Elites in Detroit, 1899–1933*. Philadelphia: Temple University Press, 1988.
– 'The "Metropolitan Thesis" and the Writing of Canadian Urban History.' *Urban History Review* 14, 3 (1985), 95–113.
Davis, Fred. *Yearning for Yesterday: A Sociology of Nostalgia*. London: Collier Macmillan, 1979.
Davis, Natalie Zemon. *Society and Culture in Early Modern France*. Stanford, CA: Stanford University Press, 1975.
Dear, M.J., J.J. Drake, and L.G. Reeds, eds. *Steel City: Hamilton and Region*. Toronto: University of Toronto Press, 1987.
DeBlasio, Donna M. 'Oral History, Deindustrialization and the Museum Exhibit: "By the Sweat of Their Brow: Forging the Steel Valley."' Paper presented to the American Oral History Association, Buffalo, New York, October 1998.
Desan, Suzanne. 'Crowds, Community, and Ritual in the Work of E.P. Thompson and Natalie Davis.' In Lynn Hunt, ed. *The New Cultural History*. Berkeley: University of California Press, 1989.
Dicken, Peter. *Global Shift: Industrial Change in a Turbulent World*. London: Harper and Row, 1986.
Dickerson, Dennis C. *Out of the Crucible: Black Steelworkers in Western Pennsylvania, 1875–1980*. Albany: State University of New York Press, 1986.
Dictionary of Canadian English: A Dictionary of Canadianisms on Historical Principles. Toronto: Gage Education Publishing Co., 1991.
Dodson, Peter Michael. 'Import Challenge, Sectoral Response and the Decline of American Integrated Steelmaking, 1959–1982.' PhD diss., University of Virginia, 1985.
Doern, Bruce, and Brian Tomlin. *Faith and Fear: The Free Trade Story*. Toronto: Stoddart, 1991.
Doezema, Marianne. *American Realism and the Industrial Age*. Cleveland: Cleveland Museum of Art, 1980.
Donaghy, Greg. 'A Continental Philosophy: Canada, the United States, and the Negotiation of the Autopact, 1963–1965.' *International Journal* (1998), 441–64.
Doro, Sue. *Blue Collar Goodbyes*. Watsonville, CA: Papier-Mache Press, 1992.
Doucet, Michael, and John Weaver. *Housing the North American City*. Montreal: McGill-Queen's University Press, 1991.
Downs, Roger, and David Stea. *Maps of Minds: Reflections on Cognitive Mapping*. New York: Harper and Row, 1977.
Drache, Daniel. *The Deindustrialization of Canada and Its Implications for Labour*. Ottawa: Canadian Centre for Policy Alternatives, 1989.

Dublin, Thomas. *When the Mines Closed: Stories of Struggles in Hard Times.* Ithaca, NY: Cornell University Press, 1998.

Dudley, Kathryn Marie. *The End of the Line: Lost Jobs, New Lives in Postindustrial America.* Chicago: University of Chicago Press, 1994.

Dunk, Thomas W. *It's A Working Man's Town: Male Working-Class Culture.* Montreal: McGill-Queen's University Press, 1991.

Ehrenberg, Ronald G., and George H. Jacubson. 'Advance Notification of Plant Closings: Does It Matter?' *Industrial Relations: A Journal of Economy and Society* 28, 1 (1989), 60–71

Eleen, John W., and Ashley G. Bernardine. *Shutdown: The Impact of Plant Shutdown, Extensive Employment Terminations and Layoffs on the Workers and the Community.* Toronto: Ontario Federation of Labour, 1971.

Eley, Geoff, and Ronald Grigor Suny, eds. *Becoming National: A Reader.* New York: Oxford University Press, 1996.

Ellem, Bradon, and John Shields. 'Making a "Union Town": Class, Gender and Consumption in Inter-war Broken Hill.' *Labour History* (Australia), 78 (2000), 116–40.

Fainstein, Susan S. 'Local Mobilization and Economic Discontent.' In Michael Peter Smith and Joe R. Feagin, eds. *The Capitalist City: Global Restructuring and Community Politics.* Oxford: Blackwell, 1987.

Faue, Elizabeth. 'Community, Class, and Comparison in Labour History and Local History.' *Labour History* (Australia) 78 (2000), 155–62.

– *Community of Suffering and Struggle: Women, Men, and the Labor Movement in Minneapolis, 1915–1945.* Chapel Hill: University of North Carolina Press, 1991.

Ferraro, Gary P. *The Cultural Dimension of International Business.* Englewood Cliffs, NJ: Prentice-Hall, 1990.

Filipelli, Ronald L., and Mark McColloch. *Cold War in the Working Class: The Rise and Decline of the United Electrical Workers.* Albany: State University of New York Press, 1995.

Fine, Lisa M. '"Our Big Factory Family": Masculinity and Paternalism at the Reo Motor Car Company of Lansing, Michigan.' *Labor History* 34, 2–3 (1993), 274–91.

Fisher, Marvin. *Workers in the Wilderness: The European Response to American Industrialization, 1830–1860.* Oxford: Oxford University Press, 1967.

Fitzpatrick, James F. *WARN Act and State Plant-Closing Handbook.* Washington: Bureau of National Affairs, 1993.

Folbre, Nancy R., Julia L. Leighton, and Melissa R. Roderick. 'Plant Closings and Their Regulation in Maine, 1971–1982.' *Industrial and Labor Relations Review* 37, 2 (1984), 185–96.

Forbath, William E. *Law and the Shaping of the American Labor Movement*. Cambridge: Harvard University Press, 1991.

Ford, William D. 'Coping with Plant Closings.' *Labor Law Journal* 36, 6 (1985), 323–6.

Foucault, Michel. *The Order of Things: An Archaeology of the Human Sciences*. 1970. Reprint, New York: Vintage Books, 1973.

Fox, Bonnie J., and John Fox. *Occupational Gender Segregation of the Canadian Labour Force, 1931–1981*. Toronto: York University Institute for Social Research, 1987.

Francis, R. Douglas. *Images of the West: Responses to the Canadian Prairies*. Saskatoon: Western Producer Prairie Books, 1989.

– 'Regionalism and the Region.' In Mel Watkins, ed. *Canada*. New York: Facts on File, 1993.

Frank, Dana. *Buy American: The Untold Story of Economic Nationalism*. Boston: Beacon Press, 1999.

French, Michael J. *The U.S. Tire Industry: A History*. Boston: Twayne Publishers, 1990.

Friedman, S. 'Discussion: IR Developments in U.S. and Canada.' In *Proceedings of the 41st Annual Meeting of the Industrial Relations Research Association*. Madison: University of Wisconsin Press.

Frisch, Michael. *A Shared Authority: Essays on the Craft and Meaning of Oral and Public History*. Albany: State University of New York Press, 1990.

Fudge, Judy, and Eric Tucker. *Labour before the Law: The Regulation of Workers' Collective Actions in Canada, 1900–1948*. Oxford: Oxford University Press, 2001.

Fuechtmann, Thomas G. *Steeples and Stacks: Religion and Steel, Crisis in Youngstown*. Cambridge: Cambridge University Press, 1989.

Fukuyama, Francis. 'The Great Disruption: Human Nature and the Reconstitution of Social Order.' *Atlantic Monthly*, May 1999, 55–80.

Futrell, Allan W., and Charles A. Willard. 'Intersubjectivity and Interviewing.' In Eva M. McMahan and Kim Lacy Rogers, eds. *Interactive Oral History Interviewing*. Hillsdale, NJ: Lawrence Erlbaum, 1994.

Gaffield, Chad. 'The New Regional History: Rethinking the History of the Outaouais.' *Journal of Canadian Studies* 26, 1 (1991), 64–81.

Gaffield, Chad, and Pam Gaffield, eds. *Consuming Canada: Readings in Environmental History*. Toronto: Copp Clark, 1995.

Gans, Herbert. *The Urban Villagers: Group and Class in the Life of Italian–Americans*. 1962. Reprint, New York: Free Press, 1982.

Garland, John H. *The North American Midwest: A Regional Geography*. New York: John Wiley and Son, 1955.

Garreau, Joel. *The Nine Nations of America*. Boston: Houghton Mifflin, 1981.

Geertz, Clifford. *The Interpretation of Cultures*. New York: Basic Books, 1973.

Giddens, Anthony *The Consequences of Modernity*. Stanford, Ca: Stanford University Press, 1990.

Gillam, Richard. 'The Perils of Post-industrialism.' *American Quarterly* 34, 1 (1983), 77–82.

Gillis, John R. *A World of Their Own Making: Myth, Ritual and the Quest for Family Values*. New York: Basic Books, 1996.

Gindin, Sam. 'Breaking Away: The Formation of the Canadian Auto Workers.' *Studies in Political Economy* 29 (1989), 63–89.

– *The Canadian Auto Workers: The Birth and Transformation of a Union*. Toronto: James Lorimer and Company, 1995.

Glassberg, David. 'Public History and the Study of Memory.' *The Public Historian* 18, 2 (1996), 7–23.

Glyde, Gerald P. 'Canadian Labour and the Free Trade Agreement.' *Labor Studies Journal* 17, 4 (1993), 3–23.

Godfrey, Dave, and Mel Watkins, eds. *Gordon to Watkins to You, a Documentary: The Battle for Control of Our Economy*. Toronto: new press, 1970.

Goldrick, M.D., and D. Holmes. *Jobs and the Metro Toronto Economy: Symposium Proceedings*. Toronto: York Urban Studies Program, 1981.

Goody, Jack. *Representations and Contradictions: Ambivalence towards Images, Theatre, Fiction, Relics and Sexuality*. Oxford: Blackwell, 1997.

Gordon, Walter. *A Choice for Canada: Independence or Colonial Status*. Toronto: McClelland and Stewart, 1966.

Granatstein, Jack. *Yankees Go Home? Canadians and Anti-Americanism*. Toronto: HarperCollins, 1996.

Grant, George. *Lament for a Nation: The Defeat of a Nation*. Ottawa: Carleton University Press, 1965.

Grayson, J. Paul. *Corporate Strategy and Plant Closures: The SKF Experience*. Toronto: Our Times, 1985.

– *Plant Closures and De-Skilling: Three Case Studies*. Ottawa: Science Council of Canada, 1986.

Guimond, James. *American Photography and the American Dream*. Chapel Hill: University of North Carolina Press, 1991.

Haas, Gilda, and Plant Closure Project. *Plant Closures: Myths, Realities and Responses*. Boston: South End Press, 1985.

Hall, Jacquelyn Dowd, James Leloudis, Robert Korstad, et al. *Like a Family: The Making of a Southern Cotton Mill World*. Chapel Hill: University of North Carolina Press, 1987.

Hall, Stuart, David Held, and Kenneth Thompson, eds. *Modernity: An Introduction to Modern Societies*. Oxford: Blackwell Publishers, 1997.

Hamper, Ben. *Rivethead: Tales from the Assembly Line*. New York: Time-Warner, 1991.

Handlin, Oscar. *The Uprooted*. New York: Grosset and Dunlap, 1951.

Hareven, Tamara, and Randolph Langenbach. *Amoskeag: Life and Work in an American Factory-City*. New York: Pantheon Books, 1978.

Harper, Michael C. 'The Scope of the Duty to Bargain Concerning Business Transformations.' In Samuel Estreicher and Daniel G. Collins, eds. *Labor Law and Business Change: Theoretical and Transactional Perspectives*. New York: Quorum Books, 1988.

Harris, Richard, and Peter J. Larkham, eds. *Changing Suburbs: Foundation, Form and Function*. London: E & FN Spon, 1999.

Harvey, David. 'On the History and Present Condition of Geography: An Historical Geography Manifesto.' *Professional Geographer* 36 (1984), 1–11.

Haskell, Robert F. *Cognition and Symbolic Structures: The Psychology of Metaphoric Transition*. Norwood, NJ: Ablex Publishing Corporation, 1987.

Hathaway, Dale A. *Can Workers Have a Voice? The Politics of Deindustrialization in Pittsburgh*. University Park, PA: Pennsylvania State University Press, 1993.

Hattam, Victoria C. *Labor Visions and State Power: The Origins of Business Unionism in the United States*. Princeton, NJ: Princeton University Press, 1993.

Hawkins, Bruce W. 'The Social Dimension of a Cognitive Grammar.' In Wolf-Andreas Liebert, Gisela Redeker, and Linda Waugh, eds. *Discourse and Perspective in Cognitive Linguistics*. Amsterdam: John Benjamins Publishing Company, 1997.

Hayden, Dolores. *The Power of Place: Urban Landscapes as Public History*. Cambridge, MA: MIT Press, 1995.

Hayes, Samuel P. *Beauty, Health, and Permanence: Environmental Politics in the United States, 1955–1985*. Cambridge: Cambridge University Press, 1987.

Heathorn, Stephen. *For Home, Country, and Race: Constructing Gender, Class, and Englishness in the Elementary School, 1880–1914*. Toronto: University of Toronto Press, 2000.

Helly, Dorothy O., and Susan M. Reverby, eds. *Gendered Domains: Rethinking Public and Private in Women's History*. Ithaca, NY: Cornell University Press, 1992.

Heron, Craig, ed. *Imperialism, Nationalism and Canada*. Toronto: New Hogtown Press, 1977.

Higgins, Benjamin. *The Rise and Fall? of Montreal: A Case Study of Urban Growth, Regional Economic Expansion and National Development*. Moncton: Canadian Institute for Research on Regional Development, 1986.

High, Steven. 'Deindustrializing Youngstown: Memories of Resistance and Loss in the Decades following 'Black Monday.'' *History Workshop Journal* 54 (2002), 100–21.

Hildebrand, Grant. *Designing for Industry: The Architecture of Albert Kahn.* Cambridge, MA: MIT Press, 1974.

Hillmer, Norman, ed. *Partners Nevertheless: Canadian–American Relations in the Twentieth Century.* Toronto: Copp Clark, 1989.

Hinshaw, John, and Judith Modell. 'Perceiving Racism: Homestead from Depression to Deindustrialization.' *Pennsylvania History* 63, 1 (1996), 17–52.

Hiscott, Robert Dennis. 'Plant Closures and Employee Displacement: A Case Study of the Beach Appliance Plant Closure,' Master's thesis, Queen's University, 1982.

Historical Atlas of the United States. Washington, DC: National Geographic Society, 1988.

Hobsbawm, Eric. *Nations and Nationalism since 1870: Programme, Myth, Reality.* Cambridge: Cambridge University Press, 1990.

Hobsbawm, Eric, and Terence Ranger, eds. *The Invention of Tradition.* Cambridge: Cambridge University Press, 1983.

Hoerr, John P. *And the Wolf Finally Came: The Decline of the American Steel Industry.* Pittsburgh: University of Pittsburgh Press, 1988.

Holmes, J., and A. Rusonik. 'The Break-up of an International Labour Union: Uneven Development in the North American Auto Industry and the Schism in the UAW.' *Environment and Planning* A 23 (1991), 9–35.

Horowitz, Roger. 'What Did Workers Want in the 1930s, Anyway?' *Labor History* 38, 2–3 (1997), 169–72.

Hounshell, David A. *From the American System to Mass Production: The Development of Manufacturing Technology in the United States, 1800–1932.* Baltimore: Johns Hopkins University Press, 1984.

Hunt, Lynn. *The New Cultural History.* Berkeley: University of California Press, 1989.

Hurt, R. Douglas. 'Ohio: Gateway to the Midwest.' In James H. Madison, ed. *Heartland: Comparative Histories of the Midwestern States.* Bloomington: Indiana University Press, 1988.

Ingham, John N. *The Iron Barons: A Social Analysis of an American Urban Elite, 1874–1965.* Westport, CT: Greenwood Press, 1977.

Jackson, Andrew. 'The Free Trade Agreement: A Decade Later.' *Studies in Political Economy* 58 (1999).

Jackson, Peter. *Maps of Meaning: An Introduction to Cultural Geography.* London: Routledge, 1989.

Jackson, Peter, and Jan Penrose, eds. *Constructions of Race, Place and Nation.* Minneapolis: University of Minnesota Press, 1994.

Jakle, John A. 'Images of Place: Symbolism and the Middle Western Metropolis.' In Barry Checkoway and Carl V. Patton, eds. *The Metropolitan Midwest:*

Policy Problems and Prospects for Change. Chicago: University of Illinois Press, 1985.

Jackle, John, and David Wilson. *Derelict Landscapes: The Wasting of America's Built Environment*. Savage, MD: Rowman and Littlefield Publishers, 1992.

Jecchinis, Chris. *Public Policy and Institutional Arrangements Concerning Redundancies in Certain West European Countries and Their Relevance for Canada in General and Ontario in Particular*. Thunder Bay: Lakehead University Department of Economics, 1978.

Jenson, Jane, and Rianne Mahon, eds. *The Challenge of Restructuring: North American Labor Movements Respond* (Philadelphia: Temple University Press, 1993), 210.

Jeszeck, Charles A. 'Plant Dispersion and Collective Bargaining in the Rubber Industry.' PhD thesis, University of California, 1982.

Johnson, Christopher H. *The Life and Death of Industrial Languedoc, 1700–1920*. New York: Oxford University Press, 1995.

Jones, Bryan D., and Lynn W. Bachelor. *The Sustaining Hand: Community Leadership and Corporate Power*. 2nd ed. Lawrence: Kansas University Press, 1993.

Jones, David C. *Empire of Dust: Settling and Abandoning the Prairie Dry Belt*. Edmonton: University of Alberta Press, 1987.

Jones, Gareth Stedman. *Languages of Class: Studies in English Working-Class History, 1832–1982*. Cambridge: Cambridge University Press, 1983.

Jones, Jacqueline. *The Dispossessed: America's Underclass from the Civil War to the Present*. New York: Basic Books, 1992.

Kasson, John F. *Civilizing the Machine: Technology and Republican Values in America, 1776–1900*. 1976. Reprint. New York: Hill and Wang, 1999.

Keith, W.J. *Literary Images of Ontario*. Toronto: University of Toronto Press, 1992.

Kelly, Edward. 'Plant Closings Legislation: The Ohio Experience.' In William Schweke, ed. *Plant Closings: Issues, Politics and Legislation*. Boston: Conference on Alternative State and Local Policies, 1980.

Kenney, Martin, and Richard Florida. *Beyond Mass Production: The Japanese System and Its Transfer to the U.S.* New York: Oxford University Press, 1993.

Kern, Stephen. *The Culture of Time and Space, 1880–1918*. Cambridge: Harvard University Press, 1983.

Kerson, Roger, and Greg LeRoy. *State and Local Initiatives on Development Subsidies and Plant Closings*. Chicago: Federation for Industrial Retention and Renewal, 1989.

Kessler-Harris, Alice. *Out to Work: A History of Wage-Earning Women in the United States*. Oxford: Oxford University Press, 1982.

Kleinberg, S.J. *The Shadow of the Mills: Working-Class Families in Pittsburgh, 1870–1907*. Pittsburgh: University of Pittsburgh Press, 1989.

Kovach, Kenneth A., and Peter E. Millspaugh. 'The Plant Closing Issue Arrives at the Bargaining Table.' *Journal of Labor Research* 4, 4 (1983), 367–74.

Kramar, Myron. *The Impact of Plant Closures on Older Workers, Consolidated Bathurst: A Case Study*. Hamilton: Social Planning and Research Council, 1984.

Lakoff, George. 'What Is a Conceptual System?' In Willis F. Overton and David S. Palermo, eds. *The Nature and Ontogenesis of Meaning*. Hillsdale, NJ: Lawrence Erlbaum Associates, 1994.

Lamonde, Pierre, and Mario Polèse. 'L'évolution de la structure économique de Montréal 1971–1981: déindustrialisation ou réconversion?' *L'Actualité économique* 60, 4 (1984), 471–94.

Lasch, Christopher. 'The Communitarian Critique of Liberalism.' In Charles H. Reynolds and Ralph V. Norman, eds. *Community in America*. Berkeley: University of California Press, 1988.

– *The True and Only Heaven: Progress and Its Critics*. New York: W.W. Norton, 1991.

Laxer, Robert, ed. *(Canada) Ltd.: The Political Economy of Dependency*. Toronto: McClelland and Stewart, 1973.

Levitt, Kari. *Silent Surrender: The Multinational Corporation in Canada*. Toronto: Macmillan, 1970.

Lewis, David L. *The Public Image of Henry Ford: An American Folk Hero and His Company*. Detroit: Wayne State University Press, 1976.

Lichter, S., Linda Robert, and Stanley Rothman. *Watching America*. New York: Prentice-Hall, 1989.

Linkon, Sherry Lee, and John Russo. *Steeltown, USA: Work and Memory in Youngstown*. Lawrence: University of Kansas Press, 2002.

Linteau, Paul-André. *Histoire de Montréal: depuis la Confédération*. Montreal: Boréal, 1992.

Lipset, Seymour Martin. *Continental Divide: The Values and Institutions of the United States and Canada*. New York: Routledge, 1990.

Lockyer, K.G. *Factory and Production Management*. 1962. Reprint, London: Pitman, 1974.

Lord, George F., and Albert C. Price. 'Growth Ideology in a Period of Decline: Deindustrialization and Restructuring, Flint Style.' *Social Problems* 39, 2 (1992), 155–69.

Lubove, Roy. *Twentieth Century Pittsburgh: Government, Business and Environmental Change*. New York: John Wiley and Sons, 1969.

– *Twentieth Century Pittsburgh*. Vol. 2. *The Post Steel Era*. Pittsburgh: University of Pittsburgh Press, 1996.

Lucic, Karen. *Charles Sheeler and the Cult of the Machine*. Cambridge: Harvard University Press, 1991.

Luebke, Frederick C. 'Regionalism and the Great Plains: Problem of Concept and Method.' *Western Historical Quarterly* 15, 1 (1984), 19–38.

Lummis, Trevor. 'Structure and Validity in Oral Evidence.' In Robert Perks and Alistair Thomson, eds. *The Oral History Reader*. New York: Routledge, 1998.

Lynd, Alice, and Staughton Lynd, eds. *Rank and File: Personal Histories of Working-Class Organizers*. Boston: Beacon Press, 1973.

Lynd, Staughton. *The Fight against Shutdowns: Youngstown's Steel Mill Closings*. San Pedro, CA: Singlejack Books, 1982.

– 'The Genesis of the Idea of a Community Right to Industrial Property in Youngstown and Pittsburgh, 1977–1987.' *Journal of American History* 74, 3 (1987), 926–58.

– *Living Inside Our Hope: A Steadfast Radical's Thoughts on Rebuilding the Movement*. Ithaca, NY: ILR Press, 1997.

– ed. *We Are all Leaders: A Collection of Essays Dealing with Alternative Unionism in the Early 1930s*. Chicago: University of Illinois Press, 1996.

McBride, Stephen. *Not Working: State, Unemployment, and Neo-Conservativism in Canada*. Toronto: University of Toronto Press, 1992.

McCann, L.D. *Heartland and Hinterland: A Geography of Canada*. Scarborough: Prentice-Hall, 1982.

McDonogh, Gary. 'The Geography of Emptiness.' In Robert Rotenberg and Gary McDonogh, eds. *The Cultural Meaning of Urban Spaces*. Westport, CT: Bergin and Garvey, 1993.

McFadden, David. *A Trip around Lake Erie*. Toronto: Coach House, 1980.

McGill, Linda D. 'State Laws Extend Warn Provisions.' *Employment Relations Today* 18, 2 (1991).

Machor, James L. *Pastoral Cities: Urban Ideals and the Symbolic Landscape of America*. Madison: University of Wisconsin Press, 1987.

MacIntyre, Alasdair. *After Virtue: A Study of Moral Theory*. Notre Dame: University of Notre Dame Press, 1981.

McKenzie, R.B. *Fugitive Industry: The Economics and Politics of Deindustrialization*. Cambridge, MA: Ballinger Press, 1984.

MacLachlan, Ian Robertson. 'Industrial Plant Closure and Competitive Strategy in Ontario, 1981–1986,' PhD diss., University of Toronto, 1990.

MacTavish, Donald J., ed. *Windsor and Essex County Blueprint for a Brighter Tomorrow* Windsor: Windsor Star, 1982, 28.

Mahon, Rianne. *The Politics of Industrial Restructuring: Canadian Textiles*. Toronto: University of Toronto Press, 1984.

Marchetti, Peter E. 'Runaways and Takeovers: Their Effect on Milwaukee's Economy.' *Urbanism: Past and Present* 5, 2 (1980), 1–11.

Marcus, Irwin M. 'The Deindustrialization of America: Homestead, a Case Study, 1959–1984.' *Pennsylvania History* 52, 3 (1985), 162–82.

Markusen, Anne, Peter Hall, Sabina Deitrick, and Scott Campbell. *The Rise of the Gunbelt*. New York: Oxford University Press, 1991.

Markusen, Anne, and Joel Yudken. *Dismantling the Cold War Economy*. New York: Basic Books, 1992.

Marx, Leo. *The Machine in the Garden: Technology and the Pastoral Ideal in America*. New York: Oxford University Press, 1967.

Marx, Leo, and Bruce Mazlish, eds. *Progress: Fact or Illusion*. Ann Arbor: University of Michigan Press, 1996.

Massey, Doreen. 'A Global Sense of Place.' *Marxism Today* (1991), 24–9.

– *Space, Place, and Gender*. Minneapolis: University of Minnesota Press, 1994.

Massey Doreen, and Pat Jess, eds. *A Place in the World? Places, Cultures and Globalization*. Oxford: Oxford University Press, 1995.

Massey, Doreen, and Richard Meegan. *The Anatomy of Job Loss*. London: Methuen, 1982.

Mather, Cotton. 'The Midwest: Image and Reality.' *Journal of Geography* 85 (1986), 190–4.

Maynes, Mary Jo. *Taking the Hard Road: Life Course in French and German Workers' Autobiogaphies in the Era of Industrialization*. Chapel Hill: University of North Carolina Press, 1995.

Milkman, Ruth. *Farewell to the Factory: Auto Workers in the Late Twentieth Century*. Berkeley: University of California Press, 1997.

Mills, C. Wright. *White Collar: The American Middle Classes*. 1951. Reprint, London: Oxford University Press, 1956.

Modell, Judith, and Charlie Brodsky. *A Town Without Steel: Envisioning Homestead*. Pittsburgh: University of Pittsburgh Press, 1998.

Moody, Kim. *An Injury to All: The Decline of American Unionism*. New York: Verso, 1988.

Moore, Franklin G. *Manufacturing Matters*. Homewood, IL: Richard D. Irwin, 1965.

Moore, James M. *Plant Layout and Design*. New York: Macmillan Company, 1962.

Moore, Sally F., and Barbara G. Myerhoff, eds. *Secular Ritual*. Assen: Van Gorcum, 1977.

Moore, Steve, and Debi Wells. *Imperialism and the National Question in Canada*. Toronto: n.p., 1975.

Morgan, Cecilia. *Public Men and Virtuous Women: The Gendered Languages of*

Religion and Politics in Upper Canada, 1791–1850. Toronto: University of
Toronto Press, 1996.

Morris, Lydia. 'Redundant Populations: Deindustrialisation in a North-East
English Town.' In Raymond M. Lee, ed. *Redundancy, Layoffs and Plant Closures: Their Character, Causes and Consequences.* London: Croom Helm, 1987.

Muszynski, Leon. *The Deindustrialization of Metropolitan Toronto: A Study of
Plant Closures, Layoffs and Unemployment.* Toronto: Social Planning Council
of Metropolitan Toronto, 1985.

Nader, Ralph, and William Taylor. *The Big Boys: Power and Position in American
Business.* New York: Pantheon Books, 1986.

Neill, J.V., and Diana Fitzsimons, eds. *Reimaging the Pariah City: Urban Development in Belfast and Detroit.* Aldershot, U.K.: Avebury, 1995.

Nelles, H.V., and Abraham Rotstein, eds. *Nationalism or Local Control: Responses
to George Woodcock.* Toronto: New Press, 1973.

Nelson, Daniel. *Managers and Workers: Origins of the Twentieth-Century Factory
System in the United States, 1880–1920.* Madison: University of Wisconsin
Press, 1995.

Nissen, Bruce, ed. *Fighting for Jobs: Case Studies of Labor, Community Coalitions
Confronting Plant Closings.* Albany: State University of New York Press, 1995.

Noble, David F. *Progress without People: New Technology, Unemployment and the
Message of Resistance.* Toronto: Between the Lines, 1995.

Nora, Pierre, ed. *Realms of Memory: The Construction of the French Past.* New
York: Columbia University Press, 1998.

Norcliffe, Glen. 'In a Hard Land: The Geographical Context of Canadian
Industrial Landscape Painting.' In Paul Simpson-Housley and Glen
Norcliffe, eds. *A Few Acres of Snow: Literary and Artistic Images of Canada.*
Toronto: Dundurn Press, 1992.

Nye, David E. *American Technological Sublime.* Cambridge, MA: MIT Press,
1994.

– *Image Worlds: Corporate Identities at General Electric, 1890–1930.* Cambridge,
MA: MIT Press, 1985.

O'Connor, Thomas Francis. 'Plant Shutdowns and Worker Attitudes: The Case
of Kelvinator.' Master's thesis, University of Western Ontario, 1970.

Ontario. Ministry of Labour. *Preferential Hiring Rights in Business Relocations
and Closures.* Toronto, 1983.

Ontario. *Ontario: Canada's Heartland of Industry, Finance, Culture.* Toronto:
Department of Travel and Publicity, 1961.

Organization for Economic Cooperation and Development. *Job Losses in Major
Industries.* Paris: OECD, 1983.

– *Job Security and Industrial Relations.* Paris: OECD, 1979.

– *Policies for Promoting Industrial Adaptation*. Paris: OECD, 1976.

– *Regional Policies in Canada*. Paris: OECD, 1980.

Ornstein, Allan C. 'Decline of the Frostbelt.' *Dissent* 30, 3 (1983), 366–74.

Orvell, Miles. *After the Machine: Visual Arts and the Erasing of Cultural Boundaries*. Jackson: University Press of Mississippi, 1995.

Osberg, Lars, Fred Wien, and Jan Grude, *Vanishing Jobs: Canada's Changing Workplaces*. Toronto: James Lorimer, 1995.

Oxford Dictionary of New Words. Oxford: Oxford University Press, 1981.

Page, Leonard, and Judith Scott. *The Law of Plant Shutdowns*. Detroit: United Auto Workers, 1981.

Palmer, Bryan D. *Capitalism Comes to the Backcountry: The Goodyear Invasion of Napanee*. Toronto: Between the Lines, 1994.

Pappas, Gregory. *The Magic City: Unemployment in a Working-Class Community*. Ithaca, NY: Cornell University Press, 1989.

Parr, Joy. 'Gender History and Historical Practice.' In Joy Parr and Mark Rosenfeld, eds. *Gender and History in Canada*. Toronto: Copp Clark, 1996.

– *The Gender of Breadwinners: Women, Men, and Change in Two Industrial Towns, 1880–1950*. Toronto: University of Toronto Press, 1990.

Passerini, Luisa. 'Work Ideology and Consensus under Italian Fascism.' *History Workshop* 8 (1979), 84–92.

Perrucci, Carolyn C., Robert Perrucci, et al. *Plant Closings: International Context and Social Contexts*. New York: Aldine de Gruyler, 1988.

Perry, David C. 'The Politics of Dependency in Deindustrializing America: the Case of Buffalo, NY.' In Michael Peter Smith, and Joe R. Feagin, eds. *The Capitalist City: Global Restructuring and Community Politics*. Oxford: Blackwell, 1987.

Phillips, Anne, and Barbara Taylor, 'Sex and Skill: Notes toward a Feminist Economics.' *Feminist Review* 6 (1980), 9–88.

Picot, Garnett, and Ted Wannell. *Job Loss and Labour Market Adjustment in the Canadian Economy*. Ottawa: Statistics Canada, 1987.

Pitegoff, Peter. *Plant Closings: Legal Remedies When Jobs Disappear*. Sommerville, MA: Industrial Cooperative Association, 1981.

Plant, Robert. *Industries in Trouble*. Geneva: International Labour Organization, 1981.

Polizzotto, Carolyn. *The Factory Floor: A Visual and Oral Record, 1900–1960*. Freemantle, Australia: Freemantle Arts Centre Press, 1988.

Portelli, Alessandro. *The Death of Luigi Trastulli and Other Stories: Form and Meaning in Oral History*. Albany: State University of New York Press, 1991.

Portz, John. *The Politics of Plant Closings*. Lawrence: University Press of Kansas, 1990.

Preston, William D. Jr., and Gerson B. Mehlman. 'The Due Process Clause as a Limitation on the Reach of State Legislation: An Historical and Analytical Examination of Substantive Due Process.' *Baltimore Law Review* 8, 1 (1978).

Proulx, David. *Pardon My Lunch Bucket: A Look at the New Hamilton ... With a Bit of the Old Thrown In*. Hamilton: City of Hamilton, 1971.

Raines, John C., Lenora E. Berson, and David McI.Grace, eds. *Community and Capital in Conflict: Plant Closings and Job Losses*. Philadelphia: Temple University Press, 1982.

Rea, K.J. *The Prosperous Years: The Economic History of Ontario, 1939–1975*. Toronto: University of Toronto Press, 1985.

Richards, John, and Larry Pratt. *Prairie Capitalism: Power and Influence in the New West*. Toronto: University of Toronto Press, 1979.

Roberts, Wayne. 'Shutdowns: Canadian Workers Are Virtually Unprotected from Take-the-Money-and-Run Multinationals.' *The Facts* 7, 4 (1985), 22–5.

Rodwin, Lloyd, and Hidehiko Sazanami, eds. *Deindustrialization and Regional Economic Transformation: The Experience of the United States*. Boston: Unwin Hyman, 1989.

Roediger, David. *Wages of Whiteness: Race and the Making of the American Working Class*. 1991. Reprint, New York: Verso, 1999.

Rogovin, Milton, and Michael Frisch. *Portraits in Steel*. Ithaca, NY: Cornell University Press, 1993.

Root, Kenneth A. *Perspectives for Communities and Organizations on Plant Closings and Job Dislocations*. Ames, IA: North Central Regional Center for Rural Development, 1979.

Rothstein, Lawrence E. *Plant Closings: Power, Politics and Workers*. London: Auburn House, 1986.

Rotstein, Abraham. 'Is There an English-Canadian Nationalism?' in *Goals for Canada*. The Walter Gordon Lecture Series. Vol. 2. Toronto: Canada Studies Foundation, 1977–8.

Rotstein, Abraham, and Gary Lax. *Independence: the Canadian Challenge*. Toronto: Committee for an Independent Canada, 1972.

Rubenstein, James M. *The Changing U.S. Auto Industry: A Geographical Analysis*. New York: Routledge, 1992.

Sack, Jeffrey, and C. Michael Mitchell. *Ontario Labour Relations Board: Law and Practice*. Toronto: Butterworths, 1985.

Safarian, A.E. 'Some Myths about Foreign Investment in Canada.' *Journal of Canadian Studies* (1971), 3–21.

Said, Edward. *Orientalism*. New York: Vintage Books, 1979.

Sangster, Joan. *Earning Respect: The Lives of Working Women in Small Town Ontario, 1920–1960*. Toronto: University of Toronto Press, 1995.

Saunders, Ronalds. *Permanent Layoffs: Some Issues in the Policy Debate*. Toronto: Ontario Economic Council, 1981.

Schauer, Frederick F. 'English Natural Justice and American Due Process: An Analytical Comparison.' In Sidney R. Peck, ed. *Due Process: Introductory Material for a Seminar on Due Process*. Toronto: Osgoode Hall Law School, 1994.

Schoenberger, Erica. *The Cultural Crisis of the Firm*. Cambridge, MA: Blackwell Publishers, 1997.

Schuler, Douglas Arnold. 'Corporate Political Involvement for Managing Industrial Decline: The Case of the U.S. Steel Industry and Steel Policy.' PhD diss., University of Minnesota, 1992.

Schumpeter, Joseph A. *Capitalism, Socialism and Democracy*. 1942. Reprint, New York: Harper and Row, 1976.

Scott, Joan. 'Gender: A Useful Category of Historical Analysis.' *American Historical Review* 91 (1986), 28–50.

Scranton, Philip. 'Large Firms and Industrial Restructuring: The Philadelphia Region, 1900–1980.' *Pennsylvania Magazine of History and Biography* 116, 4 (1992), 419–65.

– 'Many Cities, Many Hills: Production, Space, and Diversity in Pennsylvania's Urban History.' *Pennsylvania History* 59, 1 (1992).

– *Proprietary Capitalism: The Textile Manufacturer at Philadelphia*. Cambridge: Cambridge University Press, 1983.

Serrin, William. *Homestead: The Glory and Tragedy of an American Steel Town*. New York: Vintage Books, 1994.

Sexton, Jean. *Fermetures d'usines et reclassement de la main-d'oeuvre au Québec*. Quebec: Ministère du travail, 1975.

Sexty, Robert W. *Public Enterprise and Employment in Canada* (Technical Study 33). Ottawa: Labour Market Development Task Force, 1981.

Sferra, Jane. 'A Way of Life Gone Forever: The Youngstown Steel Industry.' Master's thesis, Miami University in Oxford, OH, 1993.

Shippani, Michael. 'Creative Alternatives to Plant Closings: The Massachusetts Experience.' *Labor Law Journal* 38, 8 (1987).

Shorris, Earl. 'The Empty House.' In Earl Shorris, ed. *While Someone Else Is Eating*. Garden City, NY: Anchor Press, 1984.

Shortridge, James. *The Middle West: Its Meaning in American Culture*. Lawrence: University of Kansas Press, 1989.

Smith, Anthony D. *Theories of Nationalism*. New York: Holmes and Meier, 1983.

Smith, E.G. 'Political Economy and the Canadian Working Class: Marxism or National Reform?' *Labour/Le Travail* 46 (fall 2000), 343–68.

Smith, Merritt Roe, and Leo Marx, eds. *Does Technology Drive History? The Dilemma of Technological Determinism*. Cambridge, MA: MIT Press, 1994.

Smith, Miriam. 'The Canadian Labour Congress: From Continentalism to Economic Nationalism.' *Studies in Political Economy* 38 (summer 1992), 35–60.

Smith, Neil. *Uneven Development: Nature, Capital and the Production of Space*. Oxford: Basil Blackwell, 1984.

Smith, Ruth, and Eric M. Eisenberg. 'Conflict at Disneyland: A Root-Metaphor Analysis.' *Communications Monographs* 54, 4 (1987), 367–80.

Smith, W. Rand. *The Left's Dirty Job: The Politics of Industrial Restructuring in France and Spain*. Pittsburgh: University of Pittsburgh Press; Toronto: University of Toronto Press, 1998.

Sobel, David, and Susan Meurer. *Working at Inglis: The Life and Death of a Canadian Factory*. Toronto: James Lorimer, 1994.

Spayd, Donald Paul. 'The Economic Impact of Deindustrialization on Financial Decisions of the Warren City Schools, 1975–89.' PhD diss., University of Akron, 1991.

Squires, Gregory D. *Capital and Communities in Black and White: The Intersections of Race, Class and Uneven Development*. Albany: State University of New York Press, 1994.

Stairs, Denis. 'North American Continentalism – Perspectives and Policies in Canada.' In David M. Cameron, ed. *Regionalism and Supranationalism: Challenges and Alternatives to the Nation-State in Canada and Europe*. Montreal: Institute for Research on Public Policy, 1981.

Stansell, Christine. 'Woman in Nineteenth Century America.' *Gender and History* 11, 3 (1999), 419–32.

Staudohart, Paul D., and Holly E. Brown, eds. *Deindustrialization and Plant Closure*. Lexington, MA: Lexington Books, 1987.

Stein, Judith. *Running Steel, Running America: Race, Economic Policy and the Decline of Liberalism*. Chapel Hill: University of North Carolina Press, 1998.

Steinberg, Theodore. *Nature Incorporated: Industrialization and the Waters of New England*. Amherst: University of Massachusetts Press, 1991.

Storey, Robert, and Wayne Lewchuk. 'From Dust to DUST to dust: Asbestos and the Struggle for Worker Health and Safety at Bendix Automotive.' *Labour/Le Travail* 45 (spring 2000), 103–40.

Styck, Lucien, ed. *Heartland II: Poets of the Midwest*. DeKalb: Northern Illinois University Press, 1975.

Sugrue, Thomas J. *The Origins of the Urban Crisis: Race and Inequality in Postwar Detroit*. Princeton, NJ: Princeton University Press, 1997.

Taksa, Lucy. 'Like a Bicycle, Forever Teetering between Individualism and

Collectivism: Considering Community in Relation to Labour History.'
Labour History (Australia) 78 (2000).

Tarr, Joel A. *The Search for the Ultimate Sink: Urban Pollution in Historical Perspective*. Akron, OH: University of Akron Press, 1996.

Teaford, Jon C. *Cities of the Heartland: The Rise and Fall of the Industrial Midwest*. Bloomington: Indiana University Press, 1994.

Terkel, Studs. *Hard Times: An Oral History of the Great Depression*. New York: Pantheon, 1970.

– *Working*. New York: Pantheon, 1972.

Thompson, E.P. *The Making of the English Working Class*. New York: Vintage Books, 1963.

– 'The Moral Economy of the English Crowd in the Eighteenth Century.' *Past and Present* 50 (1971), 76–136.

Thompson, John Herd, and Stephen J. Randall. *Canada and the United States: Ambivalent Allies*. Montreal: McGill-Queen's University Press, 1994.

Tiffany, Paul A. *The Decline of American Steel: How Management, Labor and Government Went Wrong*. New York: Oxford University Press, 1988.

Toffler, Alvin. *The Third Wave*. New York: William Morrow, 1980.

Tomlins, Christopher L. *The State of the Unions: Labor Relations, Law and the Organized Labor Movement in America, 1880–1960*. Cambridge: Cambridge University Press, 1985.

Torrence, William D. 'Plant Closing and Advance Notice: Another Look at the Numbers.' *Labor Law Journal* 37, 8 (1986), 461–5.

Tuan, Yi-Fu. 'Place: An Experiential Perspective.' *Geographical Review* 65, 2 (1975), 151–65.

– *Space and Place: The Perspectives of Experience*. Minneapolis: University of Minnesota Press, 1978.

Turner, Victor. *The Ritual Process: Structure and Anti-Structure*. 1969. Reprint, New York: Aldine de Gruyter, 1995.

Tweedale, Geoffrey. *Steel City: Entrepreneurship, Strategy, and Technology in Sheffield, 1743–1993*. Oxford: Clerendon Press, 1995.

Ullman, John E. *The Anatomy of Industrial Decline: Productivity, Investment, and Location in U.S. Manufacturing*. New York: Quorum Books, 1988.

United States. Department of Labor. *Major Collective Agreements: Layoff, Recall and Worksharing Procedures*. Washington: Government Printing Office, 1972.

– Office of Technology Assessment. *Plant Closings: Advance Notice and Rapid Response, Special Report*. Washington: Government Printing Office, 1986.

– Secretary of Labor. *Economic Adjustment and Worker Dislocation in a Competitive Society: Report of the Secretary of Labor's Task Force on Economic Adjustment and Worker Dislocation*. Washington: Government Printing Office, 1986.

Van der Knaap, Bert, and Richard Le Heron, eds. *Human Resources and Industrial Spaces: A Perspective on Globalization and Localization.* New York: John Wiley and Sons, 1995.

Van M. Krontseng, Richard. 'Judicial and Arbitral Resolution of Contractual Plant Closing Issues.' *Labor Law Journal* 35, 7 (1984), 393–406.

Van Nostrand, John C. 'The Queen Elizabeth Way: Public Utility Versus Public Space.' *Urban History Review* 7, 2 (1983), 1–24.

Vance, Jonathan F. *Death So Noble: Memory, Meaning, and the First World War.* Vancouver: UBC Press, 1997.

Walden, Keith. *Becoming Modern in Toronto: The Industrial Exhibition and the Shaping of a Late Victorian Canada.* Toronto: University of Toronto Press, 1997.

Walsh, John, and Steven High. 'Rethinking the Concept of Community.' *Histoire sociale/Social History* 17, 64 (1999), 255–74.

Ward, Stephen V. *Selling Places: The Marketing and Promotion of Towns and Cities, 1850–2000.* London: Routledge, 1998.

Watkins, Mel. 'Foreign Ownership and the Structure of Canadian Industry.' In Dave Godfrey and Mel Watkins, eds. *Gordon to Watkins to You: The Battle for Control of Our Economy.* Toronto: New Press, 1970.

Wayman, Tom. 'Detroit Poem.' In Tom Wayman. *Counting the Hours: City Poem.* Toronto: McClelland and Stewart, 1983.

Webber, M.J. 'Regional Production and the Production of Regions: The Case of Steeltown.' In Allen J. Scott and Michael Storper, eds. *Production, Work, Territory: The Geographical Anatomy of Industrial Capitalism.* Boston: Allen and Unwin, 1986.

Webster's Ninth New Collegiate Dictionary. Springfield, MA: Merriam-Webster Inc., 1987.

Weinstein, Bernard. 'The Divided States of America.' *Current* (July–August 1980), 52–3.

Wells, Don. 'The Impact of the Postwar Compromise on Canadian Unionism: The Formation of an Auto Workers Local in the 1950s.' *Labour/Le Travail* 36 (fall 1995), 147–73.

Westerman, William. 'Central American Refugee Testimonies and Performed Life Histories in the Sanctuary Movement.' In Robert Perks and Alistair Thomson, eds. *The Oral History Reader.* New York: Routledge, 1998.

Westfall, William. 'On the Concept of Region in Canadian History and Literature.' *Journal of Canadian Studies* 15, 2 (1980), 3–15.

Williams, Raymond. *Keywords: A Vocabulary of Culture and Society.* London: Fontana Press, 1983.

Williamson, Michael, and Dale Maharidge. *Journey to Nowhere.* Garden City, NY: Dial Press, 1985.

Worster, Donald. *Dust Bowl: The Southern Plains in the 1930s*. New York: Oxford University Press, 1979.

– *Nature's Economy: A History of Ecological Ideas*. Cambridge: Cambridge University Press, 1994.

Wright, Robert A. '"Dream, Comfort, Memory, Despair": Canadian Popular Musicians and the Dilemma of Nationalism, 1968–1972.' *Journal of Canadian Studies* 22, 4 (1987–8), 27–42.

Wuthnow, Robert. *Meaning and Moral Order: Explorations in Cultural Analysis*. Berkeley: University of California Press, 1987.

Yates, Charlotte. 'From Plant to Politics: The Canadian UAW, 1936–1984.' PhD diss., Carleton University, 1988.

– 'North American Autoworkers' Response to Response to Restructuring.' In Miriam Golden and Jonas Pontusson, eds. *Bargaining for Change: Union Politics in North America and Europe*. Ithaca, NY: Cornell University Press, 1992.

Zelinsky, Wilbur. 'North America's Venacular Regions.' *Annals of the Association of American Geographers* 70, 1 (1980), 1–16.

Zippay, Allison. *From Middle Income to Poor: Downward Mobility among Displaced Steelworkers*. New York: Praeger, 1991.

Zukin, Sharon. *Landscapes of Power: From Detroit to Disney World*. Berkeley: University of California Press, 1991.

Illustration Credits

Canadian Auto Workers: Bob White visiting Houdaille Factory.

Metropolitan Museum of Art: Criss-crossed conveyors (Ford Motor Company Collection, Gift of Ford Motor Company and John C. Waddell, 1987 (1987.1100.1))

National Archives of Canada: Molten steel being poured (Gar Lunney, PA 205828); Illustration of Dunlop Tire (John Verselest, C-092414).

Pennsylvania State University, Special Collections Library, Historical Collections and Labor Archives: Cartoon by Clarence Eaton.

Photo Archives of the Ontario Federation of Labour (Frank Rooney): Protest of the closing of Houdaille Bumper; Protesting Ontario plant closures.

David Smiley: The assembly line at Inglis; The last shift at Inglis.

Tri State Conference on Manufacturing (Steel), Archives Service Center, University of Pittsburgh: A community poster announcing a meeting. (UE/Labor 93:10. Box 65)

UE News/Fred Wright Cartoon, Labor Cartoons and Drawings, UE Archives, Archives Service Center, University of Pittsburgh: Fred Wright a pre-eminent labour (#U-48); A poster by Fred Wright (#2026); A cartoon by Fred Wright indicating who gains (#1007); A Fred Wright cartoon suggesting the reasons (#U-158); The management leaves in style (#2074) Fred Wright cartoon supporting United Electrical (#777).

Walter P. Reuther Library, Wayne State University, The Detroit News Collection: Beginning phase of Dodge Main's demolition; Demolition of Dodge Main.

Jim West: Selling out-of-town newspapers; Demolition of part of Chrysler; Closed Cadillac plant; Anti-imports signs; Labor Day Parade; Girl holds sign.

Youngstown Historical Center of Industry and Labor: Blast furnace demolition; Brier Hill Works, Blowing Engine House; Youngstown Sheet and Tube's Campbell Works; Youngstown community members wearing shirts; A procession leaves Stop 14 Gate (Gerald Dickey Collection, United Steelworkers of America Photographs); Gerald Dickey speaking (Gerald Dickey Collection, United Steelworkers of America Photographs); A flyer; Editorial cartoon from the *Brier Hill Unionist*.

Index